How to Protect Your Business, Professional, and Brand Names

David A. Weinstein

JOHN WILEY & SONS, Inc.

New York ● Chichester ● Brisbane ● Toronto ● Singapore

Library of Congress Cataloging-in-Publication Data
Weinstein, David A., 1942–
How to protect your business, professional, and
brand names / by David A. Weinstein.
    p.   cm.
  ISBN 0-471-51557-4.—ISBN 0-471-51558-2 (pbk.)
    1. Trademarks—United States—Popular works.   2. Business names—United States—Popular works.   I. Title.
KF3180.Z9W45   1991
346.7304′88—dc20
[347.306488]   90-12000
                                                                    CIP

Printed in the United States of America

90 91 10 9 8 7 6 5 4 3 2 1

To my parents
Sam and Rowena

for the values, creativity, and ethical principles
they have given their children

and to

Is and Evelyn
for their humor and kindness, and for Gayle

Preface

The names and symbols businesses and professionals use to identify their products and services are or can become extremely valuable intangible assets. They are eligible for legal protection under the area of law dealing with unfair competition. In many instances, substantial efforts are made and money spent to develop and promote them so that relevant members of the public and trade seek and patronize the products, services, and activities the names and symbols identify. When such efforts are successful, these names and symbols immediately bring to mind these products, services, and activities.

With knowledge of the fundamentals of protecting business and professional names and symbols described in this book, you will be able to select, acquire rights in, register, enforce, and permit others to use them. Furthermore, you will be aware of what steps to take to avoid conflicts with others regarding their use.

This book is for everyone who would like to know how to protect business and professional names and symbols. It is for individuals who operate small businesses as well as for multinational corporations. It is for those who operate commercial enterprises as well as for those who are engaged in noncommercial, nonprofit, and fraternal activities.

Both readers who have no knowledge of where to begin or

what is involved and readers who know a little and want to know more about this subject will find this book a useful reference tool.

With this book you will find that protecting names and symbols is not complicated. Among other things, you will learn the difference between corporate and trade (assumed or fictitious) names, as well as understand trademarks, service marks, and other types of marks. You will also learn the notations used to denote a claim of rights in a name or symbol and how to register it.

How to Protect Your Business, Professional, and Brand Names explains everything the reader needs to know in easy-to-understand language and includes forms and sample documents. The book outlines the process of checking names for potential conflicts and describes the steps necessary to acquire rights. It includes directions for registering with state agencies as well as with the U.S. Patent and Trademark Office. Approaches to licensing and transferring rights are discussed, and guidance is provided for asserting and defending infringement claims.

The information given in this book is the result of my 22 years of experience in the field of trademark law. I believe it will enable you to understand what is involved and how to proceed to protect names and symbols.

DAVID A. WEINSTEIN
Denver, Colorado

Contents

1

Terminology and Applicable Law

The first thing you should do to learn how to protect business and professional names and symbols is to become familiar with the nomenclature and with which area of law governs the legal protection available for names and symbols.

Names and symbols like "Cheerios," "Visa," "McDonald's Corporation," "GE," and an alligator emblem are used in connection with specific products and businesses. Many people know some or all of these names and symbols, but do they know whether they are corporate or trade (assumed or fictitious) names, patents, copyrights, trademarks, or service marks? Is anything used in close association with them that suggests what they are? Do the words *incorporated, inc., corporation, corp., company, limited, enterprise,* and *association* give a clue? What meaning, if any, is given to the words *patented, patent pending, all rights reserved, copyright,* and *Registered U.S. Patent & Trademark Office,* and the notations *copr.,* ©, TM, SM, and ®?

As explained later in this chapter, the way a name or symbol is used determines the appropriate terminology. This terminology changes with corresponding changes in the way the name or symbol is used. However, what does not change is the particular area of law that governs name and symbol protection.

Many people believe patent, copyright, or trademark law may be applicable but do not know which. Those who think it is patent law are wrong. And those who think it is copyright law are right only if they are focusing on pictorial or graphic symbols. Those who think it is trademark law that governs these matters are the closest.

Actually, the law of unfair competition governs. *Unfair competition* is the umbrella area of law covering legal protection for subject matter that is within the scope of copyright, trademark and patent law. The subject matter often is referred to as *intellectual property*. This area of law also covers protection for the subject matter of corporate or trade names as well as for *trade dress* (distinctive product packaging or product configuration), all of which a business may use to identify products and services.

Although unfair competition is the area of law generally applicable to name and symbol protection, the principles of trademark law typically serve as reference points to determine how rights in business names and symbols are acquired and enforced. For this reason, trademark law generally is the focal point of discussion in this book.

Trademark subject matter, the manner of acquiring rights in it, and the scope of those rights are sometimes confused with the subject matter, rights, and protection governed by patent and copyright law. Knowing the domains of these legal specialties will help you avoid misusing the terminology peculiar to each area and identify the kind of legal protection available for the intellectual property businesses commonly have.

A good way to introduce these three areas of law is to refer to the activities, products, and services of a hypothetical music recording company. This example highlights the subject matter, rights, and protection each area of law governs as well as the terminology and notations used for business names and symbols.

The hypothetical company is Music in Motion, Inc. It does business under the name "Penstemmon Music." This company is a Colorado corporation. It manufactures, advertises, and sells phonograph records, audiocassettes, and compact discs nationwide. These products embody musical compositions and are identified on labeling by the designation "Geared for Running," which features a pictorial design in association with it. The music was created with a specific tempo and pitch to sell to people who listen to music while exercising or running. Print, radio, and television advertising is used to promote these products.

The company created, owns, and uses a computer software program known as "Invetrack" for keeping track of its inventory. Also, it uses the name "Shereth" to identify the distribution services it offers to other companies for their records, cassettes, and compact discs.

PATENT PROTECTION

The machinery and technical processes the company uses to manufacture its products may be eligible for patent protection. Possibly the configuration of the cassette can be protected as a patented invention. If the chemical compound formulated to produce the tape is novel and unique, it might also be patented.

Patent protection generically denotes the limited monopoly (*patent*) given under the Federal Patent Act to something called a *patented invention*. Subject to a few exceptions, the first person to invent subject matter eligible for patent protection is the only one entitled to obtain a patent. Two or more persons who collaborate on an invention are considered co-inventors and can jointly obtain the patent for it.

Patent protection is available only if the subject matter is new and unique. It should not be known or used by others or described in a publication in the United States or any foreign country. Small improvements in eligible subject matter that would be obvious to anyone with ordinary skill cannot be patented. Furthermore, a patent cannot be obtained for anything that is publicly used or on sale in the United States one year or more prior to the date of filing an application for patent.

A U.S. patent gives the owner the exclusive right to prevent anyone else from making, using, or selling the patented invention throughout the United States, its territories, and its possessions. Protection for a U.S. patent does not extend to foreign countries. Separate patents must be obtained from the government of each country where protection is desired.

A patent can last for 17 years (for mechanical, electrical, chemical, and plant patents) or 3½, 7, or 14 years (for a design patent). The limited monopoly does not become effective on the patent application filing date. Its life begins on the date the patent is granted, which can be from two to four years or more after the filing date.

A U.S. patent grant is obtainable only from the federal government and only for

1. A new and useful industrial or technical process, machine, article of manufacture, or composition of matter (chemical compositions, mixtures of ingredients, or new chemical compounds), or any new and useful improvements for these items.
2. A new, original, and ornamental design for an article of manufacture.
3. Any distinct and new asexually reproduced variety of plant.

The U.S. Patent and Trademark Office (USPTO) is the federal agency responsible for granting patents. It is part of the Commerce Department and has offices only in Washington, D.C.

An application for patent is filed with the USPTO. Although the patent application has a prescribed format, the government does not provide a form. Each application is, in effect, custom made and contains a detailed and precise description of the invention.

Jurisdiction over patent is exclusively within the authority of the federal government and U.S. District Courts. Therefore, state and local government agencies and courts have no power to confer or regulate patent protection.

The word "Patent" (or abbreviation "Pat.") followed by a series of numbers indicates that all or an element of the subject matter is patented. The notation "Patent Applied For" or "Patent Pending" means an application for a patent has been filed. It has no legal effect.

COPYRIGHT PROTECTION

Musical compositions and the sounds resulting from their performance that are embodied in phonograph records, cassettes and discs are protected under copyright law. Similarly, copyright protection is available for the content of the company's artwork, photographs, graphics and text for its print advertising, scripts and music for its radio commercials, and the audiovisual components of its television advertising. The pictorial design on its labeling also may be protected by copyright, as may the computer software program.

Copyright protection generically denotes the kind of protection (copyright) available under the Copyright Act of 1976 for copyrightable works. Subject to a few exceptions, the person who creates such a work is entitled to this protection. If two or more persons collaborate in creating a work, they are co-owners of its copyright.

The word work is not defined in the Copyright Act but can be described as a generic term for anything that is the product of an individual's creative effort. It may be manifested as images and sounds as well as in other ways.

Copyright is available only if the particular work is embodied in a tangible medium of expression, falls within the broad categories of protected works established by the Copyright Act, is original with the creator, and exhibits at least a minimal degree of creativity.

An original work is one that has not been copied from another work. It does not have to be unique or original in terms of being novel or new, as is required for an invention to be eligible for a patent. Therefore, two people might claim copyright for identical creations as long as neither copied the other.

The owner of a copyright has five exclusive rights that establish the scope and kind of protection for a work:

1. Reproduce the work
2. Create variations of the work
3. Distribute the work publicly

4. Perform the work publicly
5. Display the work publicly

These rights may be exercised and enforced throughout the United States, its territories, and its possessions. Some or all of these rights may be exercised and enforced throughout the world.

The exclusive rights become immediately and automatically effective and enforceable on the date a copyrightable work is created and embodied in a physical object, such as words put on paper, sounds on audiotapes, and images on canvas or videotapes. Applying for a copyright registration or otherwise obtaining approval from a governmental agency is not necessary to acquire copyright.

Copyright can last for as long as the life of the creator of a work plus 50 years. Therefore, if the creator is the initial owner of copyright, the length of his or her life determines how long protection will exist.

Copyright is available for the following kind of works:

1. Literary works
2. Musical works, including accompanying words
3. Dramatic works, including any accompanying music
4. Pantomimes and choreographic works
5. Pictorial, graphic, and sculptural works
6. Motion pictures and other audiovisual works
7. Sound recordings

These works can be embodied in such things as books, magazines, newspapers, photographs, audiotapes and records, videotapes, paintings, sculpture, jewelry, and computer software programs.

Ordinarily, registration of a copyright ownership claim is required only when the owner desires to enforce copyright. Prior to March 1, 1989, registration was also required to avoid the loss of copyright for publicly distributed copies of a work that did not feature a copyright notice. United States copyright law prior to that date required placement of a copyright notice on such copies to avoid invalidation of the copyright. This action is no longer necessary.

Registration is accomplished by completing and filing a pre-printed official application form with the U.S. Copyright Office, the one and only agency responsible for copyright registration. It is within the Library of Congress and has offices only in Washington, D.C.

Jurisdiction over copyright is exclusively within the authority of the federal government and U.S. District Courts. Therefore, state and local government agencies and courts have no power to confer or regulate copyright protection.

Although a copyright notice is no longer required, using one on copies of publicly distributed works is prudent. A copyright notice on an item indicates that a claim of rights is made in its content under copyright law. This notice consists of three components: the encircled letter "C," © (or "Copyright" or "Copr."), followed by a year date and the name of the copyright owner.

When copyright is claimed for sounds embodied in an object, the first component of the notice is the encircled letter "P," ℗, rather than the word, symbol, or abbreviation for copyright.

TRADEMARK PROTECTION

Because the hypothetical company is incorporated, the name "Music in Motion, Inc." functions as a corporate name. When doing business as Penstemmon Music, it is using a name other than its chartered name. Therefore, Penstemmon Music functions as its trade (assumed or fictitious) name.

The designation "Geared for Running" and a pictorial design are used to identify phonograph records, cassettes, and discs. They function as trademarks. The designation "Invetrack" also functions as a trademark because it is used to identify the company's computer software program. The name "Shereth" functions as a service mark because it identifies the company's distribution services.

Trademark protection is the legal protection for the names and symbols a business uses to identify its products and services.

The principles of law applicable to trademark protection also are applicable to the protection of names and symbols when they serve a different function, namely, when they are used to identify a business itself.

A trademark includes "any word, name, symbol, or device, or any combination thereof used by a person, or which a person has a bona fide intention to use in commerce to identify and distinguish his or her goods including a unique product, from those manufactured or sold by others and to indicate the source of the goods, even if the source is unknown" (Trademark Act of 1946).

The function of a trademark is to indicate the origin of a product. It identifies physical commodities, whether natural, manufactured, or processed. For example, "Jell-O" identifies a gelatin dessert (General Foods Corporation); an alligator emblem identifies clothing (Izod); the slogan "This Bud's for you" identifies beer (Anheuser-Busch, Inc.); the pinch bottle shape identifies whiskey (Haig & Haig, Inc.); and a colored tag identifies clothing (Levi Strauss & Co.).

Often, the phrase *brand name* is used instead of the word *trademark* in reference to a name or symbol that identifies a product, and frequently the word *trademark* is used to refer to a name or symbol that identifies a service. The latter use is technically incorrect because a service mark means "any word, name, symbol, or device, or any combination thereof used by a person, or which a person has a bona fide intention to use in commerce . . . to identify the services of one person, including a unique service, from the services of others and to indicate the source of the services, even if that source is unknown" (Trademark Act of 1946).

In effect, the function of a service mark is to identify an activity performed by one business for another person, rather than for itself, either for compensation or otherwise. For example, "Hertz" identifies automobile rental services (Hertz Corporation); "McDonald's" identifies restaurant services (McDonald's Corporation); "NBC" identifies television broadcasting services (National Broadcasting Company, now owned by General Electric); "Exxon" identifies gasoline service station services (Exxon

Corporation); and "Sears" identifies department store services (Sears, Roebuck & Co.).

The Trademark Act states that a name or symbol is used as a certification mark when it is used to certify regional or other origin, material, mode of manufacture, quality, accuracy, or other characteristics of products or services, or that the work or labor on them was performed by members of a union or other organization. For example, "Washington" and an apple design certifies that apples were grown in the State of Washington; "UL" certifies that electrical products meet standards set by Underwriter's Laboratories, Inc.; and "United States Garment Workers of America" certifies that clothing was made by members of the United States Garment Workers of America union.

The Trademark Act provides for three kinds of collective marks: collective trademarks, collective service marks, and collective membership marks. It states that a mark is a collective trademark or service mark when it is used to identify products or services by members of a cooperative, association, or other collective group or organization, or which a cooperative, association, or other collective group or organization has a bona fide intention to use in commerce. A mark is a collective membership mark when it is used to indicate membership in a union, an association, or other organization. Examples of collective marks used to identify products and services are "PGA" for merchandise offered by members of the Professional Golf Association and the team symbols used by members of the National Hockey League to identify merchandise. Examples of collective membership marks are "The Best Western Motels," which indicates membership of motels in a national association; "Alpha Epsilon Phi" indicating membership in a fraternal organization; and "American Bar Association," indicating membership in an association of lawyers.

When a name or symbol identifies a business rather than the services offered by the business, the correct terminology for it is *corporate* or *trade* (assumed or fictitious) *name*. Whether it is a corporate or trade name depends on what it is used to identify and the way in which it is used.

A *corporate name* is the name under which a secretary of state grants a corporate charter. It is the name of the corporation.

A name other than its chartered name that a corporation uses to identify itself is called its *trade name*. For example, "Penstemmon Music" is the trade name of Music in Motion, Inc.

The term *trade name* means any name a business uses to identify itself. Sometimes a trade name is referred to as an *assumed name* or as a *fictitious name*.

When a name is used to identify the products and/or services of a business as well as the business itself, it functions as a trademark or service mark in one role and as a corporate or trade name in another. For example, the name "Coca-Cola" functions as a trademark when it identifies a soft drink and as a corporate name when it identifies the Coca-Cola Company. "Mountain Bell" functions as a service mark when it identifies telephone communication services and as a trade name when it identifies U.S. West Communications Corporation.

Even though a trademark, service mark, corporate name, and trade name differ in terms of what each identifies, the legal rights and protection are the same.

Protection for a mark exists by reason of a federal statute known as the Trademark Act of 1946 (Trademark Act or the Lanham Act), state statutes, the common law, or all three.

Subject to some exceptions, the business that first uses an identifying name or symbol is entitled to this protection. Under certain circumstances, however, two or more businesses may use the same name or symbol, and each is entitled to protection for it with limitations.

Note that the owner of a name or symbol is the business that uses it, not the person who creates it, in contrast to patent and copyright ownership, in which the creator is usually the initial owner of rights, not the user of the patented invention or copyrighted work.

As discussed in Chapters 2, 3, and 4, protection for a mark is available only for names and symbols that are distinctive. Generic names and symbols cannot be protected, and those that are descriptive may be difficult to protect.

The owner of a protected name or symbol possesses the exclusive right to use it to identify particular products or services and/or the owner's business. This right includes the right to prevent others from using a confusingly similar name or symbol to identify the same or similar products, services, or business enterprises.

Proprietary rights in a name or symbol become effective immediately and automatically on the date it is first used to identify a product, service, or business. They last as long as the name or symbol is continuously used in this way.

Although the user of a name or symbol does not have to register it with a government agency to acquire rights, a government agency's approval is usually necessary to use a corporate or trade name and to register a mark.

Generally, corporate and trade names are registered at the state level with the Office of the Secretary of State. At the local level they may be recorded with a county recorder and/or an agency that deals with tax matters, such as the Department of Revenue.

Marks can also be registered at the state level with the Office of the Secretary of State. At the federal level, marks may be registered with the USPTO.

No one governmental agency has exclusive jurisdiction over trademark subject matter, the rights associated with it, and the protection to which it is entitled. Federal law does not preempt state and local law in this area. Both the federal government and states can enact and enforce trademark laws.

Currently, the two systems in the United States under which rights in a mark can be obtained and enforced are the Trademark Act, which is the federal statute, and law enunciated by court decisions (common law) and by virtue of state statutes.

The existence of both federal and state protection for a mark does not seem to pose any significant problems because most state trademark laws are modeled on the federal law. The result is a great deal of uniformity in trademark laws throughout this country.

The notation ® is used to give notice that a mark has been federally registered by the U.S. Patent & Trademark Office. The notation "Registered United States Patent & Trademark Office" or "Reg. U.S. Pat. & Tm. Off." may be used in lieu of the ® symbol. None of these notations should be used for marks that have not been federally registered. If one of them is not used in connection with a federally registered mark, however, some of the benefits of federal registration will be lost.

The notation "TM" or "SM" may be used in close association with a mark that has not been federally registered. However, its use is not required, and no established rules prescribe the manner of its use. Nonetheless, this notation is commonly used to advise others of a claim of rights in a mark.

No notation is used to denote that a name or symbol functions as a trade name. The designations *corporation*, *incorporated*, *corp.*, *inc.*, *company*, and *limited* are commonly used in connection with a corporate name.

PROTECTION FOR IDEAS

These areas of law provide no protection for the company's idea of creating music with a specific tempo and pitch for sale to individuals who listen to music while exercising or running. Rather, protection for this idea is limited to the individual elements used to implement the idea and only for the specific way they are expressed and embodied.

As indicated previously, patent protection may apply to the equipment used to produce the phonograph records, tapes, and discs, the configuration of the cassette, and the chemical compound for the tape. Copyright protection may be available for the music, advertising and promotional material, packaging, and computer software program. Trademark protection may be relied on for the names and symbols used by the company.

Concerning the idea itself, the company can maintain it as a secret, or can impose contract limitations on its use by others through trade secret, know-how, confidential disclosure, or nondisclosure agreements. However, other companies can compete by creating and marketing the same kind of music for people who exercise and run. This is permissible as long as the company's music and advertising and promotional material are not copied, its patented subject matter is not used without its permission, and the same or confusingly similar names and symbols are not used to identify competing products.

2
Selection: Preliminary Considerations

The names and symbols a business uses may be its most valuable asset. They can determine everything from market share, amount of retail shelf space, and the selling price for the products and services they identify to the potential for one business to merge with or be acquired by another.

Names and symbols often are the main way the public and the trade readily identify and distinguish the products and services of one business from those of another. In many instances, names and symbols are the only way to identify and distinguish them.

In this book, *symbol* means a pictorial or graphic design or a logogram that may be used as a mark. *Name* means the word or words a business uses to identify itself (corporate or trade name), whether or not it is legally protected. Sometimes *name* also includes *mark*, which means here a trademark, service mark, certification mark, or collective mark that qualifies for legal protection, whether or not it is registered with a state and/or the USPTO. Later in the book, when *mark* is used to discuss registration, it can be interpreted to include a word or symbol that also can be used as a name. *Word* is used to mean a word that may or may not be eligible for federal registration and legal protection as a name or mark.

Ideally, you should select a word or symbol that can be legally protected and used without infringing anyone's rights. There-fore, it should be distinctive or capable of becoming distinctive, and it should not be the same as or similar to a name or symbol used by anyone else for the same kind of products or services.

Because names and symbols can be key factors in the success of a business, in the process of selecting them pay careful atten-tion to their strengths and weaknesses from a legal as well as a marketing viewpoint. They should not be routinely adopted. Give the same care and consideration to your names and sym-bols that you give to selecting other major assets.

Carelessly selecting a name or symbol is asking for negative legal and financial consequences. You may find that you cannot register it and cannot stop others from using it. You may find that the right to use the name or symbol may be challenged, lim-ited, or lost. Each of these consequences can be disastrous.

The costs of asserting or defending an infringement claim can be immense. If the right to use a name or symbol is limited or lost, a business may no longer be able to benefit from the repu-tation associated with it, even though it can continue to offer the same products and/or services under a modified or different name or symbol.

A name change by Adolph Coors Company for one of its beers demonstrates some of the problems that can happen. Solely for marketing reasons and not because of a name challenge by another party, Coors changed the name of its flagship beer from Banquet Beer to Original Draft. Consumers in at least two states somehow thought that the beer itself had changed. Sales slumped and Coors had to undertake an informational campaign to tell consumers that the beer was the same and only the name had been changed.

At the time a name or symbol is selected for use as a corporate or trade name, as a mark, or both as a name and mark, questions such as the following should be asked:

- Are certain kinds of words and symbols better than others from a protection standpoint?

- Can a procedure be followed to learn whether another business uses the same name or symbol?
- Does incorporation under a name or symbol or registration of it as a mark mean that no one else can use it?
- If another business uses the same name or symbol but has not incorporated under it or registered it, can someone else use it?
- What effect does another business's use of the same name or symbol in a particular city or state have on someone else's right to use it in a different geographic area?
- What effect does another business's use of the same name or symbol for particular products or services have on someone else's right to use it for different products or services?
- Will the business be adversely affected if the right to use the name or symbol is lost or geographically restricted because of a conflict with another business?

The first question concerns selection of a name or symbol that is eligible for protection. It is answered in this and the next two chapters. The other questions concern finding a name or symbol that is not confusingly similar to one used by another party and are dealt with in later chapters.

ELIGIBILITY FOR LEGAL PROTECTION

When determining the kinds of words and symbols that are preferable from a protection standpoint the standards used by the USPTO and the courts are the best reference. State agencies that register business names and marks, typically the Office of the Secretary of State, have similar standards.

As a minimum, standards used to determine eligibility for federal trademark registration require that a name or symbol be capable of identifying a product or service and that it not be confusingly similar to a federally registered mark. Generally, state standards are not as restrictive for corporate and trade names. They usually require only that the name not be the same as or deceptively similar to an existing name registered by the state.

Although state statutes concerning registration of marks typically require that the name or symbol be capable of identifying a product or service, as required for legal protection and federal registration, states do not seem to make a practice of strictly applying these statutes. As a result, most states allow registration of names or symbols as corporate and trade names and as marks that are not eligible for legal protection.

DISTINCTIVENESS

Distinctiveness is a focal point of this chapter. The standards of confusing similarity and deceptive similarity are discussed in Chapter 5.

For purposes of unfair competition law, a name or symbol is distinctive if it can be associated by relevant members of the public or trade with one source. They do not have to be able to identify the source. Relevant members of the public or trade are those individuals to whom the product or service is directed. For example, relevant members of the public and trade for a dessert food product are consumers and food distributors. If they associate "Jell-O" gelatin dessert with one source, then "Jell-O" is distinctive, even though they do not know that the source of the dessert is General Foods Corporation.

A name or symbol may be inherently distinctive when used in connection with a particular product or service. It can be immediately protected at the time of first use. In many but not all cases, a name or symbol that is not inherently distinctive may acquire distinctiveness as a result of long and/or widespread use in connection with the product or service. A name or symbol that becomes distinctive as a result of use will be protected at the time it becomes distinctive.

A business that desires federal registration and legal protection of a name or symbol it uses, must select something that is inherently distinctive or that can become distinctive. Whether a name or symbol possesses this attribute is determined by the particular products or services with which it is used. The USPTO and courts always evaluate names and symbols in reference to the products and services. For this reason, a potential name or symbol should never be considered in the abstract.

Courts and the USPTO have established four major categories for words and symbols in terms of distinctiveness and legal protection. Words and symbols in the generic category are given no protection. Those in the arbitrary/coined category and in the suggestive category are given the most protection. Those in the descriptive category can be given protection once they become distinctive.

Generic words and symbols are not and cannot become distinctive. Therefore, they cannot be legally protected or federally registered. However, as is the case with descriptive, geographic, and laudatory terms, a word or symbol that is generic for one product or service may be inherently distinctive when used for a different kind. For example, *seats* may be generic for chairs, couches, or bleachers but distinctive for travel reservation services, and *bundt* is generic for a type of ring cake but inherently distinctive for x-ray examination equipment.

Regardless of whether they are or may become distinctive, certain words and symbols cannot be federally registered. (For purposes of categorizing them they would fall in the generic category.) These include words or symbols that are immoral, scandalous, or deceptive, that disparage or falsely suggest, or that comprise the flag of a nation or state. Whether words not eligible for federal registration can be registered in a state and legally protected there depends on how the law is applied by the state where registration or protection is sought.

Arbitrary and coined words and symbols are inherently distinctive. They qualify for legal protection and federal registration at the time they are first used as marks. Arbitrary words and symbols are those whose meaning has no significance in relation to the products or services they identify ("Camel" for cigarettes and "Tide" for laundry detergent). Coined words and symbols are invented for the purpose of being used as a mark and are meaningless ("Exxon" for petroleum products and "Kodak" for film).

Suggestive words and symbols, which are those that require imagination, thought, and perception to reach a conclusion about the nature of the products or services they identify, are usually inherently distinctive when first used. They also qualify for legal protection and federal registration from the outset.

In almost all cases, words and symbols in the descriptive category are not inherently distinctive. The descriptive category is a catchall for descriptive words and symbols, surnames, laudatory expressions, colors, trade dress, product and packaging configurations, and nonutilitarian elements of products that are not inherently distinctive. However, through widespread and long use, the items in this category may become distinctive and therefore qualify for legal protection and all the benefits of federal registration.

A word or symbol that is descriptive, geographic, or laudatory for a particular kind of product or service may be inherently distinctive at the time of first use in connection with a different kind of product or service. For example, *fullview* is descriptive for vehicle rearview mirrors, *Virginia* is a geographic term for tobacco, and *exquisite* is laudatory for wearing apparel. Nevertheless, *fullview*, *Virginia*, and *exquisite* are inherently distinctive at first use for candy bars, nylon stockings, and automobile motor oil, respectively.

STRONG VERSUS WEAK NAMES AND SYMBOLS

The extent of legal protection for a name or symbol depends on whether it is weak or strong. Strength is measured in terms of the degree of distinctiveness a name or symbol possesses. Highly distinctive ones are considered strong, and those with little distinctiveness are considered weak.

Strong names and symbols are entitled to a broad scope of protection. Rights in them will be enforced against identical or similar names or symbols used for the same, similar, and often unrelated products and services.

At the other extreme, legal protection for weak names and symbols is narrow. Ordinarily, rights in them will be enforced only against identical or substantially similar names or symbols that are used for the same products or services.

Arbitrary, coined, and suggestive names and symbols are strong. Surnames as well as descriptive names and symbols are weak until such time as they acquire distinctiveness. Commonly used names and symbols also are considered weak. Strong and weak names and symbols are discussed further in Chapters 5 and 10.

THE EFFECT OF REGISTRATION

Registration of a word or symbol as a name or mark does not necessarily mean it is entitled to legal protection or that its use cannot be successfully challenged. Conversely, a refusal to register a mark by the USPTO or a state agency does not necessarily affect your right to use it.

Similarly, the right to use a name or symbol does not necessarily mean that it can be registered in a state or by the USPTO. For example, a generic word or symbol may be used as a name, but it cannot be federally registered.

In the United States, the right to register and the right to use are not synonymous. The Trademark Act and most, if not all, state trademark registration statutes are concerned only with the right to register. The right to use is a separate but related determination usually made by the courts in connection with infringement lawsuits.

State registration of your name or symbol is an indication that using it is acceptable in that state from the standpoint of the state agency. However, state registration does not mean that your use of a name or symbol cannot be successfully challenged in a civil action in that state or elsewhere on the ground that it should not be legally protected or for other reasons.

A statutory prohibition against registration of a word or symbol as a corporate or trade name is an indication that it cannot be legitimately used as such, but it does not mean that it cannot be legitimately used as a mark.

As discussed in Chapter 7, the name under which a corporation is formed or does business must be approved by the state agency responsible for incorporation. Often a trade name used by a business must also be approved. A state shows its approval by allowing incorporation under the name, accepting a change of name request, or registering a trade name. Therefore, a case can be made that the use of a name is unlawful and cannot be legally protected if it is not approved by the state as a corporate or trade name. You will have to check the law in the state or states where you want to use the word or symbol to determine if you need to acquire approval for it in this way.

State registration is not ordinarily required as a condition of using a word or symbol as a mark. Consequently, the absence of a registration for it is not an indication that it cannot be legitimately used and/or legally protected. Again, if you have a question about this for a word or symbol in this category, you should check the specific state law.

Note that the USPTO maintains both the Principal Register and the Supplemental Register for purposes of federal registration. To be registered on the Principal Register, a word or symbol must be inherently distinctive or have acquired distinctiveness. If it is not distinctive but is capable of becoming distinctive and no prohibition against registration is applicable, it may be registered on the Supplemental Register. Registration is discussed in Chapter 8.

3
Nonprotected Words and Symbols

$\mathbf{A}$s a general rule, most English and foreign language words and symbols are available for every business's use to refer to itself and to its products and services. However, depending on how a business uses them, some are not eligible for federal registration or legal protection. Some are not eligible for federal registration but may be legally protected. Some cannot be used lawfully, and some cannot be used without violating someone else's proprietary rights.

1. Words or symbols that function as the common name of or depict a product or service (that is, are generic) belong to everyone. No one can exclusively appropriate, federally register, or legally protect them.
2. The Trademark Act prohibits federal registration of words and symbols that are deceptive, disparaging, scandalous, or misleading. Depending on the circumstances surrounding their use, courts may or may not grant legal protection to them.
3. Certain words and symbols are protected by federal statutes that reserve their use to particular organizations and agencies. Others cannot lawfully use them.
4. Finally, businesses have exclusively appropriated many

words and symbols as names and marks for their own particular products and services. Unauthorized use by others may constitute infringement.

This chapter discusses words and symbols in the first three categories. Those in the last category are covered in Chapter 5.

GENERIC WORDS AND SYMBOLS

Public policy allows the unrestricted use of words and symbols that are generic for a product or service. In this capacity they function as the common descriptive name for the product or service and communicate characteristic information about it. Therefore, they must be available for everyone's use without limitation.

Because of this policy, the USPTO will not federally register generic words or symbols, although the Trademark Act does not expressly prohibit their registration. Moreover, courts will not give them legal protection and thus permit them to be exclusively appropriated. If the law were otherwise, everyone's right to free use of many words and symbols would be lost in one way or another.

For example, if a business that makes and sells pizza were entitled to claim exclusive rights in and appropriate *pizzeria* to communicate characteristic information about its activities, no other business that engages in the same activity would be able to use this word to tell the public what it does without being successfully challenged by the first user. As a consequence, all other businesses engaged in the same activity would be required to use different words to describe what they do. As each adopted a word to fulfill this function, that word would be preempted from our language. As a result, fewer and fewer words would be available to communicate information about a particular product or service. The net effect would be the absence of a generally accepted common descriptive name for a pizzeria or any other product or service.

Despite this fundamental law that generic words and symbols cannot be federally registered or legally protected, no definition for the word generic has been provided in the Trademark Act or universally adopted by the courts. As a general rule, a generic word or symbol is agreed to be one that members of the relevant public and trade use to refer (or understand that it refers) to a particular kind of product, service, or business activity without regard to its source and without regard to who makes, markets, or offers it. It is also generic if it refers to the group or class within which any of these things falls.

In effect, whether a word or symbol is generic is directly dependent on the meaning an identifiable group of people give it. For example, in this country bicycle, pharmacy, and the skull and crossbones symbol, respectively, mean a particular kind of two-wheeled self-propelled vehicle, a place where medicine is dispensed, and poison. Vehicle, store, and chemical compound signify the class of products and services within which each falls. When bicycle, pharmacy, and poison are used in connection with playing cards, an appliance repair shop, or a musical instrument, they are not generic because the relevant public does not give these meanings to these words.

A dictionary is a starting point for determining whether a word or symbol is generic from the viewpoint of the relevant public and trade. Court and USPTO determinations of genericness include consideration of dictionary definitions.

A definition that covers the product, service, or activity is a good indication that the word or symbol is generic. However, if the word or symbol lacks a definition, it still could be generic. Other factors that should be and are considered include uses of the word or symbol in consumer and trade publications and polls and surveys of relevant sectors of the public and trade. If a relevant segment of the public and/or trade considers a word or symbol generic, although other segments do not, it may nonetheless be considered generic.

Although the courts and USPTO give a fair amount of weight to dictionary definitions, a successful argument could be made that a definition is not determinative of genericness. If a substantial portion of the relevant public or trade can be shown to be unfamiliar with the meaning of the word or symbol as given by the definition even though it encompasses the product or service, the word or symbol might be protected.

Nevertheless, you are in a much better position if you select a word or symbol whose definition does not encompass the product or service. This tactic usually works, but not always.

A name or symbol may become generic because a sizable portion of the relevant public commonly uses it as the generally accepted name for a product or service. This common usage may be enough to make it generic without a dictionary definition even though it serves to identify the source of a product or service to a small segment of the public. Typically, a word or symbol that is inherently distinctive or capable of becoming distinctive loses or does not attain this status because it is commonly used as the name for the product or service.

Escalator (power-driven stairs), *cellophane* (transparent cellulose sheet), *kerosene* (flammable hydrocarbon oil), *linoleum* (floor covering), and *lollipop* (candy on a stick) became generic because they were commonly used as the names for these products. "Xerox" (process for copying), "Kleenex" (cleansing tissues), and "Jell-O" (gelatin dessert) may become generic by virtue of common usage if the relevant public continues to treat them as generic product names.

When a product or service is unique when first introduced and no known or generally accepted generic word exists for it, the mark used for it may be the only word used to refer to it. Under such circumstances, the potential for the mark to become generic is good because the relevant public and trade use it as the generic designation when referring to the product or service without regard to who makes, markets, or offers it. Also, a mark may become the generic designation for products or services when it is used to the exclusion of the generic designation or because it is easier to remember or pronounce than the generic designation. For example, no generally accepted descriptive designation is available for the cheese product identified by the mark "Liederkranz" so this mark is always used to refer to that product and could become generic for it. Many people use the mark "Popsicle" for frozen confections without regard to who

makes them because the generic designation "quiescently frozen confection" is cumbersome to use and hard to remember.
Similarly, although *aspirin* once functioned as a mark in the
United States, it is now a generic designation because nothing
was comparable and consumers found the chemical name *sali-
cylic acid* difficult to remember and pronounce.

Although a word or symbol may become generic through
common usage, making a generic word or symbol distinctive
and protectible is virtually impossible. Misspelling or hyphen-
ating a generic word does not make it eligible for legal protection, and neither does using an accepted shortened version of it.
Similarly, a foreign language word is generic if its English language equivalent is generic and vice versa. "Brezdel" is generic
for hot soft pretzels. It is a misspelling of *bretzel* which is an
alternate word for pretzel. "Al-kol" is generic for rubbing alcohol. "Ha-lush-ka" is generic for noodles because it is a variation
of the Hungarian word *haluska* meaning egg noodle. "Vinka" is
generic for wine; it is a variation of the Polish word *winka* which
means wine. "Cheno" is generic for chenodeoxycholic acid.

Ordinarily, a visual representation or image of a product or
service used in connection with it is generic. A picture of a sewing machine is generic when it is used in connection with sewing machines, and so is the representation of peanuts used on
packaging for peanuts. A drawing of a man painting the side of
a building is generic for paint-contracting services.

Initials are generic when they are generally known to stand
for generic words and are used in connection with the product
or service which the word means. "PVC" is generic when used
in connection with polyvinyl chloride and so is "CB" in reference to citizen band radios.

Combining two generic words to create a single new word
does not necessarily create a nongeneric expression. It is generic
if the resulting combination conveys a specific meaning recognized by the relevant public as a common name for the product,
service, or activity; otherwise, it is not. *Surgicenter* is generic for
an outpatient surgery center and *turbodiesel* is generic for diesel
engines combined with turbo components.

Although a generic word or symbol cannot be legally protected, function as a mark, or be federally registered with the USPTO, it may be used as a corporate and trade name. Many states allow such a word or symbol to be registered as a mark. However, one business is not entitled to use it to the exclusion of others' use when it is the common name for the product or service. Consequently, it has little or no chance of becoming a valuable business asset.

For example, "Paint Products, Inc." is a generic name for a business that sells paint products. It may be used by the business as its name and registered as a corporate or assumed name with a state agency, if it is not registered by another business. However, this name cannot be exclusively appropriated, legally protected, or federally registered as a name for a paint products business because it is generic.

PROHIBITED WORDS AND SYMBOLS

Section 2(a) of the Trademark Act prohibits federal registration of a mark that

> consists of or comprises immoral, deceptive, or scandalous matter; or matter which may disparage or falsely suggest a connection with persons, living or dead, institutions, beliefs, or national symbols, or bring them into contempt, or disrepute.

Therefore, you cannot federally register a word or symbol in this category.

If not prohibited by state law in the state where you desire registration, a word or symbol in this category may be registered as a corporate or trade name and/or as a mark. Possibly, it may also be used and legally protected as a name and/or mark. To learn whether this is the case, check the state law.

Dictionary definitions and the public's understanding of a word or symbol's meaning are used to determine whether it is immoral, deceptive, or scandalous, or disparages or falsely suggests. The USPTO uses these standards to determine if a word or symbol can be registered; it takes into consideration the product or service with which it is used.

Immoral and Scandalous Matter

Scandalous matter is variously defined as something that would be shocking to the sense of propriety, disgraceful, and offensive to morality. Consequently, in determining whether a word or symbol is scandalous, it is considered in the context of the moral values and conduct that society has deemed to be appropriate at the time. *Immoral matter* is evaluated by the same standard.

Case law indicates that a word or symbol may be immoral or scandalous even though a majority of the public does not consider it to be so. It can fall within this class if a substantial composite of the general public believes it to be immoral or scandalous.

Some words and symbols that have been held to be scandalous are "Madonna" for wine (1938); "Dowager Queen" for ladies' underwear (1938); "Agnus Dei" for safes (1943); "Messia" for alcoholic beverages (1968); "Bubby Trap" for brassieres (1971); and a photograph of a nude man and woman lying together and kissing for a newsletter devoted to social and interpersonal relationship topics (1979). However, "Week-End Sex" for a magazine (1974), a caricature of an unclothed man sitting and contemplating the unseen portion of his genitalia, for a medical device (1975), and "Badass" for stringed musical instrument bridges (1978) were not found to be scandalous.

Deceptive Matter

A word or symbol is *deceptive* when an essential and material element is misrepresented, is distinctly false, and is the element the relevant public relies on in seeking one product or service rather than another; that is, it is deceptive if it leads purchasers to believe they are obtaining something different than what they actually obtain.

How a majority of the relevant public regards a word or symbol determines whether it is deceptive, not its impact on ignorant or gullible persons. The reactions of the latter should not be persuasive because, as noted by one court:

> It is also theoretically conceivable that here and there a person may exist who assumes that there is cream in cream of tartar; milk in the pharmaceutical known as milk of magnesia; that there are edible sponges in sponge cake; that the confection known as Eskimo Pie is a pie that is either made by Eskimos or a formula obtained from Eskimos; and that there is soda in soda water.

A three part test is used by the USPTO to determine whether a word or symbol is deceptive. It is deceptive and cannot acquire distinctiveness if affirmative answers are given to all three questions.

1. Is it misdescriptive of the character, quality, function, composition, or use of the product or service?
2. If so, are prospective customers likely to believe that the misdescription actually describes the product or service?
3. If so, is the misdescription likely to affect the decision to purchase?

Affirmative answers to these questions resulted in findings that the following words are deceptive: "Syrup of Figs" for a laxative medicinal preparation that did not contain figs; "Sheffield" for stoves and ranges not made in Sheffield, England; "Dutch Boy" for flower bulbs not from Holland; "Limoges" for chinaware not made in Limoges, France; and "Lovee Lamb" for automotive seat covers made of synthetic fiber. The opposite finding was made with respect to: "Holeproof" for hosiery because no one would believe that holes would not develop in it; "Nuhide" for dungarees because it is a matter of common knowledge that they are made exclusively from cotton; and "Nippon" for radios, television sets, and tape recorders because they are made in Japan.

Matter That Disparages or Falsely Suggests

The ordinary meanings for *disparage*, *falsely suggest*, *contempt*, and *disrepute* are used to evaluate words and symbols in reference to persons, institutions, beliefs, or national symbols. Disparaging matter degrades them, falsely suggestive matter is misleading about them, contemptuous matter creates a strong dislike for them, and disreputable matter disgraces them.

The relevant public's understanding of a word or symbol in reference to a specific product or service determines whether it conveys any of these meanings. If it does, the word or symbol falls within this prohibited category.

The history of this particular prohibition suggests that its purpose is to protect a person's rights of privacy and publicity, an institution's reputation, and respect for national symbols. Case law and legislative history appear to be silent regarding what constitutes and is intended to be protected with respect to beliefs.

Persons intended to be protected include natural persons, living and dead, as well as persons recognized in law, such as partnerships, corporations, and associations. However, the prohibiton is probably not applicable to a deceased person whose survivors cannot assert the right of publicity.

The person or institution does not have to be well known, and the full or correct name need not be used. If a nickname or other designation is generally known by the public at large, its use may constitute a false suggestion.

The University of Notre Dame was not able to prevent a food business from using "Notre Dame" to identify cheese because the university could not show that it was known for such products. French fashion designer Isabelle Canova was unsuccessful in challenging another person's federal registration of "I. Canova" because the USPTO concluded she did not allege facts that her name was of sufficient fame. However, the USPTO refused to register the "National Intelligence Academy" as a mark for educational services on the ground that it falsely suggests a connection with the U.S. government. Federal registration was also refused for "U.S. Bicentennial Society" as a mark for ceremonial swords because it was held to suggest falsely a connection with the federal government.

Case law indicates that the term *national symbol* includes anything that by its appearance and sound immediately suggests to a person the name of the country for which the symbol stands. National symbols are said to be more enduring in time than government agencies and departments. They conjure up a country as a whole.

"U.S.," "Uncle Sam," the Statue of Liberty, an American or bald eagle, and a hammer and sickle were all found to be national symbols. In contrast, "Apollo," "OSS," (Office of Strategic Services), "House of Windsor," "The Union Jack," and "Boston Tea Party" were not found to be national symbols.

Flags, Coats of Arms, or Other Insignia

Section 2(b) of the Trademark Act is an absolute prohibition against federal registration of a mark that

> consists of or comprises the flag or coat of arms or other insignia of the United States, or of any State or municipality, or of any foreign nation, or any simulation thereof.

This prohibition is based on the thought that detracting in any way from the honor due these symbols is contrary to public policy. Whether this point of view is followed by the states can be determined by referring to the law of each state where a business desires to use a symbol in this category.

Case law indicates that *insignia* means emblems and devices used to represent national authority. Therefore, the category of prohibited symbols includes seals of local, state, and federal governments, including their departments, as well as the Great Seal of the United States and the Presidential Seal.

Federal registration is not possible for a symbol that literally reproduces or creates the impression of being the same as a flag, coat of arms, or other insignia. However, the possibility of federal registration is not so clear when some of the elements of a flag, coat of arms, or other insignia are included in a symbol.

If a symbol gives the appearance or effect or has the characteristics of a flag, coat of arms, or insignia, a persuasive argument
can be made that it is a simulation and cannot be federally registered. However, a symbol that contains individual features or
distorted elements that suggest one of these things can be federally registered.

The USPTO did not refuse registration of marks featuring an
eagle and shield design, a conglomeration of nondescript flags,
or a design combining representations of portions of the flags of
Denmark, Norway, and Sweden. Registration was refused, however, for a symbol simulating the flag of Italy, one that included
the Russian coat of arms, and another that closely resembled the
insignia of Great Britain.

Names, Portraits, and Signatures of Individuals

Section 2(c) of the Trademark Act prohibits federal registration
of a mark that

> consists of or comprises a name, portrait, or signature iden-
> tifying a particular living individual except by his written
> consent, or the name, signature, or portrait of a deceased
> President of the United States during the life of his widow,
> if any, except by the written consent of the widow.

The rationale for this prohibition is to protect the names of
living individuals and deceased presidents against commercial
exploitation by others. In effect, it is an attempt to safeguard an
individual's right of privacy. For this reason, it does not prohibit
federal registration of the names of deceased persons, except the
name of a deceased president under certain circumstances.
Ordinarily, the right of privacy terminates on an individual's
death.

Wyatt Earp, Davy Crockett, and Abraham Lincoln are the

names of individuals that can be federally registered. All are deceased and the widow of President Lincoln is no longer living. However, the USPTO refused registration of the name Eisenhower in 1973 when Mrs. Eisenhower was still alive.

In addition to full names, this prohibition is against federal registration of shortened names, nicknames, and pseudonyms, generally, without regard to how well known the individual is. If a person is not well known or known in reference to the product or service for which his or her name is used, the USPTO may not require that person's consent for federal registration of the name. For instance, the USPTO allowed registration of "Arnold Brand" for tomatoes without the written consent of an individual by the name of Arnold Brand. Nothing in its records indicated that Mr. Brand was engaged in a business involving the sale of such products.

Even though a deceased individual's name, portrait, or signature can be federally registered, note that the use of it may violate a legal right known as the right of publicity. If the right of publicity has attached to a deceased individual's name, portrait, or signature, unauthorized use may violate this right.

Unlike the right of privacy, the right of publicity can survive an individual's death. Various states have enacted statutes that recognize a posthumous right of publicity and grant protection to personality characteristics during the life and after the death of an individual. Also, this right may have a basis for protection under federal law through Section 43(a) of the Trademark Act, which provides that liability may arise for the use of a false designation of origin or any false description or representation, including words and symbols.

Right of publicity protection can be enforced by individuals and their families or estates when the individual's name, portrait, or signature is well known and has been commercially exploited during that person's life. For example, the unauthorized use of "Elvis Presley," "John Wayne," or "Lucille Ball" may violate the right of publicity possessed by the heirs or estates of these individuals.

NAMES AND SYMBOLS PROTECTED BY
FEDERAL STATUTES

"American Legion," "Smokey Bear," and the "Red Cross" insignia are examples of words and symbols protected by specific federal statutes. The unauthorized use of them is prohibited and may result in fines, imprisonment, or both.

Other words and symbols protected by statute are: American Symphony Orchestra League, American War Mothers, Big Brothers of America, Blinded Veterans Association, Blue Star Mothers of America, Board for Fundamental Education, Boy Scouts of America, Conference of State Societies, Coast Guard, Disabled American Veterans, Federal Home Loan Bank, FFA and Future Farmers of America, five interlocking rings (symbol), 4-H Club and emblem, Geneva Cross, Girl Scouts of America, Johnny Horizon, Ladies of the Grand Army of the Republic, Little League Baseball, National Conference on Citizenship, National Music Council, National Safety Council, National Woman's Relief Corps, Naval Sea Cadet Corps, Olympiad, Olympic, Red Cross, Sons of Union Veterans, Swiss Confederation Coat of Arms, United Spanish War Veterans, The United States Blind Veterans of the World War, and Veterans of Foreign Wars.

4

Protected Words and Symbols

All the words and symbols in the categories discussed in this chapter are eligible for federal registration and legal protection. However, some are preferable to others because of their immediate eligibility for federal registration on the Principal Register, the point in time when legal protection is available, and their strength in terms of protection.

Of the many approaches you can take to select a word or symbol for a business, product, or service, two are obvious. One is selecting the word or symbol first and then finding and learning about its category to determine how easy or difficult it may be to register and protect. The other approach is learning about each category first, deciding which includes the kind of word or symbol best suited for the contemplated business name or mark, and then selecting a word or symbol within the category.

Whatever approach you use, learning about distinctive words and symbols as well as one or more of the categories discussed in this chapter is inevitable. To make this process easier, the discussion of each category includes examples of the type of words and symbols it covers.

INHERENTLY DISTINCTIVE WORDS AND SYMBOLS

Inherently distinctive words and symbols are the best kind to use if you want a strong name or mark in terms of legal protection. As mentioned in Chapter 2, words and symbols in these categories are eligible for legal protection beginning on the day of first use, and they can be federally registered on the Principal Register without showing that relevant members of the public or trade associate them with a particular source. They can be suggestive, arbitrary, or coined.

Suggestive words and symbols are desirable because they can develop into strong names and marks. When first used, they are usually not entitled to a broad scope of protection. Until they become strong, rights in them will be enforced only against the same or substantially similar names or marks used in connection with the same or closely related products or services. Suggestive words and symbols are desirable from an advertising and marketing standpoint because they indirectly convey information about the products or services. Because they convey information, the relevant public may learn more from them about the products or services with which they are used than a word or symbol that has no meaning with respect to the product or service. Also, they may be more memorable than other kinds of words and symbols. This category is discussed more fully near the end of this chapter.

Arbitrary and coined words and symbols are desirable because they are strong names and marks at the outset. Unlike suggestive words and symbols, they do not directly or indirectly convey information. For this reason, they may not be desirable for advertising and marketing purposes when they are first used. However, balanced against this lack of information is the broad scope of protection to which they are entitled at first use. Rights in them will be enforced against similar as well as identical names and marks for the same or unrelated products or services. This category is discussed more fully at the end of this chapter.

WORDS AND SYMBOLS THAT CAN BECOME DISTINCTIVE

Words and symbols that have the potential to become distinctive are the next best kind to use. They are in the descriptive category, which includes words and symbols that are descriptive; deceptively misdescriptive; geographically descriptive; surnames; laudatory; grade, model, size, or style designations; nonfunctional trade dress, product and container configurations, architectural features of structures, and physical features of products; shapes; ornamentation; color; and sounds.

Legal protection for these kinds of words and symbols is not available if they are not distinctive. Similarly, they cannot be federally registered if they have not attained this status.

When first used in connection with products or services, words and symbols in this category are weak in terms of legal protection. Until they become distinctive it can be difficult to enforce rights in them. Even when a word or symbol in this category becomes distinctive, however, other businesses can use it for accurate and fair descriptions.

If a nondistinctive word or symbol becomes distinctive in reference to the products or services of one business, it is said to have lost its first meaning and acquired a "secondary meaning." When this occurs, the relevant public no longer views it primarily as a description, geographic indicator, surname, laudatory word, grade designation, trade dress, container, feature, shape, color, or sound (the first meaning). Instead, it is viewed as identifying the source of the product or service with which it is used (the secondary meaning). Secondary meaning is discussed further in the Chapter 6 section "Distinctiveness and Secondary Meaning."

DESCRIPTIVE WORDS AND SYMBOLS

Public policy allows everyone to use words and symbols freely to describe products and services accurately and fairly. Otherwise, depletion of our vocabulary would adversely affect the normal use of our language, as noted in the Chapter 3 discussion about generic words and symbols.

Section 2(e)(1) of the Trademark Act prohibits the USPTO from allowing Principal Register registration of words or symbols that merely describe products or services, although they may be registered on the Supplemental Register. Similarly, courts will not give them legal protection if they are not distinctive.

A word or symbol is descriptive if it immediately tells the relevant public about the qualities, features, function, purpose, use, components, ingredients, or characteristics of a product, service, or activity.

As mentioned previously, at the time a descriptive word or symbol becomes distinctive (acquires secondary meaning), it has a different function in the eyes of the relevant public. Instead of being viewed as describing the products or services of the business that uses it, the word or symbol is associated only with the particular products or services of that business. When secondary meaning is acquired in this way, the word or symbol may be exclusively appropriated, federally registered, and protected by that business. However, others have a right to continue using it in a purely descriptive sense for accurately and fairly describing their products and services. This use will not infringe anyone's exclusive rights. It is a defense to an infringement claim, as noted in the Chapter 12 section "Court Actions."

The policy of allowing free use of descriptive words and symbols applies whether they are descriptive in English or in a foreign language. If the English translation of a foreign word describes a product or service, it cannot be federally registered or legally protected. It is available for use by everyone as a product or service description.

"Le Sorbet" could not be federally registered as a mark for a restaurant that sells fruit ices on the ground that it is merely descriptive. It is the French language equivalent of "fruit ices." Similarly, registration of "Gasa" was refused as being merely descriptive of toilet paper. It is the Spanish language word for "gauze," which is a thin, transparent material. And "Selecta" was refused registration as a mark for beer because it is the Spanish language equivalent of "select," which describes a quality of beer.

Although this policy is observed by the USPTO and the courts, generally it is not followed by most state agencies. Typically, states permit registration of descriptive words and symbols as marks, corporate names, and trade names. However, state registration does not necessarily mean that legal protection is available. As discussed earlier, protection depends on whether a word or symbol has become distinctive, among other factors.

A determination of whether a word or symbol is descriptive is not made in the abstract. The specific products or services with which it is used and its possible significance in relation to them must be considered. Other factors that must be considered include the context in which it is used on labels, packages, and advertising material and the relevant public's likely reaction to it.

"Crushproof" is merely descriptive of a quality of cardboard boxes, just as "Sure Grip" describes a characteristic of nonskid coatings. "Breadspred" describes a function of jams and jellies, and "Apricot" describes a feature of fruit-scented dolls. "Parrot Jungle" is descriptive of a tourist attraction situated on lush-foliaged land that features parrots and other birds uncaged and in a natural habitat, much like a jungle. And "Lotsa Suds" is descriptive of a laundry detergent.

All qualities, features, functions, uses, ingredients, or characteristics of a product or service or only the most important of them do not have to be described for the word or symbol to be descriptive. Descriptiveness may be found when only one significant attribute is described.

Dictionary definitions and the meanings given by an identifiable segment of the public or trade come into play in determining descriptiveness, just as they do in determining whether a word or symbol is generic. The existence of nondescriptive meanings for a word or symbol will not preclude a finding of descriptiveness. Similarly, the existence of a word or symbol that may be more descriptive does not preclude a finding of descriptiveness for a different one.

If you have to go through mental gymnastics to reach the conclusion that a word or symbol is descriptive, it probably is not. If the descriptive meaning is obsolete or known only by a very small segment of the public, the word or symbol is also probably nondescriptive.

As is the case with generic words, misspelling a descriptive word will not convert it to one eligible for federal registration or legal protection. "Bikineez" is a phonetic equivalent of "bikinis" and merely descriptive of panty hose having characteristics of a bikini. Similarly, "Kwixstart," the phonetic equivalent of "quick start," is descriptive of electric storage batteries.

Federal registration and legal protection are also not available for generally known initials or abbreviations that may be readily recognized as shorthand notations for descriptive words. As an acronym for multiple listing service, "MLS" could not be federally registered for a boat listing service. Because "UV" stands for ultraviolet, it was refused registration as a mark for ultraviolet film. As a recognized abbreviation for "homogenized," "Homo" is ineligible for federal registration as a mark for milk.

Pictorial representations that describe a product or service are as descriptive as words that describe. Therefore, they cannot be federally registered on the Principal Register or protected by the courts. A graphic representation of a cue stick and ball describes billiard parlor services; a picture of a kneeling man driving a spike is descriptive of the manner of use of fertilizer sticks.

Numbers and letters that describe are also ineligible for Principal Register registration and legal protection. Therefore, "FM 107" is descriptive for radio broadcast services when the position for receiving the signal is 107 on the FM radio dial. The letter E superimposed on representations of wheat heads describes a toilet soap containing vitamin E, and "RDA" for food products is descriptive of them because it stands for "recommended daily allowance."

Combining descriptive words to form a new word may not prevent a finding of descriptiveness, even if the combination is not in a dictionary. The combined word is not registrable or protectible if it describes the product or service with which it is used. "Autofuse" is descriptive of fuses, "Sportscreme" describes a topical analgesic, and "Poopscoop" describes a hand-held collector to pick up dog excrement.

DECEPTIVELY MISDESCRIPTIVE WORDS AND SYMBOLS

As is the case with merely descriptive words and symbols, Section 2(e)(1) of the Trademark Act prohibits the USPTO from allowing a Principal Register registration of those that are deceptively misdescriptive in relation to the products or services they misdescribe. However, they can be registered on the Supplemental Register. This prohibition is against words or symbols that are deceptively misdescriptive, not against those that are merely misdesriptive.

Deceptively misdescriptive words or symbols can be registered in most states because the state agencies responsible for registration of marks do not strictly follow applicable state statutes. They might also be given legal protection, although not until they acquire distinctiveness.

Federal registration is possible on the Principal Register at the time a deceptively misdescriptive word or symbol becomes distinctive. Then the relevant public no longer views it as referring to the character, quality, or nature of the product, service, or activity with which it is used. Instead, it is viewed as indicating the source, even if the source is unknown. At this time it is said to have acquired secondary meaning.

A word or symbol is deceptively misdescriptive if it meets the following three-part test.

1. It conveys information about a particular product or service that creates a false impression that the product or service possesses certain attributes it does not have.
2. The relevant public is likely to believe the product or service possesses these attributes.
3. A decision to obtain the product or service is not likely to be based on the deceptive misdescription.

"Baked Tam" was found to be deceptively misdescriptive for a simulated ham product made of turkey. Similarly, "Crow-Tox" was held to be deceptively misdescriptive of a preparation for protecting seeds against birds that contains no poison.

A distinction is made between a word or symbol that is deceptively misdescriptive and one that is deceptive. It is deceptive if the relevant public's decision to obtain the product or service is likely to be based on the inaccurate information in a deceptive misdescription.

GEOGRAPHICALLY DESCRIPTIVE WORDS AND SYMBOLS

The USPTO and courts treat geographic words and symbols as descriptive designations. Typically, states do not take this position. As with descriptive words and symbols, states do not strictly follow applicable statutes and instead allow registration of geographically descriptive words and symbols as corporate and trade names and as marks without regard to distinctiveness.

A geographic word or symbol consists of the name of a continent, country, state, city, town, locality, region, area, river, body of water, mountain, or other geographic location, including nicknames and abbreviations for such places as well as maps and outlines of them. "North American," "U.S.," "Swisse," "West Coast," "Mid-West," "Bama," "Dixie," "Quaker State," "Lone Star," "Lackawana," "Elgin," "Columbia," "Cognac," "Gibraltar," "Antartica," "L.A.," a map of the United States, and an outline of the State of California are geographic words and symbols.

The general rule is that geographic words and symbols are free for use by everyone to the extent they indicate the geographic area where a product or service originates, is made, or where the maker or provider resides or has a place of business. Everyone conducting business in a particular geographic area has a legitimate interest in truthfully representing that their products or services originate from that area.

Federal registration on the Principal Register will be refused for words or symbols that are *primarily* geographically descriptive of products or services and nondistinctive. Similarly, registration will be refused for those that are nondistinctive and *primarily* geographically deceptively misdescriptive. Section 2(e)(2) of the Trademark Act sets forth these prohibitions but does not preclude registration of such words or symbols on the Supplemental Register.

Words or symbols that are geographic designations but not primarily geographically descriptive are eligible for federal registration and legal protection. This group includes designations that have minor or obscure geographic meanings not known to the average person, that have alternative nongeographic meanings, that cannot be associated with any specific geographic area, or that are areas not significant as areas of manufacture or commercial activity for the products or services with which they are used. Ordinarily, the legitimate interest of businesses in using these designations is not as great as for a geographic designation whose geographic meaning or products or services are generally known.

"Kem" is a geographic designation because it is the name of a river in Russia. As this meaning is not generally known, however, it should be entitled to registration on the Principal Register and legal protection. Similarly, "Jersey" is a geographic designation that is federally registrable and protectible because it also can mean a type of fabric, kind of knitted jacket, or breed of dairy cow. "Globe" and a pictorial representation of a globe are geographic designations, but they are not primarily geographically descriptive because they do not identify a particular geographic location. "Mt. Zion" is not primarily geographically descriptive of wine because this area is not known for wine.

The test for determining whether a geographic designation is primarily geographically descriptive consists of the following questions:

1. Does the designation immediately or primarily convey a geographic connotation?
2. Do the products or services with which it is used originate from that place?

If the answer to the first question is no, the designation is not primarily geographically descriptive. If the answer is yes and the products or services actually originate from the place named, the designation is primarily geographically descriptive.

"Paris" is primarily geographically descriptive for perfume because this kind of product is known to originate from that city. "Old Dominion" is primarily geographically descriptive for pipe tobacco. It is the nickname for the state of Virginia, whose largest crop is tobacco. Even though "Harwell" is not a well-known place, it is primarily geographically descriptive for nucleonic instruments because it is well known for them.

If the designation immediately suggests a geographic connotation but the products or services do not originate from there, the designation is either primarily geographically deceptively misdescriptive or deceptive.

A geographic designation is deceptive if it is primarily geographically descriptive and if its use, either planned, designed, or implied, is calculated to deceive the public as to the geographic origin of the products or services. Deception occurs because the designation bestows on products or services characteristics they do not possess that increase their salability. Deceptive geographic designations cannot be federally registered under any circumstances or legally protected.

"California Mix" is primarily geographically deceptively misdescriptive for a mixture of dried fruit and nuts not originating from California. "American Beauty" is primarily geographically deceptively misdescriptive for sewing machines of Japanese origin. However, "Sheffield" is deceptive if used on cutlery made in the United States because Sheffield is an English city renowned for its cutlery.

When words and symbols that are primarily geographically descriptive or primarily geographically deceptively misdescriptive become distinctive for a business's products or services, they are eligible for Principal Register registration and legal protection by that business. As with descriptive words or symbols, however, others can continue to use them to describe accurately and fairly the geographic origin of their products or services. As long as they are used by others in a descriptive sense and not as marks, they will not infringe exclusive rights. Such use is a defense to an infringement claim as noted in the Chapter 12 section "Court Actions."

If "San Francisco" becomes distinctive for T-shirts manufactured by a business in San Francisco, other T-shirt companies in that city can continue to use this geographic designation to indicate where their products originate. They cannot use it as a mark for their products without infringing the rights of the business that made it distinctive.

The geographic meaning of a word or symbol can be diluted by combining it with other matter to form a composite. If the resulting combination conveys a nongeographic meaning, it is immediately eligible for Principal Register registration and legal protection.

"Hawaiian Ices" for a frozen confection, "Royal Canadian" for ginger ale, and "English Leather" for men's toiletries are examples of composites whose meanings are neither primarily geographically descriptive nor primarily geographically deceptively misdescriptive.

SURNAMES

As a matter of public policy, every individual has a legitimate interest in and right to use his or her surname for a business he or she operates, whether the business is operated as a sole proprietorship, partnership, or corporation. However, this right is not absolute.

An individual is not entitled to use his or her surname if such use is likely to result in confusion and/or deception of the public. If an individual's surname is the same as that of another individual and both use it in connection with identical or similar products or services, the later user's right to use it may be restricted or prohibited. Typically, this limitation occurs when the surname has become distinctive and associated with the first user.

One way to restrict use is to require the later user to add dis-

tinguishing words to the surname. However, use will be prohibited if adding words to the surname does not protect the public
or when the later user is shown to be not acting in good faith
with respect to use of the surname.

To avoid confusion with another party's use of "Waterman"
for fountain pens, a later user of the surname was required to
use it as part of the composite "Arthur A. Waterman & Co., Not
Connected with the L.E. Waterman Co." A stricter limitation
was imposed on use of the surname Baker in connection with
chocolate. The later user was prohibited from using it as a mark
but was permitted to use it as part of the trade name "W.H.
Baker" to identify it as a manufacturer. A later user's use of the
surname Cole was prohibited altogether for pharmaceutical
products because a supplier had confused orders from it with
orders by an earlier user of "Cole" for the same products.

Surnames that have not become distinctive are treated the
same as merely descriptive and primarily geographically
descriptive words. The USPTO will not allow their registration
on the Principal Register and courts are not inclined to grant
legal protection to them.

Section 2(e)(3) of the Trademark Act prohibits Principal Register registration of a word that is primarily merely a surname,
but it does not bar federal registration of a nondistinctive surname on the Supplemental Register. As is the case with descriptive and geographic designations, states generally permit registration of surnames as corporate or trade names and as marks
without regard to distinctiveness.

Determining whether a word is primarily merely a surname
requires consideration of its principal significance to the relevant public when it is used in connection with a product or service. Telephone and other directories may be referred to in this
regard as well as dictionaries.

If the primary significance of a word is as a surname, it will
be regarded as primarily merely a surname even though it is
uncommon. Similarly, a word will be regarded as being primarily merely a surname if it has this significance but is combined
with a generic word or symbol. Furthermore, a word will be

regarded as a surname when it is recognized by the public as a surname even though initials are added to it. "Johnson," "Tiffany," and "Cellini" could be said to have primary significance as surnames as could "Sarby Clocks," "J.C. Higgins," and "S. Seidenberg & Co."

A word with a well-known meaning other than a surname will not be treated as a surname. In addition, if two surnames or a given name and surname are combined to form a composite, the combination probably will not be treated as primarily merely a surname.

"Douglas," "Cotton," and "Samson" have significance other than as surnames. Likewise, as a combination of surnames, "Schaub-Lorenz" is not considered primarily merely a surname, and neither is the full name "Andre Dallioux."

SLOGANS

Slogans, like words and symbols, are federally registrable on the Principal Register and entitled to legal protection if they are used as a mark to identify a product or service. They do not have to be unique, catchy, or rhyming to be marks. However, they cannot be registered or protected if they are generic in reference to the products or services with which they are used.

Descriptive slogans, whether in English or another language, must attain distinctiveness for Principal Register registration. Until that occurs, they may be registered on the Supplemental Register if they are capable of identifying products or services.

Ordinarily, descriptive slogans, like descriptive words and symbols, are viewed as conveying information about a product or service rather than as a source indicator. "Brand names for less" and "Why pay more" as references to retail store services are examples of the kind of slogans viewed as conveying information rather than functioning as marks. However, if they become distinctive like "This Bud's for you," "Ford has a better idea," and "Only her hairdresser knows," they can be registered on the Principal Register and given a broad scope of protection.

LAUDATORY TERMS

Laudatory words such as *best, super, finest, supreme,* and *pre-mium,* are treated the same as descriptive words and symbols. When used in reference to a product or service, they are perceived as praising it rather than identifying its source. Therefore, until distinctiveness is acquired, they are not eligible for Principal Register registration or legal protection. A word of this kind, even after becoming distinctive in reference to the products or services of a particular business, may be used by others in a nontrademark sense to describe accurately and fairly their products and services. Such use is a defense to an infringement claim, as noted in the Chapter 12 section "Court Actions."

ALPHABET LETTERS AND NUMBERS

Alphabet letters and numbers can be used as marks, federally registered, and protected if they are distinctive. The letters "G.E." function as a mark used to identify electrical appliances and other items, as does an ornamented letter W. In addition, "IBM" identifies business equipment, and "CBS" identifies broadcast services.

The number "501" identifies blue jeans, "3 in 1" is a federally registered mark for household oil, and "7-11" is a registered mark that identifies retail store services.

GRADE, MODEL, SIZE, OR STYLE DESIGNATIONS

Numbers, letters, words, or symbols that are used to differentiate among grade, model, size, or style designations or colors of products or services are deemed to be descriptive in that they describe the products or services relative to each other. This rule holds even when they are arbitrarily selected and do not directly refer to a characteristic or feature of a product or service.

As with other kinds of descriptive words and symbols, those

that function as grade, model, size, style, or color designations can be federally registered on the Principal Register and legally protected. To acquire this status, they must also be used as marks and acquire distinctiveness, even though they continue to fulfill their differentiation function.

The individual components of an alphanumeric series consisting of 71B, 72B, 73B through 78B, used by a business to differentiate the sizes of its electrical connectors, were treated as marks and granted protection on a showing of distinctiveness. Similarly, the designations "U3" and "U4" were shown to have become distinctive and therefore protected as marks for contact lenses of differing thickness that one business offered.

FUNCTIONAL VERSUS NONFUNCTIONAL FEATURES

Public policy holds that everyone has a right to use a product's trade dress or its configuration, the configuration of a product's container or packaging, the architectural features of a structure, and the physical features of a product and be free of others' proprietary rights claims if the features are functional and not protected by patent. However, if they are not protected by patent, are nonfunctional, are used as a source indicator (as a mark), and are distinctive, they or representations of them can be registered as marks on the Principal Register and legally protected.

No specific standard can uniformly and routinely determine whether trade dress, product and container configurations, architectural features of structures, or physical features of products are functional. Each fact situation must be considered individually. An affirmative answer to one or more of the following questions means that the trade dress, configuration, or feature is probably functional.

1. Will protection for the trade dress, configuration, or feature hinder competition or impinge upon the rights of others to compete effectively in selling the same or similar products?
2. Is the trade dress, configuration, or feature essential to the use or purpose of the product or affect its cost or quality?

3. Is the trade dress, configuration, or feature optimal in terms of engineering, economy of manufacture, or fulfilling a utilitarian function?
4. Is the trade dress, configuration, or feature substantially related to the product's value as a product?

If others must slavishly copy the trade dress, configuration, or feature used by one business in order to have an equally functional product, it is functional. If alternative appealing designs or presentations can be developed or the trade dress, configuration, or feature merely enables a business to market products more effectively, however, it is not functional. Likewise, it is not functional if it possesses some incidental functional aspects.

Trade Dress and Product Configuration

A product's overall design or appearance is referred to as its *trade dress*. Such features as size, shape, color or color combinations, texture, and graphics arranged together are considered as a whole rather than separately. If trade dress is nonfunctional, used as a mark, and distinctive, it may be registered and protected.

Hartford House Ltd. was able to protect as trade dress the overall appearance of its greeting cards comprising the following elements: a two-fold card containing poetry on the first and third pages; unprinted surfaces on the inside three panels; a deckle edge on the right side of the first page; a rough-edge stripe of color or wide stripe on the outside deckle edge of the first page; a high-quality, uncoated, textured art paper for the cards; fluorescent ink for some of the colors printed on the cards; lengthy poetry, written in free verse, typically appearing with a personal message; appearance of hand-lettered calligraphy on the first and third pages with the first letter of the words often enlarged; an illustration that wraps around the card and is spread over three pages, including the back of the card; and the look of the cards, primarily characterized by backgrounds of soft colors done with airbrush blends or light watercolor strokes, usually depicting simple contrasting foreground scenes superimposed on the background.

Similarly, Vuitton et Fils, S.A., federally registered and successfully asserted rights in a trade dress mark consisting of a design covering the entire surface of luggage, handbags, and related items. The mark is an arrangement of the initials "LV" superimposed one upon the other and surrounded by three floral symbols, all in a mustard color, on a brown background.

The trade dress of the following products has also been protected: Harlequin's paperback book cover design for a series of books consisting of a particular arrangement of components on a 6¾-inch glossy white background featuring specific pictorial and printed matter elements always in the same color combinations; and Service Ideas' color scheme for an insulated plastic beverage server in which the central shell of the server is one color and the top portion, lid, handle, and base portion are a common second color darker than the color of the central shell.

Product configurations protected as marks include: Zebco's profile of a closed-face spin-cast fishing reel consisting of a chrome, cone-shaped front cover, a stubby back cover, and a black and chrome finish; Good Industries' 21-inch-high beverage dispenser in the form of a replica of a 1920s-era gasoline pump; and Minnesota Mining & Manufacturing's triangular chemical cake used in a metal plating process.

Container Configurations

Principal Register registration and protection are also possible for a product's nonfunctional and distinctive container configuration or packaging if it is used as a source indicator.

The green Indian club–shaped bottle used by Perrier is protected as a mark for carbonated mineral water. A tear-shaped plastic container was granted protection as a mark for lemon juice although it possessed some functional attributes that did not dictate its configuration. Haig & Haig Limited can protect its pinch bottle as a mark for whiskey, and Mogen David's decanter-type bottle was found capable of being a mark for wine. Also, the configuration of a Texize trigger-activated spray container was found capable of being protected as a mark for household cleaners.

Architectural Features and Structures

Representations of architectural features of structures may be registered as marks on the Principal Register and legally protected if they are nonfunctional, used as a mark, and distinctive. If the features claimed as a mark comprise enough of the structure to constitute a building that houses the business that claims rights in them or otherwise primarily serve a utilitarian purpose, they are functional and are not protected. That they incidentally serve a functional purpose will not detract from their ability to be registered and protected.

The architectural features of Fotomat's freestanding kiosk structure were federally registered on the Principal Register and granted legal protection. They consist of a steeply pitched, overhanging, three-tiered, yellow roof on a rectangular base used to identify drive-up photographic developing services. Similarly, the McDonald's golden arches structure is federally registered on the Principal Register and legally protectible as a mark used to identify restaurant services. White Castle's building design, simulating a miniature castle with battlements, was granted legal protection as a mark identifying its restaurant services; and so was the orange-tiled roof and cupola structure of Howard Johnson restaurants for its services.

Physical Features of Products

A physical feature that has a defined shape and is placed at a specific location on a product can be registered as a mark on the Principal Register and legally protected if it is distinctive and used as a mark.

The rear pocket tab used by Levi Strauss & Co. is such a physical feature. It serves as a mark for blue jeans. Likewise, the statuette hood ornament and square-framed, vertically shuttered front grille used by Rolls-Royce Motors Limited are physical features that function as marks identifying a particular kind of automobile.

COMMON SHAPES

Common basic shapes such as circles, ovals, squares, triangles, bands, bars, stripes, diamonds, stars, and hearts are frequently used as background or borders for the display of words or symbols. However, they are not registrable as marks on the Principal Register or legally protected unless they are used as marks and are distinctive separate and apart from the material displayed within them. Similarly, if such shapes are not distinctive when used alone, they cannot be registered as marks or legally protected until they are used as marks and acquire distinctiveness.

To be distinctive, common shapes must be used prominently in relation to other material and be artistic or eye-catching enough to create an independent commercial impression. A curved-band design appearing at a specific location was granted protection as a mark for athletic shoes, as was a design of three parallel stripes placed on the sides of running shoes at the laces. Also found to be distinctive, registrable, and protectible were a red dot appearing on the heels of shoes, a red crown shape painted on the necks of bowling pins, and a blue band on a drum container.

ORNAMENTATION

Ornamental matter on a product can be registered as a mark on the Principal Register and legally protected if it is used primarily as a source indicator, even if it is incidentally decorative. The line between mere ornamentation and ornamentation that is merely an incidental quality is not always ascertainable. In contrast, ornamentation used primarily as an aesthetically pleasing decoration will be difficult if not impossible to register and protect as a mark.

The commercial impression created by ornamental matter, the manner in which its user promotes it, and practices of the trade are factors to consider in determining whether it functions as a mark.

The size, location, and dominance of ornamental matter on the product can have an effect on the commercial impression it creates. If it covers a large amount of surface area, the relevant public may view it as primarily decorative rather than as a mark.

Frequent advertising and promotional use and emphasis of ornamental matter as a mark for particular products may support a claim that it is a mark.

Ornamentation is commonly used as a mark for products in certain categories, such as clothing. Therefore, when ornamentation is used as a mark for a product in these categories, such as a T-shirt, it tends to be treated and accepted as a mark rather than being primarily decorative.

The display of "EXPO '74" across the front of a T-shirt was found to constitute use as a mark identifying its source rather than as ornamentation, as was use of National Hockey League team names and symbols such as Boston Bruins, Chicago Black Hawks, and Philadelphia Flyers embroidered on cloth patches. Similarly, a loop design functions as a mark used to identify Calvin Klein jeans, and artwork of a football helmet featuring the word "Broncos" on the front of T-shirts functions as a mark identifying them, as does artwork on hats that is identical to a Coors beer label. The seal of the University of Colorado on ceramic mugs functions as a mark identifying their source.

COLOR

Color applied to a product in a definite, arbitrary way or design such as a circle, triangle, or star, can function as a mark if it is used in the manner of a mark. Color is capable of functioning as a mark and can be federally registered on the Principal Register when the overall color of a product does not serve a primarily functional purpose and is distinctive, and no competitive need requires the color to remain available to all competitors. Owens-Corning Fiberglas Corporation federally registered the color pink as a mark for its fibrous glass residential insulation. This color is uniformly applied to the product as its overall color.

If a color describes a product or service, it is subject to the same criteria as descriptive words and symbols. To be registrable and protectible, it must acquire distinctiveness. Because color is usually perceived as ornamentation, most businesses that use color as a mark must show that it has become distinctive for the particular product or service with which it is used.

Eastman Kodak has been able to protect the yellow background in combination with red and/or black as used on packaging for its film products because the color has become distinctive. Mishawaka Rubber & Woolen Mfg. Co. was able to enforce rights in a red ball design embedded in a shoe heel as a mark for shoes because it became distinctive.

When color performs a primarily utilitarian function for a product or service, it is not subject to federal registration or legal protection. The blue dot on Sylvania flashbulbs was found to be functional because it changes color if the bulb leaks air. Likewise, Diamond Match Company was not able to enforce rights in the colors red and blue for match heads because the blue tip functions as an indicator of the striking portion.

SOUNDS

Sounds can function and be protected as marks if they are not functional, are used as a mark, and become distinctive for a particular product or service. National Broadcasting Company acquired rights in the musical note sequence G-E-C as a mark used to identify its broadcast services. The producer of the radio program "Inner Sanctum" used a creaking door sound to identify its programming service.

SUGGESTIVE WORDS AND SYMBOLS

Unlike words and symbols that are generic, descriptive, geographic, or surnames, those that are suggestive are deemed to be inherently distinctive. They are eligible for Principal Register registration and legal protection at the time they are first used in connection with a product or service.

This category of words and symbols is between the category for those that are descriptive and the category for those that are arbitrary or coined. Suggestive words and symbols do not exactly describe but have some element of description, enough to make the suggesting process work. At the same time, suggestive words and symbols are not wholly arbitrary because they give hints about the products or services with which they are used.

Suggestive words and symbols have been said to require imagination, thought, and perception to reach a conclusion as to the nature of the products or services with which they are used. They differ from descriptive words or symbols because those that are descriptive immediately convey an idea of the qualities, features, function, purpose, use, components, ingredients, or characteristics of a product or service.

When determining whether a word or symbol is descriptive or suggestive is difficult, the courts and USPTO often make the distinction on an intuitive basis rather than by logical analysis. Affirmative answers to the following questions tend to support a finding that the word or symbol is suggestive rather than descriptive.

1. Is the meaning of the word or symbol so remote and subtle that it is fanciful and not needed by all businesses that market the same or similar products or services?
2. Is the meaning of the word or symbol incongruous?
3. Is a multistage reasoning process necessary to determine what product or service characteristics the word or symbol indicates?

Because suggestive words and symbols are not product or service descriptions, the policy of allowing their appropriation does not lessen the number of words and symbols in our vocabulary that can be used for description. Therefore, no reason exists for a suggestive word or symbol to be available for use by everyone with respect to particular products or services when one business claims exclusive rights in it for those products or services. If a business uses a suggestive word or symbol to identify particular products or services, no other business can use it for the same or similar kind of products or services.

Two descriptive words or symbols can be combined to form a new one that is suggestive. "Flexiseal" was found to be suggestive of a caulking compound, "Unisole" was found to be suggestive of a one-piece molded sole and heel unit, and "Stronghold" was found to be suggestive of steel nails.

In addition, the following words and symbols represent the kind found to be suggestive: "Money 24" for automatic teller machine services, a steer head design for a restaurant that serves beef, "Roach Motel" for insect traps, "Coppertone" for sun tanning products, and "Seventeen" for a monthly magazine directed to teenage girls.

ARBITRARY OR COINED WORDS AND SYMBOLS

From the standpoint of federal registration and legal protection, words and symbols classified as arbitrary or coined are ideal names and marks. They are inherently distinctive, the strongest of all names and marks, and entitled to the broadest scope of protection. Like those that are suggestive, they are immediately eligible for federal registration on the Principal Register and for legal protection on the date of first use.

Words and symbols are considered arbitrary or coined when their dictionary or other accepted meanings have no significance in reference to the products or services with which they are used. They do not in any way directly or indirectly convey information about the products or services or their configuration or packaging.

Arbitrary words and symbols differ from those that are coined. An arbitrary word or symbol is a common word or symbol whose meaning bears no relationship to the product or service. A coined word or symbol is created solely for use as a name or mark. It is invented and therefore has no dictionary definition or accepted meaning other than as a name or mark.

"Crest" (toothpaste), "Camel" (cigarettes), "Chevron" (petroleum products), "Domino" (pizza), and "Tide" (detergent) are examples of arbitrary words. "Kodak" (cameras and film), "Exxon" (petroleum products), "Yuban" (coffee), "Oreo" (cookies), and "Tylenol" (analgesic) are examples of coined words.

The negative aspect of an arbitrary or coined word or symbol is its value as an advertising tool during the initial period of its use. Because it does not convey information about the product or service, the relevant public probably will not readily know what the product or service is by referring to the word or symbol alone. More effort is required to tell potential customers about a product or service identified by an arbitrary or coined word or symbol than is the case with one that is suggestive, descriptive, or geographic. In many cases, a long period of time and/or a great deal of advertising may be required to accomplish this objective. However, once the public associates the word or symbol with the product or service, the association lasts for a long time and easily carries over to a wide variety of products and services offered by the same business. For example, if "Kodak" were used in connection with candy bars, members of the public would be likely to think they are produced by the company that offers Kodak film, namely, Eastman Kodak.

5

Searching for Potential Conflicts

The process of selecting a name or mark begins by deciding on a word or symbol to use. However, it does not end after that decision is reached. More is involved. The next step is to learn whether anyone else uses, has filed an application to federally register, or registered a name or mark that is the same as or similar to your choice.

In addition to knowing its strengths and weaknesses from the standpoint of registration and legal protection, you need to know whether the word or symbol can be used as a corporate name, trade name, or mark without infringing someone else's rights. You also need to know whether it can be registered with one or more states and/or the USPTO.

The law in this country generally provides that the first user of a corporate name, trade name, or mark (whether or not registered) in a particular geographic area has the exclusive right to use it there in connection with the business, products, or services it identifies. That person usually has a legitimate basis to challenge another party's subsequent use of a confusingly similar name or mark in the same geographic area if it is used to identify the same or similar products or services.

Most states will not permit incorporation under a word or registration of a trade name or mark if it is deceptively similar to a registered corporate name, trade name, or mark. Similarly, a state will not allow a foreign corporation to qualify to do business under a word deceptively similar to a corporate or trade name it has registered. (A foreign corporation is one that is incorporated under the laws of one state and transacts business in another state.)

The USPTO will refuse registration of a mark confusingly similar to an existing registered mark.

WHERE TO SEARCH

If someone else is known to be using the selected word or symbol as a corporate name, trade name, or mark for the same or similar products or services, selecting another one may be appropriate. Deciding whether you should do so involves considering several factors that are discussed in this chapter and Chapter 6.

When you do not know whether the selected word or symbol is being used by another person, you should conduct an investigation. This kind of investigation is commonly referred to as a corporate name, trade name, or trademark search, depending on how the word or symbol will be used. Sometimes it is called "clearing" a name or mark.

A search can disclose information that will indicate whether use of the selected word or symbol is likely to be challenged if it is used as a corporate name, trade name, or mark. The information a search generates can also indicate the chances of registering it in one or more states and/or with the USPTO.

Depending on how and where the word or symbol will be used, the search can involve checking state and local government files, USPTO records, and other information sources. The objective is to see if someone else is using it as a name or mark for the same or similar products or services in the locality or region where its use is contemplated or elsewhere in this country. You also want to see if it is the subject of an application for federal registration or has been registered in one or more states and/or the USPTO.

Ordinarily, your investigation does not have to include files and records of a foreign country. Registration and/or use of a name or mark by another person in a foreign country is of no concern unless the products or services to be identified by the selected word or symbol will be marketed there. If so, you should conduct a search in each country where it will be used.

SEARCHING IS A GOOD BUSINESS PRACTICE

No law requires a search as a condition of acquiring proprietary rights in a word or symbol, whether as a corporate name, trade name, or mark. Nor is a search prerequisite to filing articles of incorporation, qualifying to do business as a foreign corporation, or registering a trade name or mark. However, conducting a search to avoid infringing the rights of another is a good business practice whether the word or symbol will be used and/or registered locally, regionally, or nationally.

If you know in advance that a word or symbol may be faced with registration obstacles and present infringement risks, you can prudently avoid wasting time, effort, and money on it. Instead, you can select and search other words or symbols until you find one that is registrable and can be used without such risks.

In many cases, a search should cover the entire country and especially the USPTO records rather than only the area where the word or symbol will be used. That no one uses it in a particular geographic area does not mean that no one has exclusive rights in it for that area. The use of a word or symbol as a name or mark in one geographic area is often enough to give the user exclusive rights in that area and elsewhere. For example, a business that claims exclusive rights in and uses a word as a mark for snow skis in Colorado may possess rights in Colorado as well as in Minnesota, New York, Ohio, Montana, California, and other states because it has federally registered the mark and/or used it in those states.

A business that owns a federally registered mark or one that is the subject of an application for federal registration may have the exclusive right to use it nationwide for the products or ser-

vices covered by the registration or application, even though it
is used in only two states. The constructive use provisions of the
Trademark Act make this possible. Federal registration is discussed further in Chapter 8. The effect of constructive use is discussed in the Chapter 6 section "When Rights Come into Existence: Federal Registration."

A business that owns an unregistered mark can also possess
the exclusive right to use it beyond the geographic area where
it offers products or services. Rights in unregistered names and
marks exist throughout the geographic area where they are publicized as well as where products or services are offered under
them. Thus, if the Colorado business sells snow skis under its
mark in Colorado, Minnesota, and New York and has established a reputation for them in Ohio, Montana, and California
by advertising and publicity, it may be able to claim exclusive
rights in the mark in all those states.

Without question, a business that is or may become involved
in franchising should conduct a nationwide search. This search
is especially important if the name or mark is an essential ingredient of the franchise. If someone else uses it or something similar in any of the proposed franchise areas, the name or mark
will not be available for use there. As a result, you might not be
able to grant a franchise for that area.

The right to use names and marks like "McDonald's, "Century 21," and "Baskin-Robbins" free of challenge throughout
this country is a significant element in the success of these fran-
chises. They were most likely searched before commitments
were made to use them. The same is true for names and marks
like "Kraft," "Ramada Inn," and "Texaco." They would not
have their present value if they could not be used everywhere
in the United States.

Another reason for conducting a search is to learn whether a
word or symbol is strong or weak in terms of how many other
businesses use it. Search information that discloses many businesses using a particular word or symbol or something similar is
a good indication that it is weak and will be difficult to protect.
In such a case, selecting and searching a different one may be
desirable if a strong name or mark is preferred. Conversely, if

the search discloses no one or only a few other businesses using the word or symbol, it may be strong and entitled to a broad scope of protection.

If you weigh the few days or weeks needed to conduct a search and the cost involved against the possible adverse consequences of using a name or mark that may be infringing, you will see that there are definite advantages to including a search as part of the selection process.

STANDARD TO APPLY WHEN SEARCHING

The Trademark Act sets forth the standard to be used to evaluate whether a word or symbol is available in terms of being non-infringing and registrable. This standard or a variation of it is used by trademark attorneys and applied by courts as well as the U.S. Patent & Trademark Office. A business can and should use it to evaluate search information.

> A word is infringing and should be refused registration if it so resembles a registered name or mark, or one that is unregistered and previously used by another but not abandoned, as to be likely, when used on or in connection with products or services, to cause confusion, or to cause mistake, or to deceive.

Actual confusion is not an element of this standard, nor is the possibility of confusion. The requisite kind of confusion, mistake, or deception is what exists in the minds of customers for the products or services with which the word or symbol is or will be used. Consequently, when you evaluate search information to determine "likelihood of confusion," you must always keep in mind your products or services and those that are identified by the names or marks your search discloses. You cannot make this determination by comparing the word or symbol to a name or mark in the abstract.

Ordinarily, a likelihood of confusion will be found if relevant customers of average intelligence and experience, who are buying under the usual conditions and exercising ordinary care, are likely to believe the products or services of one person are made, offered, sponsored by, or in some other way connected with those of another person because the same or a similar name or mark is used to identify them.

Your word or symbol does not have to be identical to someone else's name or mark for a likelihood of confusion to be found, and the products or services with which it is used do not have to be identical to those identified by the name or mark. Similarity between the word or symbol and name or mark can result in a likelihood of confusion. It can also result when the products or services are closely related or of the kind that are known or may be assumed to be produced or offered by the same source.

No requisite number or percentage of persons must be determined to be likely to be confused. An appreciable number or percentage is sufficient, but a very small number usually is not. Because resolution of the question involves a subjective determination rather than application of an objective standard, no prescribed set of factors must be considered and no any one factor has more importance than another. Consequently, each determination of likelihood of confusion must be decided on the facts applicable to it by using various factors developed by the courts and the USPTO. They are set forth and discussed later in this chapter in the section "How to Evaluate Search Information."

SEARCHES CONDUCTED BY STATES AND THE U.S. PATENT AND TRADEMARK OFFICE

Regardless of whether a business conducts a search prior to filing for incorporation or seeking registration of a name or mark, a search will be conducted. The states and USPTO search their respective records as part of the incorporation, trade name, and mark registration processes.

A state searches its records to determine whether your word or symbol is deceptively similar to an existing one it has previously allowed and/or registered. If so, the proposed name or mark will not be accepted.

The USPTO also searches its records as part of its application-examining process to determine whether the mark you seek to register is confusingly similar to an existing registered mark. It uses the standard mentioned in the preceding section of this chapter. If it finds a confusingly similar mark, registration is refused.

In terms of learning about third party users of similar names or marks and whether they may be the basis of infringement claims by others, state and USPTO searches are of little or no value for reasons noted in the following paragraphs.

An applicant whose name or mark is accepted is not told what names or marks the search disclosed. An applicant whose name or mark is refused registration is told only the specific name or mark that is the basis for the refusal.

These searches consider only registered or applied-for names or marks in the records of the particular state or the USPTO. They do not take into account names or marks that are registered elsewhere or unregistered, even if they are similar to the selected word or symbol. This omission is significant from the standpoint of infringement because the case law in this country provides that rights in a name or mark depend on use and not on registration. Consequently, the infringement evaluation process must consider as many names or marks similar to the selected word or symbol as practical, without regard to where or if they are registered in the United States.

Furthermore, state and USPTO searches are used only to decide whether an applicant has a right to register the selected word or symbol. They do not determine your right to use it. A decision that a word or symbol can be registered does not necessarily mean that the applicant is the only person who has a right to use it or that its use will not infringe the rights of a third party. The right to register as distinguished from the right to use is discussed in Chapter 6.

In fact, if a word is infringing, state or USPTO registration ordinarily is not a valid defense and does not preclude a decision in favor of the challenging party. As an integral part of your selection process you need to determine whether a word or symbol can be registered *and* used without infringing another person's rights.

So although the states and USPTO conduct their own searches, a business should not rely on the results of such a search to learn whether others use a name or mark that is the same as or similar to the selected word or symbol. In addition, the results of such a search should not be relied on to determine whether the selected word may infringe the rights of another person. You should conduct an independent search before you use it and file for registration.

WHEN TO SEARCH

Although you may conduct a search at any time, the ideal time is shortly after selecting a word or symbol and before filing applications for registration or making commitments for its use, such as designing, developing, and purchasing stationery, business cards, labeling, packaging, or advertising featuring it.

Without question, a business has to search a word or symbol to be used as a corporate name prior to filing articles of incorporation to make sure it is acceptable to the state agency responsible for incorporation matters. If a search is not conducted and articles of incorporation are filed under a name deceptively similar to an existing corporate name, trade name, or mark, the articles probably will not be accepted and time will be lost. In such a case, you will then have to refile the articles under an acceptable name. In the intervening period, someone else may incorporate under the name.

A search should also be conducted prior to filing an application for trade name registration. As is the case for a corporate name, your purpose is to avoid the necessity of refiling such an application if the name is not acceptable.

If a conflicting name or mark is disclosed prior to using a word or symbol as a corporate name, trade name, or mark, all you lose are the time, effort, and money spent to select and search it. Ordinarily, this loss is less than that incurred if a search is not conducted, the word or symbol is used, and its use is successfully challenged as infringing. Typically, once a name or mark is found to be infringing, any stationery, business cards, labeling, packaging, advertising, and other materials featuring it can no longer be used. In addition, the goodwill associated with it is also lost because the business, product, or service is no longer identified by it.

Although conducting a search prior to using a word or symbol as a name or mark is best, failure to do so at that time does not mean that conducting a search later is merely academic. You are always wise to conduct a search when you plan to extend use of a name or mark beyond the geographic area where it is being used. As indicated in the section "Searching Is a Good Business Practice," you need to know if the name or mark can be used without conflict in other geographic areas.

You should also conduct a search when a word or symbol will be used in connection with an expanded line of business, or new products or services. Your use of it free of conflict in connection with one kind of business, product, or service does not necessarily mean it will not infringe someone else's rights when you use it for a different kind of business, product, or service.

Another time to conduct a search is when you are purchasing the names or marks of a business along with all or some of its other assets. Sometimes a seller's records are incomplete and/or inaccurate. A search can determine the registration status of the names or marks and verify that they are registered in the seller's name. You can also determine whether the seller owns more than the names or marks listed in the purchase documents and if the seller has disclosed all potential conficts associated with their continued use.

You should also conduct a search if an infringement claim is asserted against your use of a word or symbol as a name or mark. Knowing the strength or weakness of the claimant's name or mark can be useful in making an argument against the claim. If the same or a similar name or mark has been used by others, such information can be used to show that it is weak and entitled to a very narrow scope of protection. The search may also disclose that the owner of the name or mark claimed to be infringed has not successfully challenged others.

In addition, search information can be valuable during the process of registering a mark. If an application for registration has been refused on the basis of a registered mark owned by another person, information about other registered marks may be helpful. In response to the refusal, you may be able to show that the mark constituting the obstacle was registered despite registrations for similar marks. This argument may be persuasive in showing that the mark is weak and should not preclude your registration.

WHAT TO SEARCH

Information about registered names or marks used by businesses in this country is maintained by the states, the USPTO, and other government agencies. Such records include state, city, county, and local government records concerning corporate names, trade names, and marks and the taxation, regulation, and/or licensing of businesses.

At the state level, information about corporate names, trade names, and marks is usually maintained by the group responsible for corporation matters, typically the Corporations Section, Corporations Office, Division of Corporations, Business Registration Division, or a similar unit within the Office of the Secretary of State.

Trade name information may also be in the records of a state agency responsible for tax matters, such as a department of revenue or taxation. At the city and county level, it may be found in the recorder's office. It can also be found in the records of state, city, county, and local agencies responsible for licensing, such as those that issue real estate, restaurant, liquor store, nightclub, employment agency, trade school, and sales tax licenses.

Information about unregistered names or marks can be found in business, product, and other types of directories and publications. Computer data bases are another source. Specifically, this kind of information appears in telephone directory white and yellow page listings, trade association directories and publications, trade name and trademark indexes, and business directories. It also appears in consumer, commercial, and industrial product catalogs and in computer data bases comprising trademark and trade name listings. One particular source of information about industrial products and services is the multivolume publication *Thomas Register of American Manufacturers*. A source of information about periodicals is *Ulrich's International Periodicals Directory*. Sources of information about consumer products and company names are the *Trade Names Dictionary*, the *Trade Names Dictionary: Company Index*, and the *Business Organizations, Agencies, and Publications Directory*. Also, manufacturers' directories are published for most states. Many public libraries carry these publications.

At least two companies publish a printed listing of marks registered by the USPTO. They are updated on an annual basis, at a minimum. The Trademark Register of Washington, D.C., publishes *Trademark Register of the United States*, and Compu-Mark U.S. of Bethesda, Maryland publishes *Compu-Mark Directory of U.S. Trademarks*.

The extent to which a directory or publication is helpful in learning about names and marks depends on the kind of information it contains. Those that contain only listings of names and marks, application or registration numbers, and dates of registration are not as helpful as those that disclose information about the owner, the products or services with which the name or mark is used, and the date each was first used.

HOW TO SEARCH

Every business can conduct its own search. The procedure is not difficult. However, it can be time consuming, involve reviewing numerous records and publications, and cost a relatively large amount of money depending on the extent of the search, yet not disclose the information you need.

For these reasons and others, you might more efficiently utilize the services of a private search company. In some instances, however, first conducting your own search and then using a private search company to obtain additional information may be preferable.

In this book, *limited search* refers to a search a business conducts on its own. Ordinarily, this kind of search is limited because it does not review as much information or as many sources as a private search company reviews. Nevertheless, the information obtained is still useful.

If the results of a limited search do not rule out use of the selected word or symbol, you can retain the services of a private search company. This approach can save some costs and time. If the limited search discloses risks associated with use of a word or symbol, you can eliminate it as a candidate and save the cost (a few hundred dollars and more) of having a private search company conduct a search. Frequently you will also save time because normally a private search company takes ten to fourteen business days to provide search results and you can complete a limited search within a few days.

A limited search can involve checking government records for information about registered names or marks. In addition, it can involve checking many sources that disclose information about unregistered names or marks. It is a good way to obtain a feeling for whether a word or symbol can be used and registered as a corporate or trade name, registered as a name under which a foreign corporation can qualify to do business, or registered as a mark.

To determine registrability of a word or symbol with a state, you can conduct this kind of search by contacting each state group responsible for corporation, trade name, or trademark matters, usually within the Office of the Secretary of State and/ or the Department of Revenue. In many cases you can telephone or write to ask the agency if the word or symbol can be registered. In other cases you can examine relevant records at state offices; most, if not all, are open for public inspection.

If you are searching a word or symbol to determine its availability for use as a corporate name, you may be able to use a corporate services organization to do the search. Companies such as CT Corporation Systems and Prentice-Hall Legal and Financial Services can do this work for a nominal cost in one or more states. Their addresses and telephone numbers can usually be obtained in local telephone directories.

An advantage of a limited search is that it can be used for a number of words or symbols in a number of states in a day or so for the price of long distance telephone charges and/or postage. Generally, filing an application or paying a fee is not necessary to obtain the desired information.

A disadvantage of a limited search is that the information obtained may not be up-to-date or completely accurate, depending on how frequently new information is placed in state records and how current they are. It also depends on the judgment of the government employee who responds to the availability inquiry. An opinion in this regard is subjective. He or she may or may not cite a registered name or mark that is confusingly similar.

Another disadvantage of this kind of search is that it may have little or no value for learning about third-party claims to rights in unpublicized and unregistered names or marks that are the same as or similar to the selected word or symbol. A search that indicates an absence of obstacles to registration in one or more states and/or federally does not mean that no relevant names or marks exist in terms of infringement. This disadvantage is present with searches conducted by states and the USPTO and with those that you conduct by telephone or written inquiry because the state is, in effect, conducting the search.

Generally, this disadvantage may not be as great when you personally examine state records and when a limited search includes computer data bases such as TRADEMARKSCAN, Compu-Mark On-Line Trademark Searching, or Dun's Electronic Yellow Pages. A personal examination will usually disclose many names and marks, some of which may be the same as or similar to the selected word.

The TRADEMARKSCAN and Compu-Mark On-Line Trademark Searching data bases consist of information about names and marks registered by states and the USPTO as well as many but not all unregistered names and marks. They are compiled by private companies and are directly accessible by everyone for a fee payable to the company. TRADEMARKSCAN is available through Dialog Information Services, Inc. Also, these data bases may be accessed through a do-it-yourself type of computer search service available in many public libraries for a very low fee.

Information in the USPTO records can be obtained by a limited search but not directly from that agency. The USPTO will not provide information about registrability of a word or symbol in response to a telephone or written inquiry. To get this information, you have to inspect its records in the public search room in Washington, D.C. Another way to obtain it is through a search using the TRADEMARKSCAN or Compu-Mark On-Line Trademark Searching computer data bases or other data bases.

Another objective of a limited search is to learn about as many unregistered names and marks as possible. Therefore, you should make every effort to review all available sources of information about them. Public libraries are good places to find many of these sources, but their records are not all-inclusive.

Unlike information about registered names and marks found in government records, no federal, state, or local government clearinghouses exist for information about unregistered names and marks. Generally, this information appears in a variety of telephone and other directories, trade publications, catalogs, and name and mark compilations, but it is not together in one place or a few locations. Many of the sources are not updated on a regular basis; therefore, the information in them is not current and does not include newly used names and marks. Finding and examining each source can take a long time and no established criteria determine which of them should be reviewed or are most relevant.

For these reasons, among others, learning about as many relevant unregistered names and marks as possible is difficult. Consequently, this part of a limited search may not help you learn about rights claimed by third parties. As mentioned earlier, to improve your odds, you can review the TRADEMARKSCAN or other computer data bases in combination with and in addition to reviewing the kind of publications and material mentioned earlier.

In certain instances, using the services of a private search company may be easier, less time-consuming, less expensive, and more meaningful for information gathering than conducting a limited search. However, the ideal approach is to conduct a limited search to the extent reasonable and then supplement or confirm your information by using a private search company. Almost all large corporations and other businesses that regularly search words and symbols rely on information generated by private search companies in reaching a decision about their use and registrability.

PRIVATE SEARCH COMPANIES

Many private search companies specialize in providing information about registered and unregistered names and marks. Everyone can use their services. Most attorneys whose practices emphasize trademark matters use information generated by such companies as the basis for their opinions.

Some of these companies have collected information from state and USPTO records concerning corporate names, trade names, registered marks, and marks sought to be registered. It constitutes their own data base and is continually updated as new applications are filed and registrations are granted by state agencies and the USPTO. In addition, these companies have compiled from telephone and other directories, business listings, and similar material substantial information about unregistered names and marks, which they also update on a regular basis.

Three private search companies who provide name or mark information are

Compu-Mark U.S.
7201 Wisconsin Avenue
Suite 400
Bethesda, MD 20844

Thomson & Thomson
1 Monarch Drive
North Quincy, MA 02171–2126

Trademark Research Corporation
300 Park Avenue South
New York, NY 10010

Corporate service organizations that will check the availability of corporate names include CT Corporate Systems and Prentice-Hall Legal and Financial Services.

In addition to private search companies who use their data
bases to provide information, some businesses review USPTO
and state records by directly examining their records on a
search-by-search basis. They do not compile or maintain their
own data bases.

Representative of such companies is

Daphne Hammond & Associates
2518 Ft. Scott Drive
Arlington, VA 22202

The names, phone numbers, and addresses of other private
search companies may be found in many telephone directory
yellow page listings and other publications. Often they are found
under the heading "Trademark Agents and Consultants."

The fees charged for a search depend on whether it covers
state registrations only, USPTO records only, unregistered
names and marks only, or a combination of these sources. In
1990, fees ranged from below $100 to more than $225 per word
or symbol, depending on the kind of search conducted.

A private search company can take as little time as 24 hours
to obtain search information or as long as ten or more business
days. Generally, it adds a surcharge for providing search information more quickly than the normal course of a search, which
is usually five to ten business days.

You may order a search by telephoning or writing to the
search company and giving the exact word to be searched. In

addition, you have to provide a description or listing of the products and/or services with which the word or symbol is or will be used. If a symbol is to be searched, you must send a copy.

In addition to indicating the word or symbol to be searched, you should instruct the company about the kind of search you desire. That is, the company should be told to limit the search to state, unregistered, or federally registered names and marks or to cover all information sources. In many cases, a complete search should be ordered because it provides the most information about relevant names and marks. However, a full search may not always be necessary.

A separate search should be conducted for each word or symbol under consideration, even if two or more of them are somewhat similar. Sometimes a small variation between two words or symbols yields somewhat different search results for each.

Normally, information about relevant names and marks is provided by the search company in the form of a printed list, copies of application drawing sheets and registration certificates, or combinations of them. This material contains names and marks found by the search company that are the same as or similar to the word or symbol that is the subject of the search. Information about them usually includes the name of each registrant and/or user, its address, a description of the products or services with which the name and mark is used, the date of first use, and an application or registration number. Appendix A includes a copy of a representative search report.

Few, if any, search companies render an opinion about the availability of a word or symbol from the standpoint of registration or infringement. All they provide is information that can be used to evaluate its registrability or the risks associated with its use. If you want an opinion, you should obtain it from an attorney experienced in the field of trademarks who can use the search company information to render it.

Although searches conducted by private companies may be preferable to the limited searches you can conduct, they too are not flawless in their information disclosure.

LIMITATIONS ON SEARCH INFORMATION

A search is one of the best ways to evaluate a word or symbol for registration and infringement, but favorable results are no guarantee that it can be registered and/or will not infringe the rights of another person. Accordingly, search information should be viewed as an indication that the prospects for registration are reasonable and that use of the word or symbol will be noninfringing, rather than as an absolute statement in this regard.

A search has some inherent weaknesses for a number of reasons. It will not disclose unregistered names and marks that are not publicized or disclosed in material ordinarily reviewed by a search company or a business conducting a limited search. Consequently, it may not contain information about all relevant names and marks.

In addition, a search company may overlook, not find, or not report all relevant names and marks in its data base.

Finally, search information usually is accurate only on the date the search is actually conducted. A search reflects information in the data base only as of that date; that is, it discloses only unregistered and registered names and marks included in the data base when it is examined. Names and marks that are first used, listed in directories and publications, or the subject of newly filed applications after the date of the search are not disclosed. Thus, a name or mark may be submitted for registration, registered, or rights in it acquired by another person during the period between the date the data base is examined and the date the search information is provided. If you do not first use a word as a name or mark upon receiving search information, you would be prudent to conduct an updated search to confirm the prospects of noninfringing use and registration prior to making commitments to use it.

In summary, search information is accurate within the limits of the search methods utilized, the data bases available for searching, and the timeliness of updates to the data bases searched. Nonetheless, a search should be conducted to minimize the possibility of infringement and to ascertain the prospects of registration.

HOW TO EVALUATE SEARCH INFORMATION

Ideally, an attorney experienced in the field of trademark law should evaluate the results of a search. A trademark attorney has knowledge of court and USPTO case law concerning infringement and the registration of names and marks. This knowledge is needed to give a meaningful opinion about the prospects of registering a word or symbol and using it without infringing the rights of another person.

A trademark attorney applies the likelihood of confusion standard referred to in the section in this chapter on "Standards To Apply When Searching" and considers the first use date for every name and mark disclosed by a search. He or she also takes into account the geographic area where each name and mark is used and registered, as well as the application filing date for federal registration. In addition, he or she evaluates search information by using a number of other factors developed by court and USPTO case law.

If you evaluate the search information yourself, you should know that your conclusions may not be the same as a trademark attorney's opinion based on the same information. To improve the accuracy of your evaluation, you can follow the numbered steps given below, which is what a trademark attorney is likely to do to evaluate search information. Also as a trademark attorney might do, if a search discloses a mark that may be an obstacle to use and/or registration of the selected word or symbol, you should consider obtaining additional information about it to learn whether it has been abandoned or its use limited in any way. Sometimes, a mark that a search discloses is no longer in use or its use has been limited to less than all the products or services disclosed by the search. You can learn more about this aspect in the Chapter 12 section "Steps Preliminary to a Challenge."

1. Refer to Search Information

Material received from a search company, printouts from computer data base searches, and information obtained by a limited search should be used to generate a list of relevant names and marks. Note each relevant name and mark mentally or in writing. You can then evaluate this list to determine whether it contains any names and marks that may present an obstacle to use and registration of the selected word or symbol.

2. Look for Identical and Similar Names and Marks

Note all names and marks that are identical to the selected word or symbol as well as those that are similar in terms of sound, appearance, and meaning. Names and marks that are phonetic equivalents or transpositions of the selected word or symbol are also relevant. In addition, note symbols that communicate the same thing as the selected word as well as names and marks that create the same commercial impression.

Reason: The likelihood of confusion standard requires a comparison of names and marks in terms of whether they resemble each other. They should be considered in their entireties, and not analyzed part by part. If one element is more prominent than others the way it is shown, its meaning, or otherwise, however, more emphasis may be placed on it than on the other components to make the comparison.

Marks found to be confusingly similar include

Tornado	Cyclone
Pledge	Promise
Kind Touch	Gentle Touch
Response	Response Card
Lafontski	Adolphe Lafont
Ultracashmere	Ultrasuede
Pedi-Care	Pedi-A-Care

Ritz A Dish	Rinse A Dish
Buenos Dias	Good Morning
Humanomics	Humana

Marks found to be not confusingly similar include

Nutri-Trim	Nutri/System
Bami	Ami
Zips	Zip N Go
Yoplait	Yocreme
Lean Cuisine	Lean Living
Peyote	Payot
Corn Patch Pigs	Cabbage Patch Kids
Sea & Turf	Seven Seas
Miss World	Mrs. of the World
Taster's Choice	Diner's Choice

3. Note the Products and Services

For each noted name and mark, add the products or services it identifies if they are the same as, similar, or related to the products or services for which your selected word or symbol is or will be used.

Reason: The likelihood of confusion standard requires a comparison of names and marks in terms of the products or services they identify.

Products and services found to be the same or closely related include

prenatal vitamins	cosmetics for pregnant women
mustard	restaurant services
cowboy boots	men's and women's shirts
printed circuits	computer programs
salt	chemical sweetener
caramel corn	peanut butter
automobiles	winches and hoists
whiskey	preserved fruits

steak knives   razor blades
tennis rackets   skis and boots

Products and services found to be dissimilar include

vacuum cleaners   ball bearings
news transmittal   information analysis software
entertainment   space ship models
box sealant   skin care products
telephones   capital equipment
shears   haircutting salons
ceramic tile   wood doors
dehorning shears   power mower attachments
thermal paper   transfer printing paper
toy store   restaurant

4. Note the Date of First Use, Application Filing Date, and Registration Date

For each noted name and mark, add the date of first use (if this information is available), the date an application for federal registration was filed, and the date it was federally registered. If you do not know the first use date, you should obtain it. In some cases you can contact the user of the name or mark and ask for this information or check reliable sources who may have it, such as Dun & Bradstreet. If you still do not have the first use date, you can check other sources. However, the information you obtain from them may not be accurate. Often only the user of a name or mark knows when it was first used, and only a few individuals employed by the user, who may be reluctant to disclose it, have this information.

Reason: The date of first use and/or the filing date of an application for federal registration can determine who has the exclusive right to use a mark. The law in this country provides that the first use date determines priority of rights in a name or mark in connection with the products or services offered under it for each geographic area where it is first used. The filing date of an application for federal registration can also determine priority of rights in a mark but throughout the country rather than only in the geographic area where it is first used. Refer to Chapters 6 and 8 for more information about the significance of the first use date and the filing date of an application for federal registration, as well as the date of federal registration.

5. Note Where Used and Registered

For each noted name or mark, add the geographic area where it is used (if this information is given) and the places where it is registered.

Reason: The exclusive right to use a name or mark exists where it is used and known. If it is federally registered, this right may be nationwide. The first user of a name or mark in a geographic area usually possesses superior rights in it throughout the area where it is used for the products or services it identifies. In addition, that person may have rights in other areas where products or services it identifies are advertised and promoted. Federal registration can mean that rights in the mark extend throughout this country without regard to where actual use occurs. State registration may mean that rights extend throughout the state. Again, refer to Chapters 6 and 8 for more information about the significance of where a mark is used and registration.

6. Tentative Conclusion

In theory, each name and mark you listed presents a potential obstacle to the use and registration of your selected word or symbol if you have not used it or if you first used it after the first use date of the other name or mark. You cannot state whether such an obstacle actually exists with certainty for several reasons. First, evaluations of the likelihood of confusion between names and marks are frequently subjective in nature, and two persons may reach different conclusions. Also, a name or mark may not be currently in use or may not be used for the products or services disclosed by the search. Moreover, how the owner of a name or mark feels about use of the same or a similar name or mark by others is not known.

7. Other Considerations

In addition to the elements previously mentioned, the courts and the USPTO consider a number of other factors to determine whether a likelihood of confusion exists in each case.

a. The similarity or dissimilarity of trade channels through which products and services are offered, the price of the products or services, the conditions under which sales are made, and whether the products or services are sold to ordinary or discriminating customers.

   Reason: The chances of confusion may be greater if the products or services offered under the selected word or symbol and those identified by a relevant mark are: (1) marketed through the same trade channels (increases the likelihood intended customers will find them in the same stores or they will be offered by the same kind of distributors, sales agencies, or service providers); (2) purchased on an impulse basis or sold at a relatively low price (little or no time is taken to distinguish between the marks identifying such products or services); or (3) directed to ordinary customers who do not need to be discriminating in their purchases (they do not need to evaluate carefully and analyze what they buy to the same degree required in purchasing high-priced items, equipment, and services).

b. The fame of the prior name or mark (sales, advertising, length of use).

   Reason: A well-known name or mark is usually given a greater degree of protection than one that is not widely known. "Kodak" is so well known that it is likely to be given protection against a third-party use for car batteries, even though it is primarily used to identify film and related products marketed by Eastman Kodak.

c. The number and nature of similar names or marks in use for the same or similar products and services.

   Reason: A large number of similar names or marks suggests that they are weak and given a narrow scope of protection. Usually they coexist because each is distinguishable in some way from the others, either by their individual elements or by the products or services offered under them. In many cases a weak name or mark will be protected only against another's use of the identical name or mark to identify the same products or services.

d. The variety of products or services for which a mark is used.

Reason: Often, use of a mark that identifies a variety of products may be expanded to additional product lines, which may be the same as or include those identified by the selected word. Ordinarily, the owner of a mark has the right to expand business this way, which is recognized and given effect by the courts.

e. Whether the owner of the name or mark has taken action against other users of the same or a similar name or mark.

Reason: A history of infringement actions involving a particular name or mark indicates that you can reasonably expect the owner to challenge everyone who uses the same or a similar name or mark.

8. Reaching a Conclusion

When your evaluation of the search information suggests infringement liability may exist if you use or continue to use the selected word or symbol, you can select a new word or symbol and conduct a search to determine whether it is available. Another option is seeing if the infringement liability can be eliminated or reduced by directly or indirectly approaching the owner of each relevant name or mark, as suggested in the next section of this chapter. If this course of action does not lead to favorable results, a new word or symbol can be selected and searched.

ELIMINATING OR REDUCING INFRINGEMENT LIABILITY

In some cases, you can eliminate or reduce the infringement liability arising from another person's superior rights in a name or mark that is confusingly similar to your word or symbol. You can contact the owner of rights in the conflicting name or mark to negotiate: the purchase of all or some of the rights in it; the owner's consent to your use of the selected word or symbol; or a license to use the conflicting name or mark. The last alternative is the least preferable because usually a license can be terminated. When a license is terminated, typically the right to use a name or mark it covers ends, which means the selected word or symbol cannot be used after the termination date without violating the licensor's rights. Licenses are discussed in Chapter 13.

6

How and Where Rights Are Acquired and Maintained

Rights in a mark in the United States are easy to acquire. Just selecting the mark is not enough to acquire, nor is discussing it with others or preparing to offer products or services identified by it. However, all you need to do is a make a bona fide use of it in the ordinary course of business in connection with a product or service.

The date a mark is first used, how it is first used, the products or services with which it is first used, where it is first used, and whether an application for federal registration is filed before or after it is first used all have an effect on acquiring rights. Once acquired, rights in a mark are affected by the manner it is used, any expansion of the product line or services it subsequently identifies, the geographic area where it is used, and whether it is federally registered.

For the reasons given in this and following chapters, you ought to use a mark and file an application for federal registration of a mark as soon as possible after you complete the selection process.

WHEN RIGHTS COME INTO EXISTENCE: FIRST USE

In accordance with prevailing law in the United States, proprietary rights in a mark are based on its use in connection with products or services. They come into existence on the date it is first used if the use is lawful and made on a bona fide basis in the ordinary course of business.

The breadth of these rights in terms of the products or services a mark identifies is explained in the section "Protected Products and Services," where these rights can be asserted is in the section "Geographic Extent of Rights," the section "Duration of Rights and Abandonment" explains how long rights last, and when these rights can be asserted is in the section "Distinctiveness and Secondary Meaning."

If first use is followed by infrequent, nominal uses of a mark, such use may be challenged as being ineffective to bring rights into existence. To refute this kind of challenge you would be wise to keep records and undertake activities that manifest an intent to develop an ongoing regular business under the mark. Do this especially if delays occur or are expected in using a mark on a continuous basis.

Generally, the first user of a mark acquires exclusive rights for the products or services with which it is used, and not the first person who applies for or obtains a registration. For an exception to this rule, refer to the next section, "When Rights Come into Existence: Federal Registration."

Registration, whether state or federal, does not establish initial rights in a mark and is not necessary to acquire or maintain them because they are based on use. In fact, a mark will not be registered by the USPTO or by most states unless it has been used. Moreover, that a mark is not registered does not mean that the first user does not possess rights in it or will lose those rights or that a subsequent user will automatically defeat the first user's rights by registering it. However, as noted in the next section, registration by a later user can affect a first user's rights.

Reservation of a corporate name, incorporation of a business, and registration of a trade name that has not been used do not create rights even though you may be able to do any one of these things before a mark is used. Again, the first user of a corporate or trade name acquires rights in it, not the first person who reserves it, incorporates under it, or registers it.

The first use date is critical not only because it determines when rights come into existence but also because it can determine who is entitled to exclusive use of a mark when two or more businesses are using confusingly similar marks in the same geographic area. Generally, the person with the earliest first use date is entitled to prevail. Also, when two or more businesses seek federal registration of confusingly similar marks, the first use date can determine which of them is entitled to registration. For these reasons, the first use date is commonly referred to as a *priority date*.

Making arrangements for or featuring a mark in advertising and promotional material, referring to it in correspondence or discussing it with others, or otherwise using it in reference to products or services not yet produced or offered usually does not constitute a bona fide use in the ordinary course of business. Therefore, a business engaging in these kinds of activities will not create rights in a mark for itself.

Single-product shipments of products, one-time offerings of services, and other token uses made solely to establish a first use date to reserve rights in a mark are not bona fide uses in the ordinary course of business. Usually they can be successfully challenged as the basis for acquiring rights in a mark. Therefore, sending a product with a mark on it to a friend or to one division of a company from another, featuring a mark in advertising for services not fully available at the time, and similar token uses are ineffective in terms of bringing rights into existence.

Conversely, if first use of a mark is genuine and made as part of a regular transaction involving customary industry practices, it will be bona fide even though products are given away or leased rather than sold or services are offered free. Under these circumstances, the quantity of products given away, leased, or sold, the extent of services offered, and the size of the geographic area of first use have no bearing on whether the use is bona fide.

Besides token first uses, first uses that are not lawful may be challenged. All laws and regulations applicable to the products or services identified by a mark must be complied with for the use to be lawful. Federal, state, and local laws concerning labeling as well as product content, use, and safety are representative of laws that require compliance. They include the Consumer

Product Safety Act, Hazardous Substances Act, Federal Insecticide, Fungicide and Rodenticide Act, Meat Inspecting Act, Poultry Products Inspection Act, Federal Seed Act, Toxic Substances Control Act, Occupational Safety and Health Act, Federal Alcohol Administration Act, Fair Packaging and Labeling Act, Federal Food, Drug and Cosmetic Act, and various state dairy and bakery product labeling laws.

First use of a mark in a foreign country does not create rights in the United States unless a treaty with that country specifies these rights. Therefore, unless an exception is applicable, rights in a mark cannot be acquired in this country until it is used here.

Although rights in a mark can be acquired if its first use is in intrastate commerce, interstate use is preferable if federal registration is desired. A mark must be used in interstate commerce to be eligible for federal registration.

Interstate use occurs when products are sold or transported in commerce that may be lawfully regulated by Congress. This commerce includes giving away, lending, or leasing products that cross state lines, and intrastate sales of products to interstate travelers, as well as other product sales that affect such commerce.

Interstate use of a mark in connection with services occurs when the mark is used or displayed in the sale or advertising of services that are rendered in more than one state or in commerce that may be lawfully regulated by Congress. This commerce includes offering services at a location in one state to persons from other states, such as those offered by restaurants, gasoline service stations, hotels and motels, broadcasters, publications, and department stores.

Because the first use date is critical, it should be documented. It must be proved in an infringement action. Therefore, evidence referring to it should be created at the time it occurs and it should be maintained. You can note the date in business records and keep copies of all substantiating material, such as bills of lading, invoices showing dates products are shipped or services rendered, checks from customers for sales, and similar documentation that includes the mark(s) for the products or services.

WHEN RIGHTS COME INTO EXISTENCE: FEDERAL REGISTRATION

Although federal registration does not itself establish initial rights in a mark, the federal application filing date, like a first use date, can determine who has exclusive rights when a conflict arises over use of confusingly similar marks. For this reason, it too can be referred to as a "priority" date. However, unlike a priority date attributable to first use, which is effective only for the geographic area where use occurs, a priority date attributable to a federal application filing date is effective nationwide, even though it is not used everywhere.

The Trademark Act provides that filing an application for federal registration on the Principal Register constitutes constructive use of a mark, nationwide in effect. This provision makes the filing date a priority date. *Constructive use is a use created by statute without regard to whether it actually occurs. It has the same legal effect as actual use.*

Because federal registration offers another way to obtain a priority date (one that can be relied on nationwide at relatively low cost without need to immediately use a mark everywhere rights are desired) many businesses should pursue this avenue promptly upon selecting a mark. You do not need to wait until the mark has been used.

An application can be filed after interstate use of a mark, and it can also be filed based on an *intent to use* a mark in interstate commerce if it has not been used or has been used only in intrastate commerce.

The acquisition of a priority date in this way is an exception to the general rule, but it is possible only if an application is filed for federal registration on the Principal Register. Filing an application for the Supplemental Register or for state registration does not have the same result.

Although the priority date is the application filing date, it is not effective and cannot be relied on until the applied-for mark is federally registered. Federal registration cannot happen until a mark is used, subject to an exception for a mark based on a foreign application or registration. For information about foreign applications and registrations, refer to "Foreign Application and Registration-Based Application" in Chapter 9.

A mark used in interstate commerce before an application is filed can be registered immediately on completion of the application process. At that time the application filing date can be relied on as a priority date. However, a mark covered by an intent to use application cannot be registered on completion of the application process. The mark must first be used in interstate commerce as a condition of registration.

The requisite use for an intent to use application must be made no later than three years from the time the USPTO issues a notice that the applied-for mark is entitled to registration. If the USPTO does not receive satisfactory evidence that bona fide use has occurred within this period, the mark will not be federally registered based on the intent to use application. In that event, the application filing date will not be treated as a priority date for the mark. Refer to the Chapter 9 section "Intent to Use Application" for more information about intent to use applications and federal registration.

HOW A MARK SHOULD BE USED

The way a mark is first used in association with products and services is another factor that determines whether rights come into existence. It must be in accordance with prevailing standards, such as those established by the Trademark Act. Otherwise it will be insufficient to create rights.

The Trademark Act says a mark is used in commerce for *products* when it is placed in any manner on them, their containers, displays associated with them, tags or labels affixed to them, or, if their nature makes such placement impracticable, then on documents associated with their sale. Representative of the kind of displays and documents that may be acceptable are:

restaurant menus if the mark refers to a specific menu item; packing slips, shipping documents, shipping labels affixed to bulk containers, and invoices that use the mark to identify the product(s) covered by them; instructional materials and sales brochures that feature the mark; and stand-up counter displays and store window displays that contain the mark for the product displayed. Memoranda, correspondence, advertisements, and other documents that mention a mark but which are not associated with the products it identifies are generally not acceptable uses.

A mark is used in commerce for *services* when it is used or displayed in their sale or advertising. The kinds of materials that support a service mark use include signage, promotional material, brochures, circulars, stationery, business cards, print and media advertisements, information sheets, and similar items that feature the mark and refer to the services it identifies.

RULES OF USAGE

In addition to affixing a mark properly, you must use it correctly in the way you identify your product or service. Correct usage not only affects whether rights come into existence but also affects whether rights in a mark will be lost, as happened with *aspirin*, *escalator*, and *cellophane*. Over the years various corporate trademark owners have developed some general rules to provide assistance in this regard. If you follow them, the chances are good that your rights in a mark will not be challenged on the ground that it is improperly used.

1. Always use a mark as an adjective and never as a noun. Whenever possible, it should modify a noun, that is the name of the product or service it identifies. Do this at least once on labeling or in advertising, at the most prominent appearance of the mark.
   Proper usage: Buy Cracker Jack candied popcorn
                      Jell-O gelatin dessert tastes good

Improper usage: Cracker Jack is a favorite snack
Some people like candy better than Jell-O

2. Try to use the generic name of the product or service in association with the mark. Again, do this at least once at its most prominent appearance.
Proper usage: Levi's jackets
Kodak film

3. Do not use a mark in the plural or possessive form.
Proper usage: Chevrolet cars are high in quality
Kraft salad dressings are good
Improper usage: Chevrolets are quality cars
Kraft's dressings are good

4. The mark should be used in a manner that distinguishes it from surrounding text by depicting it in italics, capital letters, or initial capital letters, or by underlining it, using quotation marks around it, or displaying it in bold-face type.
Proper usage: CLIFFS study guides
Karman western wear
Imperial headwear
"IPI SPORTS" videotapes
Improper usage: cliffs study guides
karman western wear

5. Use a trademark notice in connection with the mark. If it is federally registered the notice is ®, or the designation "Reg. U.S. Pat. & Tm. Off." should be used. If unregistered or registered only by a state, the notice "TM" may be used.
Proper usage: KASHIWA ® teriyaki sauce
TEM TEX * blouses
* Reg. U.S. Pat. & Tm. Off.
Shereth ™ records

6. Always spell the mark correctly and consistently. Do not use variations.

WHO IS THE FIRST OWNER?

Ordinarily, the first owner of a mark is the person who legitimately exclusively controls the nature and quality of the products or services the mark identifies. In many instances this person is the first user, but not always. When first use is controlled by someone other than the user, the first owner is the person who exclusively controls that use, not the user. Under these circumstances, the use is for the benefit of the controlling party, and the user is a related company. The Trademark Act defines *related company* as

> any person whose use of a mark is controlled by the owner of the mark with respect to the nature and quality of the goods or services on or in connection with which the mark is used.

Typically, a related company relationship is manifested and should be documented by a written agreement that one of the parties has a right to exclusive control of the use of the mark by the other. This kind of agreement can cover first use of the mark for the purpose of bringing rights into existence for the benefit of the controlling party. It can also cover use of a mark after rights have been brought into existence by the owner's first use or by a related company. Such an agreement is commonly referred to as a *license*. Refer to Chapter 13 for information about licenses.

A designer or creator of a mark is not its owner unless that person legitimately exercises exclusive control over its use. For example, an advertising agency or logo designer does not own rights in a mark (except when copyright protection applies) if it is designed or created for a client who first uses it. Likewise, a distributor or reseller of a product manufactured by another person, as well as a broker for a service rendered by someone else, is not the owner of the mark unless it has an exclusive right to exercise legitimate control over the nature and quality of the products or services. For example, a sporting goods distributor does not own rights in "Volant" snow skis manufactured by Volant Ltd. by reason of distributing them nor does a restaurant own rights in "Pepsi-Cola" beverages it serves by reason of reselling them.

However, a person can be the first owner of rights in a mark without manufacturing the products or performing the services. As long as that person controls the nature and quality of the products or services by some means, such as selecting and/or purchasing only those that are acceptable, and makes a first use of the mark to identify them, they can be manufactured or performed by someone else. This situation happens when the manufacturer or service provider does not use its own mark for the product or service. This situation is distinguishable from the related company relationship, in which the person who owns the mark does not make first use of it. For example, a supermarket chain such as Safeway Stores can be the owner of "Town House" for jams that are produced by another company in accordance with Safeway's specifications. Similarly, an office cleaning services company can be the owner of "Top Brass" to identify such services when it contracts with others to provide cleaning that conforms to its standards.

When a mark is first used by two or more persons in business together as a partnership, joint venture, association, or other organization capable of existing as an entity, the mark is owned by people as a group, not by the individual who created the mark or registers it. They are co-owners as joint tenants or as tenants in common, depending on their agreement. If they have no agreement, ownership is determined by their legal relationship under the law of the state having jurisdiction over them. For example, members of a musical group, such as the Credence Clearwater Revival, who perform together under a mark they first use together are co-owners of it unless an agreement provides otherwise. Its registration in one member's name would not create exclusive rights for that person if it is first used by the group.

PROTECTED PRODUCTS AND SERVICES

When a mark is first used in connection with a particular product or service, ordinarily the owner obtains an exclusive right to use the mark to identify that kind of product or service. However, this right does not automatically place the owner in a

strong position to stop others from using the same mark to identify different kinds of products or services that are different
enough to present no likelihood of confusion. Relevant customers for a particular kind of product or service are considered to
be unlikely to assume that different kinds of products or services
originate from, are connected with, or are sponsored by the same
source. Consequently, at the outset the owner's exclusive right
in a mark is usually limited to the particular kind of products or
services the mark is used to identify. For example, the owner of
"Penstemmon" for audiocassettes is in a good position to suc-
ceed in challenging another person's use of the same mark for
cassette tapes as well as phonograph records, compact discs, and
related products, but not such things as candy bars, car batteries,
and computer software programs. The theory holds that purchasers of cassette tapes are not likely to believe that candy bars
or other unrelated items come from the same business that offers
cassette tapes.

In light of this theory, two or more persons can use and possess rights in the same mark to identify different kinds of products or services and coexist with each other in this relationship.
For example, the mark "Domino" is used by different companies
to identify pizza and sugar, and "Triumph" is used by different
companies to identify automobiles, women's stockings, and
calendars.

The extent to which two persons can use the same mark
depends on whether the products or services in question are or
are not sufficiently related to cause a likelihood of confusion.
Typically, this determination is made by considering the factors
the courts and the USPTO use. They involve an evaluation of
the strength of the earlier used mark, the degree of similarity
between the marks, the proximity of the products or services,
the likelihood the earlier user's line of products or services will
be expanded to include those offered by the later user, the quality of the later user's products or services, actual confusion, and
the later user's good faith in adopting the same mark.

Until a mark is used to identify a broad variety of products or
services, rights in it may not be so broad as to give the owner a
valid basis to stop another person's use of it for unrelated prod-

ucts or services. When a mark is used to identify many kinds of products or services or a broad spectrum of them, the owner can more easily show that relevant customers are likely to believe that almost any product or service generally related to them comes from the same source. For example, Philip Morris, Borden, Inc., and other conglomerates that market a broad variety of products and services under a particular mark are in a good position to claim that the exclusive right to use it extends beyond the actual range of products or services the mark identifies.

If a mark is well known, however, even though used only for a particular product or service, the owner may be able to stop others from using it to identify different products or services. This ability is based on the theory that famous marks are entitled to a broader scope of protection than unknown or weak marks. For example, marks like "Kodak," "Exxon," and "Tiffany" are so well known that their owners can reasonably assert rights in them for more than just the products they identify.

GEOGRAPHIC EXTENT OF RIGHTS

The geographic area where the exclusive right to use a mark exists depends on both where it is used and when it is first used there. Also, it depends on whether it is federally registered as well as the priority date attributable to registration.

In accordance with U.S. case law precedent (common law), the exclusive right to use a mark generally exists only throughout the area where it is used or otherwise known if it has the earliest priority date there and the owner has not federally registered it. As a consequence, two or more persons can have an exclusive right to use the same mark for the same products or services in different geographic areas, without infringing each other's rights. This situation can exist only if each area is remote from the other and the relevant public in each area is not likely to be confused by use of the same mark by someone else in another area. Simultaneous use of a mark under these circumstances is referred to as *concurrent use*. For information about federally registering a mark that is concurrently used, refer to the Chapter 9 section "Concurrent Use Application."

For example, under common law principles the owner of "Penstemmon" for audiocassettes has the exclusive right to use it in Colorado if it has the earliest priority date (e.g., June 15, 1990) in that state and no one has federally registered it or filed an application for such registration before June 15, 1990. Similarly, two different owners of "Penstemmon" who use it in Washington (first use July 1, 1990) and Connecticut (first use September 16, 1990), respectively, can acquire an exclusive right to use it in their states for the same products as concurrent users so long as they do not know about each other's use or that by the Colorado user. They have these rights even though their first use dates are later than the Colorado user's priority date. None of these owners is automatically entitled to exclusive use in other states without having the earliest priority date or being known there. To acquire this right in each and every other state, an owner must use the mark and have the earliest priority date in the state.

The rule that the exclusive right to use a mark is limited to the geographic area where use is made or it is otherwise known has two exceptions. The first, the exception of the zone of natural expansion, derives from case law precedent and is itself subject to an exception (noted in the next paragraph). The second exception is federal registration of a mark. The first user can use either or both to prevent others from obtaining a right to concurrent use of the same mark in geographic areas where the first user is not doing business.

Under the zone of natural expansion concept, courts can affirm a first user's exclusive rights in a mark against later users in areas beyond where the mark is actually used. These expanded rights are possible when the first user's business under the mark can be shown to be likely to expand geographically. Under these circumstances, the first user is entitled to a zone of natural expansion encompassing geographic areas where the first user can show that it will probably do business under the mark at some time in the future. This likelihood may be evidenced by internal memoranda, published information, negotiations with salespeople, distributors, and retailers, franchise plans, and other manifestations of the owner's intent to develop a business under the mark in states beyond where sales presently occur. This exception is attributable to the relative ease in doing business regionally or nationally by telemarketing, direct mail, and through television, cable, and radio advertising. A business can promote and offer products or services almost everywhere through licensing and franchising, among other ways, without having offices or branches throughout the country.

For example, the owner of "Penstemmon" may be able to use it exclusively in Michigan, Wisconsin, Illinois, Ohio, Pennsylvania, Kentucky, and other states in 1992 although the owner is marketing audiocassettes only in the states of Colorado, Oklahoma, Nebraska, Missouri, Kansas, and Minnesota. This expansion of rights depends on whether the owner can show that distribution of the cassettes is expanding geographically and that the states in question are targets for expansion.

An exception to the zone of natural expansion concept is possible when a later user in an area remote from the first user obtains a federal registration before the first user. If the later user was not aware of the first user's mark and the first user does not sufficiently prove an expansion program, the later user may be able to obtain nationwide rights excepting those areas where the first user has made use. Some courts have given a later user exclusivity along these lines.

For example, a person may be able to obtain the exclusive right to use "Penstemmon" nationwide, excepting Colorado, by federally registering it, even though that person first used the mark in Utah, California, Oregon, Montana, and Arizona after the Colorado user, if the Colorado user did not federally register the mark and cannot show expansion plans.

The Trademark Act exception gives the owner of a federally registered mark nationwide exclusivity despite use of the mark in less than all the states. However, this exclusivity is applicable only against persons who first file an application for federal registration or first use the same mark after the owner's application filing date. As to earlier users, exclusivity exists but only where the registrant's mark has the earliest priority date. For example, if "Penstemmon" audiocassettes are first offered for sale in Colorado and Texas (but nowhere else) on June 15, 1990, and an application for federal registration is filed December 20, 1990, the owner has the exclusive right to use the mark in Colorado and Texas as well as other geographic areas where no one else has first used it before December 20, 1990.

In one other situation, federal registration may not give nationwide exclusivity. It concerns foreign trademark applications. The Trademark Act provides that a person who files an application for federal registration of a mark based on an earlier application for the same mark filed in a foreign country is entitled to rely on the foreign filing date for priority date purposes in the United States. This exception is mandated by various trademark treaties and conventions that the United States has signed. For information about foreign applications and registrations, refer to the Chapter 9 section "Foreign Application and Registration-Based Application."

Nationwide exclusivity can be challenged by a foreign applicant whose priority date is earlier than the priority date given another person's federal application based on use. The foreign applicant can claim exclusivity in all areas of this country where others have not used the mark earlier than the foreign applicant's priority date. As a result, the mark will be concurrently used by the foreign applicant and others who have earlier priority dates in particular geographic areas.

For example, if a Belgian national files an application in Belgium on June 30, 1990, to register "Penstemmon" in that country for audiocassettes and then files an application for federal registration of this mark in the United States on January 15, 1991, based on the Belgian application, June 30 is the priority date. Because that date is earlier than the December 20, 1990, filing date of the Colorado user in the preceding examples, when the Belgian national federally registers its mark it is entitled to exclusivity in all areas other than Colorado and Texas. Because the June 30 date precedes the first use dates of others in Washington (July 1, 1990) and Connecticut (September 16, 1990), the Belgian national is entitled to exclusivity in those states.

A foreign applicant can also challenge nationwide exclusivity based on an intent to use application. The priority date for an intent to use application is the application filing date. If the foreign applicant's priority date is earlier than the intent to use filing date, the intent to use applicant will not be able to obtain exclusivity anywhere in this country.

DURATION OF RIGHTS AND ABANDONMENT

The exclusive right to use a mark is not dependent on or equal to the duration of a state or federal registration. It has no specific period of existence. This right is based on use and can last indefinitely so long as the mark continues to be used properly to identify the products or services with which it was initially used. If the mark is not used altogether or the mark is not properly used, the exclusive right to use it comes to an end. At this point the mark and corresponding right are said to be abandoned. However, if nonuse occurs for some but not all the products or services a mark identifies or the mark is improperly used for them, this right may cease only for the products or services no longer offered or for those for which the mark is improperly used. At this point, the mark and right are abandoned for those products or services.

The Trademark Act definition of *abandonment* of a mark sets forth the kind of nonuse and generally describes what constitutes improper use that will result in loss of the exclusive right to use a mark.

A mark shall be deemed to be "abandoned" when either of the following occurs:

(1) When its use has been discontinued with intent not to resume such use. Intent not to resume may be inferred from circumstances. Nonuse for two consecutive years shall be prima facie evidence of abandonment. "Use" of a mark means the bona fide use of that mark made in the ordinary course of trade, and not made merely to reserve a right in a mark.

(2) When any course of conduct of the owner, including acts of omission as well as commission, causes the mark to become the generic name for the goods or services on or in connection with which it is used or otherwise to lose its significance as a mark. Purchaser motivation shall not be a test for determining abandonment under this paragraph.

Because intent is an element of abandonment arising from nonuse of a mark, nonuse alone may be insufficient to establish abandonment even if nonuse occurs for two consecutive years. Showing that a mark has been abandoned based on nonuse usually requires showing overt acts by the owner that manifest an intent to give up rights, which can be very difficult to do. Otherwise, abandonment may be inferred through acts of the owner reflecting an intent to give up rights. The following acts usually will not be sufficient to show this intent: failing to renew a registration, offering products or services on a limited basis, and discontinuing use due to strikes, equipment breakdown, shortage of supplies, economic conditions, or other circumstances beyond the owner's control. However, dissolution or going out of business, discontinuing use for one of multiple product lines, or making a material change in a mark can be enough to establish abandonment.

A mark can become generic if the majority of the relevant public treats it as the common name for the product or service. This happened to kerosene, aspirin, cellophane, and escalator. To avoid this result, the owner of a mark should properly use it, protest misuses of it, and, where feasible, implement advertising and programs to educate the relevant public that the mark identifies the owner's products or services and does not function as their common name. The owners of "Xerox," "Teflon," "Kleenex," "Levi's" and other marks that identify products first offered only by them take these precautions.

Rights may also be abandoned by permitting others to use a mark without conditioning the use on the owner's right to control the nature and quality of their products or services offered under it. In addition, rights may be abandoned when an owner does not protest third party unauthorized uses of a mark.

DISTINCTIVENESS AND SECONDARY MEANING

Although use of a mark is enough to give the owner proprietary rights on the date this use first occurs, the owner is not necessarily in a position to enforce rights against other users in every instance. When a conflict exists with respect to users of confusingly similar marks, the owner with the earliest priority date usually prevails but only if the first user's mark is distinctive when the conflict occurs.

If a mark is inherently distinctive, the owner's first use date is the priority date for purposes of deciding who is entitled to prevail. However, the owner of a mark that acquires distinctiveness may not be able to rely on its first use date as a priority date. Instead, for purposes of resolving the conflict, the priority date for such a mark ordinarily will be the date it becomes distinctive. When that date is before a later user's first use date, the owner can prevail. If not, the later user may be allowed concurrent use of the mark.

Suggestive, arbitrary, and coined marks are inherently distinctive. As noted in Chapter 4, they are entitled to protection from the time they are first used. Thus, when a conflict arises about use of this kind of mark, the owner with the earliest priority date usually prevails.

Marks that are descriptive, geographically descriptive, surnames, and others that have the potential to become distinctive, as discussed in Chapter 4, are difficult to protect on or soon after their first use date. Protection for this kind of mark must wait until it acquires a secondary meaning (distinctiveness), which is what establishes its priority date.

For example, because "Screenwipe" is descriptive of television and computer screen cleaning wipes, the first use date of June 21, 1989, will not be considered for purposes of determining priority if secondary meaning is not acquired for it until January 1990. If another person begins using the same mark in November 1989, the first user is unlikely to be able to stop the later use. The January 1990 priority date is subsequent to the other person's first use.

No generally accepted objective standard is used in deciding whether and when a mark acquires a secondary meaning. The courts and the USPTO evaluate all facts relevant to the question of whether this status has been attained on a case-by-case basis. Normally, the person claiming secondary meaning presents the facts and has the burden of proving secondary meaning. If the relevant public can be shown to regard the mark as indicating a particular source for products or services rather than the product or service itself, this burden is met.

In many cases, secondary meaning can be acquired by advertising and promoting a mark over a period of time. The USPTO often accepts proof of substantially exclusive and continuous use of the mark in commerce for five years as prima facie evidence that a mark has acquired secondary meaning.

Generally, the longer the use and the greater the amount of advertising and promotion, the more likely that secondary meaning will be acquired. Substantial sales, extensive advertising, exclusivity of use, and ownership of a federal registration are other factors that can create a presumption that secondary meaning has been acquired.

7

Corporate and Trade Name Registration

Rights in corporate and trade names are protected under the same general principles of law that are applicable to marks. Like those in marks, rights in corporate and trade names are based on use. They come into existence when a corporate or trade name is first used in connection with a business, just as rights in a mark begin when it is first used in connection with products or services. Differing from a mark, however, a corporate name must be registered to be legitimately used as such. This requirement does not hold for a trade name. As with a mark, a trade name may be registered after use, but, unlike a mark, it cannot be registered in the USPTO. Trade names are registered in accordance with state statutory law.

Although registration is required for a corporate name and may be required for a trade name, it does not confer on the owner rights or benefits that are equivalent to those obtained by federal registration of a mark. Corporate and trade name registration does not give the owner a priority position in a conflict concerning its use by another person. It is not always an obstacle to another person's registration of a confusingly similar name, and it has no effect outside the jurisdiction of the state granting it.

The law applicable to corporate and trade name registration

varies from state to state, with many similarities and differences. For this reason, this chapter discusses the subject in general terms. It is not a comprehensive review of applicable law.

CT Corporation Systems regularly prepares charts that provide information about trade (assumed or fictitious) name registration as well as corporate name registration in each of the states. You can contact the local CT Corporation Systems office in your area to learn what each state requires. Because the information is subject to change, however, the relevant law of each state should be checked just prior to filing for incorporation and/or registering a name.

CORPORATE NAMES

Registration

Corporate name registration is a matter of concern for every business intending to operate as a corporation and for every business operating as a corporation that intends to transact business in more than one state. You must have a name that can be registered as a corporate name in every state where business will be conducted. If you cannot register a name, articles of incorporation or an application to transact business will not be accepted, even though all other matters are in order.

In accordance with the law of most if not all states, articles of incorporation will not be accepted if the name used by a business is not approved by the state agency responsible for corporation matters. Similarly, if an existing corporation's name is not acceptable in the state where it desires to transact business, it cannot qualify to transact business in that state under that name. If it operates there anyway, it may not be able to prosecute or defend lawsuits in that jurisdiction until it qualifies.

As a general rule, a corporate name cannot be the same as or deceptively similar to the name of an existing domestic corporation, foreign corporation authorized to transact business in the state, or reserved name. In addition, some states do not allow registration of a name that is the same as or deceptively similar to the name of an existing limited partnership, foreign limited partnership authorized to transact business, or trademark or trade name registered by the state.

As indicated, corporate name registration is unlikely for a name that is the same as an existing registered name. If a name is similar to an existing registered name, however, registration often depends on the experience, opinion, and knowledge of the state employee(s) given responsibility for accepting articles of incorporation and applications to transact business. The determination is subjective. As a consequence, two people may reach different conclusions about whether a particular name is deceptively similar to an existing registered name.

In some instances, a name is accepted for registration even though it is substantially similar to a registered name. Sometimes the examining employee feels that a difference of one or two words is enough to distinguish the names. Ordinarily, the state finds this situation acceptable because it is concerned only with being able to distinguish one registered name from another and not with whether one name infringes another.

For example, "Shereth Music, Inc." might be accepted despite a registration of "Shereth Record Company." An examiner may feel that *music* and *record* are different enough to justify acceptance, whereas the owner of "Shereth Record Company" would probably disagree. Its position would be that these words create the same commercial impression and that, therefore, the names as a whole are confusingly similar. From an infringement standpoint, the owner is right. However, the state is not concerned about infringement. As a result, if the owner of "Shereth Record Company" believes it will be damaged by another person's registration of "Shereth Music, Inc.," the owner will have to institute a civil court proceeding against the newcomer to prevent use of the name. The owner has this right despite registration of the name by the state. The "Substantive Rights" section in this chapter explains that name registration does not give a corporation immunity from challenge.

Despite a statutory prohibition against registration of a deceptively similar name, many states allow registration of such a name. Ordinarily, this registration has two conditions: The owner of the existing registered name must give written consent to its use by another person, and one or more words must be added to the name presented for acceptance to make it distinguishable from the existing name. Alternatively, a deceptively similar name may be registered if the person presenting it for acceptance files a certified copy of a final court decree establishing the prior right to use it.

Although an existing corporation might consent to the use of a deceptively similar name, a business has no corresponding right to file objections with the state concerning registration of a name. A business has to institute a court proceeding challenging the right to use it rather than the state's decision to register it.

Typically, the procedure for registering a newly formed corporation's name is simple. When a business is incorporated, its name is automatically registered by a state as an integral part of the incorporation process. The name is set forth in the articles of incorporation. When they are accepted, so is the name. Consequently, filing separate documents or paying additional fees is not necessary to register a new corporation's name. Also, a separate renewal of registration of the name is not required. It is automatically renewed at the time the corporation files its annual or biannual report with the state.

The procedure for registering an existing corporation's name in states other than where it is incorporated is not complicated. Usually all that is required is to file an application with and pay a fee to the state where you desire registration. You can obtain the application form or format from the state. It typically asks for the name of the applicant corporation, its state and date of incorporation, and a brief description of its business. The application usually is to be signed by an officer of the corporation and accompanied by a certificate issued by an official of its state of incorporation to indicate that it is in good standing under the laws of that state. Once issued, the registration remains in effect and must be renewed annually or at some other interval by filing a renewal application and, in many cases, paying a fee.

Name Reservation

Although registering an available corporate name as soon as possible is important to prevent another person from doing so, in many instances filing articles of incorporation immediately after learning that the name is available may not be possible or practical. Similarly, immediately filing applications to transact business in every state where a newly formed or existing corporation plans to operate may not be possible or practical.

If neither can be done immediately, another action can prevent another person's registration of the name. Most, if not all, states have a procedure for reserving a corporate name for a specific time period. The person who reserves the name has an exclusive right to register it during this period, and the state agency responsible for corporation matters will not allow another person to incorporate a business or qualify to do business under it while it is reserved.

Typically, the reserved period ranges from 60 to 120 days. You obtain a reservation by filing an application as well as paying a fee. In some states the name reservation cannot be renewed, but in others it can be renewed or extended for an additional period of the same length beginning either immediately after the initial period expires or one day or more after expiration of the initial period.

Many states allow the transfer of a reserved name by the person who reserves it. Usually, you must file a notice of transfer with the state, which identifies the transferee.

Reservation of a name is recommended, but in most states it is not prerequisite to incorporation or filing an application to transact business.

Nameholder Corporations

Another way to prevent someone else's registration of a desired name is to form a nameholder corporation. To do so, you have to form a separate corporation under the name in each state where it will be used or else form a corporation under the name in one state and then file applications for it to transact business in other states where you intend to use it.

This approach is useful when a name reservation is about to expire and cannot be renewed. By forming the nameholder corporation, you can register and reserve the name on a longer lasting basis.

Usually, a nameholder corporation is minimally capitalized and does not conduct business. In effect, it is inactive and serves the purpose only of reserving a corporate name until an active corporation is formed or the nameholder corporation becomes active.

Use of "Corp.," "Inc.," "Ltd.," and Similar Terms

Most states require that the name of a corporation contain the word *corporation, company, incorporated, limited,* or a similar term. Abbreviations of these words are acceptable alternatives.

Many states prohibit as part of corporate names the use of words such as *trust, bank,* and *savings,* unless qualified to conduct such a business under provisions of statutes; those that denote a branch of the government; or others that indicate or imply that the corporation is organized for a purpose other than that permitted by its articles of incorporation.

Substantive Rights

As a general rule, corporate name registration does not give the owner substantive legal rights in the name. All that registration means is that a state has accepted a name because it has determined the name is not the same as or deceptively similar to an existing registered name. Rights in a name are based on use, as discussed in Chapter 6.

Acceptance of a name for registration is not a conclusive

determination that the name does not infringe another person's rights in the same or similar name, whether the other name is registered or unregistered. In other words, registration does not make a registered name immune from an infringement challenge by a person who has superior rights in the same or a similar name.

For example, notwithstanding incorporation of "Shereth Music, Inc." in Colorado on April 9, 1989, "Shereth Record Company," a Colorado partnership, is in a good position to challenge use of that name where the partnership first engaged in business under its name on December 20, 1986.

Note that registration does not have the effect of defeating a prior user's rights in the same or a similar name, whether that name is registered or unregistered. That is, the first person to register a corporate name does not acquire the exclusive right to use it by doing so, although the first registrant's name may be the basis for a state to refuse acceptance for registration of the same or a similar name by a prior user. Incorporation of "Shereth Music, Inc." does not place the corporation in a good position to challenge use of "Shereth Record Company" by the partnership.

Although registration may be the basis for a state to refuse acceptance for registration of a later user's name, usually it will not be a basis to prevent a later user from using the name if the owner of the registered name is an inactive corporation that is not conducting business or offering products or services under it. Even though the corporation is not engaged in any activities, registration of "Shereth Music, Inc." may be a basis for the Colorado Secretary of State to refuse incorporation of "Shereth Song Company" because it is deceptively similar to "Shereth Music, Inc." However, "Shereth Music, Inc." may not be in a good position to challenge use of "Shereth Song Company," although it is a later user, because "Shereth Music, Inc." can be claimed to have abandoned its rights in the name by nonuse. Refer to the Chapter 6 section "Duration of Rights and Abandonment" for discussion of abandonment.

TRADE NAMES

Registration

Many states require the registration of every trade name used by an individual, partnership, corporation, or other business organization doing business in the state. Generally, a trade name is understood to mean a name other than the true name of an individual, partnership, corporation, or other organization. In some states it is referred to as an *assumed name* or *fictitious name.*

A trade name is used by a business to identify itself. It differs from a trademark, which is used to identify the products or services offered by a business, as distinguished from identifying only the business. You can register in most states in accordance with similar yet separate procedures. However, the effect of registration is different for each. Another difference between the two is that only trademarks can be registered in the USPTO. When a name is used both as a trade name and as a mark, however, which is possible, it can be federally registered as a mark. Refer to Chapter 8 for information about state and federal registration of marks.

For example, when "Penstemmon Music," the trade name of The Shereth Group, Inc., identifies the corporation, it functions as a trade name and is registrable as such. However, when it is used to identify audiocassettes marketed by The Shereth Group, Inc., it functions as a mark and can be registered as such in a state as well as in the USPTO.

The primary reason for trade name registration is to give notice to the public of the actual names of the people using the name. Consequently, almost all states require trade name registration. Failure to register or supplying false information for a registration may be a misdemeanor and can subject the user to civil and/or criminal penalties.

Because trade name registration is required primarily to give notice, many states are not concerned whether the same or a similar name is registered by two or more persons. In states where this position is taken, all trade names presented for registration are accepted. In states that are concerned about the registration of deceptively or substantially similar names, those that fall within this category are refused registration.

In states where similarity of names is of no concern, obtaining a consent to register a trade name that is the same as or similar to a registered trade name is not necessary. In most states, moreover, the owner of a registered trade name has no right to object to state registration of the same or a similar name by another person.

The procedure for registering a trade name is not complicated. Ordinarily, it involves filing an application for registration with the proper government agency and paying a nominal fee. Depending on the state, the application may be filed with the secretary of state, Corporations Division, Department of Revenue, county clerk and recorder, or another agency.

In some states registration of a trade name involves filing an application plus publishing a copy of it or a notice of intention to register it. Any publication requirement can be satisfied by publishing the application or notice in a newspaper of general circulation in the state for a specified number of times consecutively. Some states require renewal of the registration at periodic intervals; others register trade names on a perpetual basis.

Trade Name Reservation and Use of Particular Words

None of the states appears to have a mechanism for reserving trade names. Furthermore, states do not appear to have statutory prohibitions against use of particular words as part of trade names or requirements that particular words be included as components of a trade name.

Substantive Rights

Unlike corporate name registration, which in most states does not create any substantive legal rights in a name, trade name registration in some states leads to a presumption that the registrant has the exclusive right to use the name in the state. Whatever position is taken, unless a statute provides otherwise, rights in a trade name, like those in a corporate name and mark, are based on use.

To a certain degree, registered trade names, like corporate names, are protected by the states. In states where registration of a name is not allowed if a deceptively or substantially similar name is already registered, in effect the registered name is given exclusivity. For example, the registered trade name "Penstemmon Music" is given exclusivity if the state where it is registered refuses to accept another person's application for registration of the identical name.

Notwithstanding the exclusivity a registered name receives in terms of registration, as is the case with a corporate name, acceptance of a trade name for registration ordinarily is not a conclusive determination that the registrant possesses the exclusive right to use the name or that it does not infringe rights claimed by a prior user whose name may or may not be registered. Also, as is the case with a corporate name, registration of a trade name does not mean the registrant's use is immune from attack by a prior user of the same or a similar name or that the first person to register can defeat the rights of a prior user of the same or a similar name.

8

State and Federal Registration

Contrary to what many people believe, registering a mark with the USPTO or a state is not required to obtain rights and does not create rights. Furthermore, the first person to register a mark does not necessarily thereby obtain the exclusive right to use it, if it is used by others. Rights in a mark in the United States are based on and maintained by its bona fide use to identify products or services, as discussed in Chapter 6. In fact, bona fide use is so important that insufficient use or lack of use makes the procedural and legal advantages given to a registered mark ineffectual. The validity of registration can be successfully challenged on the ground that it is not supported by use.

Federal registration cannot occur until a mark has been used, but an application for registration can be filed before then. With few exceptions, states require use of a mark as a condition of registration and before you can file an application to register.

Even though rights in a mark depend on use and are enforceable only if use is sufficient and continuing, state and/or federal registration is desirable. Both offer a mark's owner procedural and legal advantages that the owner of an unregistered mark does not have and cannot acquire. Without state or federal registration, the owner of a mark must rely on the common law to protect and enforce rights. For these reasons, you should file an application for federal and/or state registration as soon as practical after a mark is selected. Delay may permit the acquisition of concurrent use rights in all areas where someone else first uses the same mark.

In terms of procedural and legal advantages, federal registration offers more to the owner of a mark than state registration. Accordingly, if a mark is eligible for federal registration, usually your best interests require obtaining it rather than or in addition to a state registration.

FEDERAL REGISTRATION

Why Obtain a Federal Registration?

Many of the reasons for federal registration of a mark are obvious. They are the procedural and legal advantages expressly set forth in the Trademark Act (and listed in the next section of this chapter). Other procedural and legal advantages are not as immediately apparent.

One advantage resulting from federal registration is the information it makes available to the public. Registration of a mark is public information that is available in the USPTO files. It can be obtained by inspecting them at its offices in Arlington, Virginia. The same information also can be obtained through data base searches of the kind referred to in Chapter 5 and through the services of search companies who compile such data for their records or who inspect those files to obtain this information when requested. This can be helpful to a registrant. A search that discloses the registered mark may be enough to discourage a potential later user from using the same mark. In this case, you will never have to challenge that person's use or registration of the mark. In the event a search is not conducted and an application for federal registration is filed, the USPTO can refuse registration and thereby make a challenge to registration unnecessary.

Another advantage of federal registration is the nationwide rights it can give to a later user of a mark, in contrast to those of the first user. A registrant can obtain the nationwide exclusive right to use the mark although someone else uses it first in a limited geographic area. These rights occur by reason of the constructive use provisions of the Trademark Act, subject to some exceptions. Refer to the section "When Rights Come into Existence: Federal Registration" in Chapter 6.

If the first user of a mark federally registers it, that person obtains constructive use with nationwide effect regardless of where the mark is used. However, when the first user does not obtain a federal registration and a later user registers the same mark, the later user may be able to limit the first user's zone of natural expansion. In this case the first user's rights in the mark are limited to the area where use is made and the later user obtains exclusive rights throughout the rest of the country. Refer to the Chapter 6 section "Geographic Extent of Rights."

For example, Scooter, Inc. can probably obtain nationwide rights to use "Scoots" for restaurant services, excepting California, despite the Morris Company's earlier use of the same mark for the same services, based on the following fact situation: Morris Company first used the mark in California on December 20, 1987, but did not subsequently use it elsewhere or file an application to register it federally. Scooter, Inc. first used the mark in Colorado and Missouri on September 16, 1988, without knowledge of its earlier use by Morris Company and federally registered it on June 21, 1989.

One more advantage of federal registration is the basis it gives a registrant who is a U.S. citizen or resident to register the mark in a foreign country. The United States is a party to various treaties that provide for this right. The federal registration application filing date can be a priority date for rights in a foreign country. For example, the owner of an application for "Scoots" filed in the United States on September 16, 1988, is entitled to rely on this date for rights priority in Australia based on a registration granted in that country resulting from an application filed there on January 31, 1989. For more information about foreign protection, refer to Chapter 14.

Procedural and Legal Advantages

Federal registration gives a registrant several procedural and legal advantages, that are expressly set forth in the Trademark Act. Some are applicable to all registered marks, whether on the Principal or Supplemental Register, others are available only for marks on the Principal Register. For information about the two registers, refer to the next section "Principal versus Supplemental Register." The following sections of the Trademark Act are applicable to all registered marks:

(a) Litigation involving infringement, unfair competition, registration of a mark, cancellation of a registration, and damages for wrongful registration can be instituted in a federal district court rather than a state court, without regard to the amount in controversy or the citizenship of the parties.

Ordinarily, litigation involving a mark must be instituted in a state court unless a basis for federal court jurisdiction exists, in which case you can choose to institute litigation in either state or federal court. Federal jurisdiction exists only where the matter in controversy involves a constitutional question; the parties are citizens of different states and the amount in controversy is more than $50,000; or a federal statute expressly supports such jurisdiction. The Trademark Act is one of those statutes.

In some cases you may have a preference or find an advantage to being in one court rather than the other. For example, being in a federal court is advantageous for enforcing an injunction prohibiting trademark infringement. An injunction granted by the U.S. District Court, Southern District of New York, is immediately fully enforceable by the U.S. District Court, Colorado, as if it had been granted by that court. To the contrary, such an injunction granted by a New York state court would not be as easy to enforce in a Colorado state court. Among other things, the Colorado court would first have to recognize the validity of the injunction and then take action to enforce it in accordance with procedures prescribed by the Colorado court.

(b) A mark confusingly similar to a registered mark will be refused registration.

When a mark is federally registered, whether on the Principal or Supplemental Register, the USPTO may rely on it as a basis to refuse someone else registration for a confusingly similar mark. The Trademark Act states that registration will be refused a mark that so resembles a registered mark as to be likely to cause confusion. This provision is an advantage to a registrant. If the USPTO refuses registration to another user of the mark, the registrant will not have to challenge that person's right to registration. However, a court challenge to that person's right to use the mark may be necessary if the applicant elects to use it as an unregistered mark.

(c) A registrant who is successful in an infringement lawsuit is entitled to an order granting injunctive relief, destruction of infringing articles, the infringer's profits, up to three times the amount of the registrant's damages, costs of the lawsuit, and attorney fees in exceptional cases.

For more information about infringement, refer to Chapter 12.

(d) No governmental agency, federal or state, can require alteration of a registered mark, or require that additional trademarks, service marks, trade names, or corporate names associated with or incorporated into the registered mark be displayed different from the display contemplated by the registered mark as shown in the registration certificate.

The intent of this section of the Trademark Act is to prohibit a governmental agency from interfering with uniform use and display of federally registered marks. For example, a state cannot require a licensed real estate broker who uses a registered mark under a franchise ("Century 21") to display the broker's name as prominently in advertising as the franchisor's registered mark.

The following sections are applicable only to Principal Register marks:

(a) An application to register can be filed based on a bona fide intention to use a mark in commerce regulated by Congress.

You gain significant advantage by filing an application to register based on intent to use, which means filing it before using a mark or before using it in commerce regulated by Congress. You are given the opportunity to reserve nationwide rights in a mark as of the application filing date without regard to where it will be or is actually used. This advantage is possible by reason of the nationwide priority date that is effective as of the filing date. With this date the owner of a mark is treated as first using it everywhere in the United States as of the filing date, without regard to where actual use occurs at the time of first use. As a result, the owner obtains the exclusive right to use it everywhere with a corresponding right to prevent a later user from acquiring a right to use it. However, all of this is possible only if a bona fide use of the mark is made in commerce regulated by Congress and a registration is granted based on the application. Moreover, it is subject to exceptions. For more information about how use affects rights in a mark and where rights exist, refer to Chapter 6. For information about filing an intent to use application, refer to the Chapter 9 section "Intent to Use Application."

(b) On registration, the filing date shall constitute constructive use of the mark, conferring a right of priority, nationwide in effect, on or in connection with the products or services specified in the registration.

For information about constructive use, refer to the Chapter 6 sections "When Rights Come into Existence: Federal Registration"and "Geographic Extent of Rights" and the Chapter 9 section "Intent to Use Application."

(c) Registration shall be constructive notice of the registrant's claim of ownership of the registered mark.

On the registration date, a legal presumption concerning a registrant's right to use the mark becomes effective. On this date everyone in the United States is said to have knowledge of the registrant's ownership of the mark (even though not every person actually does know). In effect, the mark is treated as having been first used everywhere on this date. The result is that a person who first uses a confusingly similar mark after the registration date cannot claim that the later use was made in good faith and without knowledge of the registrant's mark. If the registrant institutes an infringement action against the later user, the defenses of good faith, innocence, and lack of knowledge are not available to the later user. For information about exceptions to the constructive notice advantage, refer to the Chapter 6 section "Geographic Extent of Rights."

(d) A certificate of registration shall be admissible in evidence and shall be prima facie evidence of the validity of the registered mark and of the registration of the mark, the registrant's ownership of the mark, and of the registrant's exclusive right to use it on or in connection with the products or services specified in the certificate.

A registration certificate is treated as legally sufficient evidence to establish these facts unless they are disproved. This desirable legal advantage relieves a registrant from having to introduce evidence to establish these facts in an infringement lawsuit or USPTO proceeding. In the absence of a registration, the owner of a mark has to introduce evidence supporting these facts.

(e) If a registered mark has been used for a period of five consecutive years after registration and an affidavit confirming this is timely filed in and accepted by the U.S. Patent and Trademark Office, the registration will be incontestable, subject to certain exceptions.

A registration that becomes incontestable cannot be canceled or successfully challenged on the ground of invalidity because the mark is confusingly similar to another mark or because it is claimed to be descriptive, geographically descriptive, or a surname. For information about unregistrability based on these grounds, refer to the section "Federally Registrable Marks: Principal Register" in this chapter. An incontestable registration can be successfully challenged on certain other grounds, as explained in the Chapter 12 section "USPTO Opposition and Cancellation Proceedings."

Another desirable attribute of an incontestable registration is that it is conclusive evidence of the validity of the registered mark, of the registrant's ownership, and of the registrant's exclusive right to use it in commerce on or in connection with the products or services specified in the registration certificate. *Conclusive evidence* means these facts are irrebuttable and do not need to be proven. Despite this kind of evidentiary weight given to an incontestable registration, it is subject to certain defenses and defects, which are discussed in Chapter 12.

(f) A registration can be recorded with the United States Treasury Department, which entitles the registrant to the provisions of Section 526 of the Tariff Act and Trademark Act that are a basis for the United States Customs Service to bar the importation of products bearing infringing marks.

When a copy of the certificate of registration for a mark is filed with, and as directed by, the secretary of the Treasury, the United States Customs Service is authorized to refuse the entry into this country of imported merchandise that bears a copy or simulation of the registered mark. This merchandise can be seized and forfeited for violation of the customs laws. Merchandise that accompanies an individual is exempted when it is intended for personal use and not for sale, subject to certain exceptions.

Principal Versus Supplemental Register

The USPTO maintains two different registers for marks as provided for by the Trademark Act. They are the Principal Register and the Supplemental Register. They differ in the procedural and legal advantages each offers the owner of a mark, the kinds of marks eligible for registration on each, and the registration process itself.

To be eligible for either register, a mark must first be used in commerce regulated by Congress. One exception is that you can file an application for registration on the Principal Register based on intent to use.

Registration on the Principal Register is preferable. Unless a mark is clearly not eligible for registration on this register, you should seek registration on it. As the list of advantages in the preceding section indicates, this register gives the owner of a mark certain desirable procedural and legal advantages that are not available to a mark on the Supplemental Register.

To be eligible for registration on the Principal Register, a mark must *identify and distinguish* products or services. If it has not been used, it must be able to perform this function. In other words, the mark must be distinctive. For a discussion of distinctiveness, refer to the Chapter 2 section "Distinctiveness" and the Chapter 10 section "How To Establish Distinctiveness."

A distinctive mark is immediately eligible for the Principal Register after first use, unless it falls within one of the categories of marks that can be refused registration as provided by the Trademark Act, which is explained in the section "Federally Registrable Marks: Principal Register" in this chapter.

A mark that is clearly eligible for the Principal Register cannot be registered on the Supplemental Register. However, registration of a mark on the Supplemental Register will not prevent registration on the Principal Register later if it becomes distinctive, despite the USPTO practice of refusing to issue registrations that are in all respects identical to each other. In accordance with this practice, you can obtain only one registration for a mark for each use format covering the same products or services.

An application to register a mark on the Principal Register can be amended to one for registration on the Supplemental Register when registration on the Principal Register is refused on the ground that the mark is nondistinctive because it is merely descriptive, deceptively misdescriptive, primarily geographically descriptive or deceptively misdescriptive, or primarily a surname. A mark that is *capable of distinguishing* products or services (as differentiated from identifying and distinguishing them) is eligible for registration on the Supplemental Register but not on the Principal Register. This kind of mark is said to be nondistinctive. More information about marks in this category is in the section "Federally Registrable Marks: Supplemental Register" in this chapter.

A mark is not registrable on the Supplemental Register if it can qualify for registration on the Principal Register or if it is unregistrable (see the next section for a definition of *unregistrable* marks). Furthermore, you cannot file an application for registration on the Supplemental Register based on intent to use. You must make a bona fide use of the mark before you can file an application for Supplemental Register registration. After first use, you can register it immediately.

The process for registering a mark on either register is the same up to a point. In terms of similarity, the USPTO examines applications to determine whether statutory formalities are met, the mark is eligible for registration, and the mark is confusingly similar to a registered mark. If a mark is in this way found to be registrable, the applications are then handled differently.

A Supplemental Register mark is promptly registered, and notice is given to the public in the *Official Gazette* of the USPTO, which it publishes weekly. A Principal Register mark is also published in the *Official Gazettte* but not to give notice of registration. Rather, notice of a Principal Register mark advises the public that the mark will be registered if no one files objections to the registration with the USPTO. If no objections are filed within 30 days after the publication date, or a timely request for an extension of time to object is not filed and granted, the mark will be registered on the Principal Register. Notice of registration is then given in the *Official Gazette*. For more information about publication, refer to the section "Approval For Registration" in Chapter 11.

Federally Registrable Marks: Principal Register

Section 2 of the Trademark Act states that all marks that identify and distinguish products or services are registrable on the Principal Register unless they consist of or comprise a mark in categories *a* through *e* below.

(a) Immoral, deceptive, or scandalous matter; or matter which may disparage or falsely suggest a connection with persons, living or dead, institutions, beliefs, or national symbols, or bring them into contempt, or disrepute;

(b) The flag or coat of arms or other insignia of the United States, or of any State or municipality, or of any foreign nation, or any simulation thereof;

(c) A name, portrait, or signature identifying a particular living individual except by his written consent, or the name, signature, or portrait of a deceased President of the United States during the life of his widow, if any, except by the written consent of the widow;

Marks in the above categories are unregistrable. Generic words and symbols are also unregistrable because they are incapable of identifying and distinguishing a product or service. Chapter 3 contains discussion about unregistrable marks.

(d) A mark which (1) when used on or in connection with the products of an applicant is merely descriptive or deceptively misdescriptive of them, or (2) when used on or in connection with the products of an applicant is primarily geographically descriptive or deceptively misdescriptive of them, except as indications of regional origin (which may be registered as collective or certification marks), or (3) is primarily merely a surname.

Section 2(f) of the Trademark Act provides that a mark in category *d* may be registered if the owner can show that it has become distinctive. The Chapter 2 section "Distinctiveness," the Chapter 6 section "Distinctiveness and Secondary Meaning," and the Chapter 10 section "How to Establish Distinctiveness" contain information on this topic.

> (e) A mark which so resembles a mark registered in the Patent and Trademark Office, or a mark or trade name previously used in the United States by another and not abandoned, as to be likely when used on or in connection with the products or services of the applicant, to cause confusion, or to cause mistake, or to deceive.

A mark in category *e* may still be registered. The Trademark Act provides

> if the Commissioner determines that confusion, mistake, or deception is not likely to result from the continued use by more than one person of the same or similar marks under conditions and limitations as to the mode or place of use of the marks or the products or services on or in connection with which such marks are used, concurrent registrations may be issued to such persons when they have become entitled to use such marks as a result of their concurrent lawful use in commerce.

> Concurrent registrations may also be issued by the Commissioner when a court of competent jurisdiction has finally determined that more than one person is entitled to use the same or similar marks in commerce.

This language means that the USPTO can allow two or more persons to register the same mark without regard to who used it first. This permission is possible if the later user first used the mark prior to the filing date of an application for federal registration by an earlier user and without knowledge of an early use by anyone else. It is also possible when the owner of the earlier filed application consents to a concurrent registration by the later user. It can happen only if the Commissioner of Patents and Trademarks or a court determines that a likelihood of confusion does not exist because each person uses the mark in a different geographic area, to identify products or services distinguishable from those offered by the other, or in different trade channels.

A registration granted under these circumstances is in accordance with a procedure prescribed by the USPTO or by court order. It is referred to as a *concurrent use* registration. The registration certificate specifies the conditions of the concurrent use, such as the geographic area and/or the products or services it covers. The "Concurrent Use Application" section of Chapter 9 explains the procedure to follow to obtain a concurrent use registration.

For example, a concurrent use registration might be granted based on the following hypothetical situation: Shereth Music, Inc. first used "Penstemmon" for audiocassettes on July 4, 1989, in Colorado, Utah, California, and Texas without knowledge of anyone else's use. Music in Motion, Inc. first used the same mark for the same products on October 21, 1988, in New York, Pennsylvania, Ohio, Kentucky, Virginia, and West Virginia but did not file an application for federal registration. If Shereth Music subsequently learns about Music in Motion's mark and elects to file an application for a concurrent use registration, it must disclose Music in Motion's use so that the USPTO can institute a concurrent use proceeding. Both parties may be able to register this mark federally as concurrent users. If registrations are granted, the certificate will indicate where each user has rights to the mark.

Federally Registrable Marks: Supplemental Register

The Trademark Act states that for the Supplemental Register a mark may consist of any word, name, symbol, label, package, product configuration, slogan, phrase, surname, geographical name, numeral, or device, or any combination of them but only if the mark is capable of distinguishing products or services.

Within this category are nondistinctive, nonfunctional shapes of products and product packaging as well as trade dress. Supplemental Register registration is possible for marks that are primarily merely descriptive and for those that are primarily geographically descriptive.

STATE REGISTRATION

Why Obtain a State Registration?

Most states have enacted legislation concerning marks that is modeled on the Trademark Act. Consequently, in most cases state registration gives a registrant certain procedural and legal advantages over the owner of an unregistered mark. However, state registration offers fewer advantages than federal registration and cannot be relied on nationwide or beyond the jurisdiction of the state granting the registration.

Generally, state registration is desirable when a mark cannot be federally registered and, in some cases, as an interim measure until a mark can be federally registered. In particular situations, state registration may be desirable for advantages it offers over a federal registration.

As noted in this chapter, federal registration is not possible for a mark that is not used in commerce regulated by Congress and may not be possible because a confusingly similar mark is already registered. Although state registration does not depend on use of a mark in commerce regulated by Congress, you must use the mark in the state where you seek registration before an application can be filed. As a general rule, states do not allow applications to be filed based on an intent to use a mark.

Because trademark legislation varies from state to state, the law of each state where registration is desired should be reviewed to determine the available procedural and legal advantages.

Procedural and Legal Advantages

Generally, the following advantages of state registration are available in most states.

One advantage is that information about a registered mark becomes a matter of public record. This publicity is to the advantage of the mark's owner because it may be enough to dissuade another person from using the same mark. Someone who learns about the registered mark through a search of a state's trademark records probably will not use a mark that is confusingly similar to a registered mark.

The same result is possible when a person desiring to use and register a mark does not conduct a search. Usually, the state refuses registration when the same or a similar mark is already registered. Because a refusal to register is not a ruling on the right to use a mark, however, the owner of a registered mark will be required to challenge another person's use of an unregistered mark.

Most state statutes modeled on the Trademark Act expressly provide that use of a registered mark without the registrant's consent makes the unauthorized user liable to the registrant for the user's profits and registrant's damages. In addition, a registrant ordinarily is entitled to injunctive relief and destruction of the infringer's reproductions, copies, counterfeits, and colorable imitations of the registered mark. Some states also give the registrant a right to recover attorney fees incurred by enforcing rights in a registered mark. State courts are the proper courts for lawsuits concerning infringement of a registered mark.

Most states refuse registration to marks that are confusingly similar to marks it has registered. Some state statutes also provide that registration can be refused if the mark is deceptively similar to a registered corporate or trade name, and some go further by providing that registration can be refused to a mark that is confusingly similar to a mark registered by the USPTO. Few, if any, state statutes provide that registration of a mark constitutes constructive notice of the registrant's exclusive right to use a registered mark. The evidentiary weight many states give to registration certificates is no more than that they are competent and sufficient proof of registration. In these states a registration certificate is not treated as prima facie evidence of ownership of the mark, validity of the registration, or the registrant's exclusive right to use the mark.

Nothing comparable to the federal registration concept of incontestability appears to hold for a state registration. State registration has no legal significance to the U.S. Treasury Department or the U.S. Customs Service concerning barring importation of products that bear infringing marks.

One Register

State registration of a mark is not made in terms of being on a particular register. Typically, all registrations are given the same benefits and procedural and legal advantages.

Registrable Marks

State statutes modeled on the Trademark Act contain the same prohibitions concerning unregistrable marks as those in the Trademark Act. For information about these prohibitions, refer to the sections on federally registrable marks in this chapter.

9

Types of Applications

The registration process begins with filling out an application form with the mark to be registered plus other required information. The USPTO requires use of either its form or a typewritten application that provides the same information in the same format and order. Most states require use of a state-provided form.

States typically have only one form that can be used without regard to the kind of mark to be registered, but the federal government has more than four different application forms, each for a particular kind of mark. Consequently, you have to select and use the proper form for the mark to be registered.

FEDERAL REGISTRATION

At least four kinds of marks can be federally registered. The Trademark Act provides for registration of trademarks, service marks, certification marks, and collective marks.

Each of these marks can be the subject of a Principal Register or Supplemental Register application. Moreover, depending on an applicant's right to exclusive use of the mark, each of these marks may be the subject of an application for concurrent use registration.

Each kind of mark and each kind of registration has its own

application form and each kind of application has two versions: one seeks registration based on use of the mark prior to filing the application, and the other seeks registration based on an intent to use the mark.

Copies of application forms for each kind of mark, register, and use claim are included in Appendix B. They are similar in format, with differences attributable to the information they must contain and the material that must accompany them. This information and material is discussed in this chapter and in Chapter 10.

Each application form can be adapted to suit the kind of legal entity seeking registration. As discussed in Chapter 10, an application may be filed by an individual, firm, joint applicants, corporation, association, and other kinds of legal entities. In addition, any one of these persons can file based on ownership of a foreign application or registration.

Trademark

A trademark application seeks registration of a mark for products. The products may be natural or manufactured. Some examples of trademarks are "Coca-Cola" for beverages, "Post" for cereals, "Gant" for clothing, "Max Factor" for cosmetics, and "Monsanto" for chemicals.

Service Mark

A service mark application seeks registration of a mark for services one person performs for a person or persons other than the service mark owner. Services may be performed for pay or otherwise. Trademark and service mark applications are very similar in information required. Some examples of service marks are "TWA" for airline transportation, "United Parcel" for package delivery, "Lord & Taylor" for department stores, "Disney World" for entertainment, and "MCI" for long distance telephone services.

Certification Mark

An application for a certification mark registration covers a mark used on or in connection with products or services of people other than the owner. This kind of mark is used to certify regional or other origin, material, mode of manufacture, quality, accuracy, or other characteristics of such products or services. It may also be used to certify that work or labor on products or services was performed by members of a union or other organization.

Ordinarily, marks used under franchise agreements and other licenses function as trademarks or service marks rather than as certification marks. In these situations the owner controls the nature and quality of products or services offered by a franchisee and does not certify that they meet standards or possess certain characteristics.

Some examples of certification marks are "Underwriter's Laboratories," which certifies that products meet certain electrical standards; "Good Housekeeping," which certifies that products meet certain quality standards; and "Roquefort," which certifies that a particular cheese comes from a specific geographic area.

A certification mark differs from other kinds of marks in two ways. The owner cannot use it to identify products or services and it does not identify or distinguish the products or services of one person from those of someone else.

A mark that is used to identify the owner's products or services cannot also function as a certification mark if it is identical to or so nearly alike the proposed certification mark as to constitute essentially the same mark. However, the owner of a mark for products or services can also be the owner of a certification mark. As long as the marks are different, the same person can own them. The differences must be meaningful and not inconsequential, such as different sizes or styles of lettering. The "Good Housekeeping" trademark for magazines and the "Good Housekeeping Institute Seal of Approval" certification mark are examples of marks used by the same owner that are sufficiently different to function as a trademark and as a certification mark, respectively.

Because the purpose of a certification mark is to certify, it should not be used to indicate that the products or services originate from a particular person. Instead, it should be used only to indicate that the products or services with which it is used have been examined, tested, inspected, or in some way checked by someone other than the person who offers them. In other words, it should be used to indicate that the products or services meet certain qualifications or standards established by someone other than the person who offers them.

The owner of a certification mark is the person who determines the qualifications, standards, or requirements for certification; has responsibility for certifying that products or services meet them; and exercises legitimate control over other's use of the mark. The user of a certification mark is not its owner and cannot be an applicant.

Frequently, a governmental body or a body operating with governmental authorization is the owner of a mark that consists solely or essentially of a geographic name and certifies regional origin. Under the circumstances that many or all persons in a region want or need to indicate that their products or services originate there, the mark does not identify or distinguish the products or services. Rather it indicates their regional origin. An example of this kind of mark is "Grown in Idaho" which identifies potatoes from a specific geographical area.

A certification mark that consists of a geographical term, alone or as a component, will not be refused registration on the ground that it is primarily geographically descriptive. The Trademark Act expressly provides that this basis for refusal does not apply to an indication of regional origin.

A certification mark's qualifications, standards or requirements can be original with the owner, or they can be another person's that the owner adopts. Regardless of who establishes them, the owner of a certification mark cannot discriminately refuse to permit its use by a person who can meet them. If the owner does discriminate, a registration can be canceled. Registration can also be canceled if the owner does not control or is not able to exercise legitimate control over use of the mark, per-

mits use of it for purposes other than to certify, or uses it to identify products or services.

Certification mark applications are examined in the same way
as other applications and can be refused registration for the
same reasons. However, they differ from other kinds of applications with respect to certain required statements.

The application must state that the owner "is (intends to exercise) exercising legitimate control over use of the mark" rather
than state that the owner uses or intends to use the mark. The
kind of things the mark is or will be used to certify may be
described in general terms, such as insurance agency services,
agricultural commodities, or printed material rather than specifically, as automobile insurance agency services, corn, or
monthly magazines.

A certification mark application must also state that the
owner is not and will not be engaged in the production or marketing of the products or services to which the mark is applied.
Furthermore, it must specify the manner in which and the conditions under which the mark is or will be used. For example, it
may state that the mark certifies (or will certify) that the apples
of those who are authorized to use it come from Washington
State.

Specimens submitted with the application should evidence
use of the mark by persons other than the owner. They may be
tags, labels, advertising, and promotional material that feature
the mark, or they may be other things that are acceptable to
show use of a trademark or service mark. The Chapter 10 section "Specimens" contains more information about this topic.

Collective Mark

A collective mark application seeks registration of a mark that
members of a cooperative, an association, or other collective
group or organization use as a trademark or service mark to
identify and distinguish their products or services from those of
non-members, or, in the case of a collective membership mark,
to indicate membership in a union, association, or other organization. Some examples of collective trademarks and service

marks are "PGA" for golf instruction services and for golfing exhibitions, the team emblems of the National Football League used to identify various products, and "Boy Scouts" which is used to identify pocket knives. Collective membership marks are "Rotary International" for a public service organization, "ZBT" for a fraternal organization, and "U.S. Jaycees" for an association of chambers of commerce.

Although the members of an organization use or intend to use a collective mark and registration is based on their use, they do not own the mark and cannot be applicants. The owner is the person who controls the use of the mark. Typically, this "person" is the organization to which the members belong.

The organization's right to control use of a collective mark does not give the organization itself a right to use the mark to identify products or services it may offer. A collective membership mark can be used only to identify membership. This limitation on the collective mark owner's right does not apply to the right of an owner of a trademark or service mark. The owner of a trademark or service mark can use it without adversely affecting any rights in the mark, although the owner may permit others to use the mark under license.

Collective mark applications are examined in the same way as other mark applications and may be refused for the same reasons. However, some different statements are required for collective mark applications. A collective mark application is different in terms of identifying who uses or intends to use the mark. This kind of application requires a statement that the applicant "is exercising (or intends to exercise) legitimate control over the use of the mark" instead of stating that the applicant is using (or intends to use) the mark.

The use statement also differs from the usual trademark or service mark application in terms of stating who uses the mark. It states that the mark was first used or will be used by members of the applicant, not by the applicant.

If members are to use the mark as a trademark or service mark, the application must state the products or services with which it is to be used. If it is used as a collective membership mark, the application must state that the mark is used to indicate membership, describe the general nature of the organization (for example, social club, trade association, labor union), and specify the class of persons entitled to use the mark and the nature of the applicant's control over its use.

Specimens for a collective mark that is used as a trademark or service mark must show use of the mark by members and not by the organization. They can be tags, labels, advertisements, promotional material, or other items acceptable as evidence that a mark is used to identify a product or service. For collective membership marks, the specimens can be membership cards and certificates, plaques, decals, or copies of stationery that feature the mark. For more information, refer to the Chapter 10 section "Specimens."

Principal or Supplemental Register Application

An application may seek registration of a mark on either the Principal or Supplemental Register. Each kind of mark can be registered on either register, and the applications are substantially identical in format, required information, and material.

Concurrent Use Application

A concurrent use application seeks registration of a mark for a particular geographic area instead of nationwide, for specific products or services, or for particular channels of trade. It must indicate that the applicant's right to use the mark is not exclusive. In addition, it must identify everyone unrelated to but known to the applicant who concurrently uses the mark.

As a general rule, to be eligible to obtain a concurrent use registration, you first must have used the mark before the filing date of an application owned by someone else who used the mark earlier than you. Your use must have been without knowledge of the earlier use, lawful, and not infringing. Typically, lawful use occurs when your mark is used in a different geographic area from where the earlier user's mark is used. An infringing use would be in the same geographic area.

For example, Shereth Music can obtain a concurrent use registration for "Penstemmon" under the following facts: Shereth first used it on July 4, 1990, in Colorado and Utah without knowledge of an earlier use in New York, Virginia, and Washington, D.C., by Scooter, Inc., which filed a federal application on October 21, 1990.

If your mark was first used after another person's application filing date, you can still obtain a concurrent use registration in two ways. The owner of the application based on an earlier use may consent to the grant of such a registration, in which case the USPTO will issue the registration if it determines that confusion, mistake, or deception is not likely to result. A concurrent registration may also be obtained if a court determines that more than one person is entitled to use the same or similar marks.

A concurrent use application must provide the names and addresses of all known concurrent users, any applications filed or registrations issued to them, the geographic areas of their use, the products or services with which they use the mark, the way they use the mark, and the periods of such use. In addition, it must state the geographic area, products or services, and the mode of use for which the applicant seeks registration.

Concurrent use applications are examined in the same way as other applications and are subject to the same grounds for refusal. If the USPTO determines that confusion, mistake, or deception is not likely to result from your continued use of the mark, it will institute a concurrent use registration proceeding.

Because the concurrent use registration process can be complicated, I recommend that you retain a trademark attorney's services for this kind of application. Concurrent use rights are discussed in the Chapter 6 section "Geographic Extent of Rights."

Intent To Use Application

An intent to use application can be filed for each kind of mark. It is examined in the same way as other kinds of applications and is subject to the same grounds for refusal. It differs from other applications primarily with respect to the use statement, submission of specimens with the application, and the way it is processed after the USPTO determines that the proposed mark is registrable.

Instead of alleging use of the mark, the use statement indicates that the applicant has a bona fide intention to use the mark in commerce regulated by Congress. Specimens are not filed with the application. Instead of being registered after the mark is found to be registrable, the application remains as a pending application until an acceptable use statement and specimens are filed in the USPTO.

If you first use a mark in commerce regulated by Congress at any time while the USPTO is examining an intent to use application, you may amend the application to claim such use. Then the application will be treated the same as an application based on use.

You must file the use statement and specimens within six months of the date the USPTO issues you a notice of allowance. This notice is issued after the mark has been published for opposition and the USPTO determines that it is registrable because no opposition has been filed or because the mark has survived opposition. For information about publication for opposition and opposition proceedings, refer to the Chapter 11 section "Approval for Registration" and the Chapter 12 section "USPTO Opposition and Cancellation Proceedings."

If, for one reason or another, you cannot file the use statement and specimens within the six month period, you can obtain a six month extension to file this material by submitting a written request before the first six month period expires. In addition, you must pay a fee for the extension and provide a verified statement that you have a continued bona fide intention to use the mark and the products or services to be identified by the marks.

You can obtain further extensions of time to file the use statement and specimens beyond the first 12 months after issuance of the notice of allowance. For all extensions after the first, you must submit additional written requests. Each request must be filed prior to expiration of the then current extension and each request must show good cause why a further extension should be granted. You must pay a fee with each extension request.

Requests for extensions can be made and granted for a period of time adding up to no more than 24 months after the first extension. Therefore, the use statement and specimens must be filed no later than three years after the notice of allowance is issued. Failure to file the use statement and specimens within the first six months after the notice of allowance or within an extension period results in abandonment of the application.

The Trademark Act expressly provides that an intent to use application cannot be assigned by the applicant prior to the filing of the use statement, except to a successor to the applicant's business or to the portion of the business to which the mark pertains.

Foreign Application and Registration-Based Application

A mark can be federally registered in the United States without being used in this country if the USPTO application is based on a foreign application for the same mark or if the mark covered by the USPTO application is the subject of a foreign registration.

To do so, the applicant's country of origin and the United States must be parties to a convention or treaty concerning marks or the applicant's country of origin must extend reciprocal registration rights to U.S. nationals. An applicant's country of origin is the country where the applicant has a bona fide and effective industrial or commercial establishment. In the absence of such an establishment, the applicant's country of origin is where the applicant is domiciled or the country of which the applicant is a national, if the applicant does not live in a treaty country.

If the USPTO application is filed within six months of the foreign application filing date, the USPTO effective filing date is the foreign application filing date. As a result, the priority date for the mark in the United States is a date earlier than the USPTO application filing date. For example, a United States priority date of February 17, 1990, can be relied on for a USPTO application filed by a Japanese national when the following facts exist: The applicant filed an application to register "Shereth" in Japan on

February 17, 1990. Five months later the same applicant files a USPTO application for the same mark. Upon registration of the mark in Japan on September 18, 1990, a certified copy of the Japanese registration certificate is filed in the USPTO.

Filing a copy of the foreign application in the USPTO or including a statement in the application to the effect that the foreign filing date is claimed for priority purposes is not necessary. However, the filing date and country should be disclosed. For the previous example, the USPTO application should include a statement that the mark is the subject of a Japanese application filed February 17, 1990.

A certified copy of the foreign registration resulting from the foreign application must be filed. Until a copy of the foreign registration is filed, the USPTO will not register the mark or publish the mark for opposition or registration on the Supplemental Register. Rather, action on the USPTO application will be suspended pending receipt of the foreign registration.

A USPTO application based on a foreign registration must be filed with a certified copy of that registration. Also, the foreign registration must be in force and effect when the USPTO application is filed. Otherwise, a filing date will not be given to the USPTO application.

A USPTO application based on a foreign application or registration must allege use of the mark and be accompanied by specimens evidencing use. This use does not have to be in the United States or in commerce regulated by Congress. An application that does not allege use or is not accompanied by at least one specimen will not be assigned a USPTO filing date.

An English-language translation of a foreign registration is required. The drawing in the USPTO application must correspond to the mark shown by the foreign registration. The products or services covered by the USPTO application must correspond to those in the foreign application or registration. Moreover, a foreign applicant must appoint a domestic representative.

A foreign application-based or registration-based application is subject to the same requirements as other kinds of applications concerning classification and the description of the goods or services it covers. Furthermore, it is examined in the same way and can be refused registration for the same reasons.

If the mark covered by the USPTO application is used in commerce and also is covered by a foreign application, it is entitled to the earlier priority date if it is registered based on the foreign registration. If it is registered based on use in commerce, the applicant does not have to file a certified copy of the foreign registration.

If a USPTO application is based on both use in commerce and a foreign application, which is possible, the foreign registration certificate must be filed to take advantage of the earlier priority date.

STATE REGISTRATION

The kinds of marks that can be registered in a state vary from state to state. Some states register only trademarks, some register only trademarks and service marks, and some register all kinds of marks. When you want registration in a particular state, check the law of that state to see whether registration is possible for the kind of mark to be registered.

Many states have only one prescribed application form to use for applying to register a mark. Typically, it is preprinted and provided by the state free of charge on request to the state agency responsible for registering marks. Some states accept an applicant-prepared application. Contact each state where you seek registration to learn whether a particular form is prescribed for the kind of mark to be registered and whether a state-provided form must be used. A copy of the application form for Colorado is reproduced in Appendix C.

10

Application Content

Preparing and filing an application to register a mark is not complicated. As noted in Chapter 9, each kind of mark that can be registered as well as each kind of registration has a generally accepted form. After you choose the proper form, complete it with the information required by the USPTO or the state. Federal and state application forms have blanks for the insertion of this information.

This chapter discusses the required information as well as the kind of material that must be submitted with an application when it is filed with the USPTO or a state.

FEDERAL REGISTRATION

Required Information and Material

If a mark has been used, the required information consists of a specification of the mark to be registered, the applicant's name, address, domicile and citizenship, date the mark was first used, date the mark was first used in commerce, a listing of the products or services on or in connection with which the mark is (or will be) used, and how it is used. Also, the applicant must select either Principal or Supplemental Register.

This required information, as well as a standard statement

that forms part of the application, must be verified by the applicant. The statement is to the effect that the applicant is the owner of the mark and that it is in use in commerce. In addition, it says that, to the best of the applicant's knowledge and belief, no one else has the right to use the mark on or in connection with the other products or services that would cause confusion, mistake, or deception.

The verification can be an affidavit or declaration. A declaration must be in accordance with the USPTO prescribed format which is included in Appendix B.

The application must be accompanied by material showing the mark as actually used, that is, "specimens" of the mark. In addition, it must include a separate page featuring the mark to be registered (the "drawing" of the mark) plus a filing fee. If the applicant has retained an attorney in connection with the application, a power of attorney also should be submitted as part of the application.

If the application is based on an intent to use, the same kind of information, statement, fee, drawing, and power of attorney must be provided. Specimens are not submitted, however, and instead of dates of use the application must indicate that the applicant has a bona fide intention to use the mark in commerce. Also, at other points in the application referring to use, the applicant's intent to use rather than actual use replaces information about actual use of the mark.

Who Can Register

The owner of a mark is the only person entitled to file an application for federal registration. The owner is the person who has the right to control the nature and quality of the products or services offered under the mark at the time the application is filed. For information about ownership of a mark, refer to the Chapter 6 section "Who Is the First Owner?"

An owner is not required to be a citizen or resident of the United States but must be a natural or juristic person. A *natural person* is an individual and includes the legal representatives of an individual. The Trademark Act states that a *juristic person* includes a firm (partnership or joint venture), corporation, union, association, or other organization capable of suing and being sued in a court of law.

A local, city, county, state, or federal government agency also may apply to register a mark, as can a foreign government or its subdivisions. Furthermore, joint owners of a mark can apply to register it.

An application filed in the name of someone who is not the owner will be void. For this reason, an application should not be filed by a licensee, sales representative, or distributor of the owner or by an officer, director, or shareholder of a corporation that owns a mark, even if that individual is the sole shareholder or has the right to control the corporation.

If the owner files an application with a mistake in how the owner's name is given, the mistake can be corrected by amendment. However, an application filed by a person other than the owner cannot be amended to correct the identity of the owner. Instead, a new application must be filed.

If ownership of a mark changes while an application is pending, the application can be assigned. In this case, a document evidencing the ownership transfer should be recorded in the USPTO, and notice of the change in ownership, a copy of the transfer document, and all required information about the new owner should be given to the examining attorney. When this information is provided before the mark is accepted for registration, the certificate shows the name of the new owner as the registrant. If this information is provided later, the certificate shows the name of the prior owner as the registrant, and amendment of the registration is necessary if the new owner is to be shown as the registrant.

Individual

An individual as the owner should be identified as the applicant by giving his or her name, address, and country of citizenship. An individual doing business under a trade name should add to his or her name "also known as" or "doing business as" and then the trade name.

Joint Owners

Two or more persons who own a mark jointly and not as members of a partnership or joint venture should be identified by giving each owner's name, address, and country of citizenship. For example, the names of a husband and wife should be given as joint applicants if they use a mark outside the context of a partnership and desire to register it as joint applicants.

Partnership or Joint Venture

If a partnership or joint venture is the owner, the name of the partnership or joint venture should be given, followed by a statement such as "a partnership composed of" or "a joint venture composed of." After this statement is a list of the names of the general or active members who compose the partnership or joint venture. Each member's country of citizenship should also be given. If the partnership or joint venture does not operate under an assumed name, then the names of its members should be given. The state under whose laws the partnership or joint venture is organized or exists should be given, as well as the business address of the partnership or joint venture.

Corporation or Association

When a corporation is the owner, the official name of the corporation should be given, followed by the statement "a [state or country where incorporated] corporation" and the corporation's business address. If a corporate division is using the mark, the division name should not be given as the name of the applicant. If a subsidiary corporation owns the mark and desires to register it, however, the name of the subsidiary should be given as the applicant.

If an association is the owner, its official name should be given, followed by the statement "an association organized and existing under the laws of [state or country where organized and existing]" and the association's business address.

Domestic Representative

Regardless of citizenship, an owner who is not domiciled in the United States must designate a domestic representative in the United States who can be served notices or process in proceedings affecting the mark. The domestic representative can be a natural or juristic person.

The designation is made by including in the application a separate statement giving the name and address of the domestic representative by providing this information in a document that accompanies the application. Appendix B contains a statement that appoints a domestic representative.

One Mark Per Application

A separate written application is required for each mark. The format as prescribed by the USPTO is shown in Appendix B. If a mark is used in materially different formats, a separate application must be filed for each format to be registered. For example, a separate application should be filed for the mark "Penstemmon" if one version depicts it in script lettering and another depicts each letter as a different shape, such as mountain peaks for each m and the top view of a phonograph record for the o.

Although an application can cover only one mark, it can seek registration of the mark for all the products and/or services the mark is used to identify or will identify when it is used. However, only those that are specified in the application will be covered by the resulting registration. Those not specified or later identified by the mark can be the subject of a separate application.

Specifying Products and Services

The Trademark Act requires that an application specify the products or services on or in connection with which a mark is or will be used. Specifying is done by clearly and concisely describing products and services by common names and descriptions that are generally recognized and currently used in the marketplace, or by succinct language when no commonly used names or descriptions exist. This description is referred to as the "identification of goods (services)."

In addition to specifying the products and/or services covered by an application, you should separate them into international classes when they fall in more than one class. Also the class number, if known, should be designated for each grouping. If you do not provide the class number, the USPTO will insert it in the application and notify the applicant. Appendix C includes a copy of the USPTO international classification schedule, which gives a brief description of what is covered by each class.

An applicant who does not have access to information about the international classification system can call the USPTO trademark classification unit to learn the international class of particular products and services. To facilitate early registration of a mark, determine this information before filing the application. Questions about classification that arise after an application is filed can cause delays in the registration process.

If an application incorrectly classifies products and/or services or their description is not clear, the USPTO may request clarification, correct the classification by amendment, or request the applicant to amend the application in accordance with its suggestions. If you feel a USPTO-requested or -suggested description is not accurate, you should bring it to the USPTO's attention and discuss it rather than routinely adopt it. If the description is inaccurate, the validity of the registration may be affected.

The USPTO uses the classification system solely for its own convenience in administering the registration of marks. This system does not limit or extend an applicant's rights in a mark. However, it does affect the filing fee for the application. Each class is considered as a separate application for filing fee purposes. The 1990 fee per class is $175.00. For example, for an application that covers one class, the fee is $175.00; if it covers three classes, the fee is $525.00. The filing fee for at least one class must be submitted before a filing date will be assigned to an application.

A court or USPTO determination of whether a likelihood of

confusion exists does not necessarily consider the class given a mark. Consequently, a likelihood of confusion may exist when two persons use the same mark even though it identifies products and/or services in different classes. For example, likelihood of confusion may exist if "Penstemmon" is used by one company for phonograph records and by another company for sheet music, despite classification of records in International Class 9 and sheet music in International Class 16.

Multiple-Class Applications

An application that seeks registration of a mark for products and/or services in more than one class is referred to as *combined* or *multiple class*. It can cover products in different classes, services in different classes, and/or products and services. However, only one registration certificate is issued for this kind of application. Appendix B includes a copy of a multiple-class application.

A multiple-class application is substantially similar in format to a single-class application. It differs in the manner of setting forth the products and/or services and the date of first use in commerce for them.

The identification of goods (and/or services) for each class must be listed in numerical order beginning with the lowest class number. Each identification should be given in a separate paragraph. Following the paragraph listings for the identification of goods or services are separate paragraphs for the dates of first use for products or services in each class. Again, the list begins with the lowest class number.

You can use the earliest date of first use for any product or service in each class rather than first use dates for every product or service in the class. If the dates of first use are the same for all classes, you can use one paragraph indicating the date applies to all classes.

You can amend a multiple-class application during the examination process to change, add, or delete information about classification. You can similarly amend a single-class application to add one or more classes. However, amendments cause delays in the entire application process.

The USPTO can refuse to register the mark in one class without affecting registration of the mark in the remaining classes so long as the applicant satisfactorily deals with the refusal. An applicant may, for example, delete the class that is the basis for the refusal.

Dates of First Use and Intent to Use

Regardless of whether a mark has been used before or after filing for registration, an applicant must make a statement of use as part of the application. The timing for this statement depends on the kind of application filed.

When an application is for a mark that has been used in commerce regulated by Congress before filing, the statement must be in the application at the time of filing. If the mark is the subject of an intent to use application, the statement must be submitted within six months after the date the USPTO issues a notice of allowance that the mark can be registered. If the time for submitting the statement is extended by the USPTO based on an applicant request, however, the statement must be submitted prior to expiration of the extended period. For information about filing the use statement, refer to the Chapter 9 section "Intent to Use Application." The Chapter 11 section "Approval for Registration" contains information about the notice of allowance for an intent to use application.

The statement has two parts. It must provide the date the mark was first used on or in connection with the applicant's products or services, either in intrastate commerce or in commerce regulated by Congress. It must separately give the date the mark was first used in commerce regulated by Congress and specify whether the commerce is interstate or territorial, or commerce between a foreign country and the United States. Even if these dates are the same, they must be separately stated.

If the first use of a mark was by a related company, the following language should be included as a separate statement in the application, usually below the clause referring to the mode or manner of use.

> The mark is used by applicant's related company and such inures to applicant's benefit. Applicant controls the nature and quality of the products [services] to which the mark is applied.

Ordinarily, you may but do not have to give the name of the related company. For information about a related company's use, refer to the Chapter 6 section "Who Is the First Owner?"

When a mark has been first used by a prior owner who is a predecessor in title of an applicant, the following language should be included in the use statement.

> The mark was first used on or in connection with the goods [services] on [insert date of first use] by applicant's predecessor in title; was first used on or in connection with the goods [services] in [insert type of commerce] on [insert date of first use] by applicant's predecessor in title.

Usually you can but do not have to name the predecessor(s) of the applicant.

A mark that is used only in intrastate commerce is not eligible for federal registration. However, an intrastate sale may qualify as use in commerce regulated by Congress if it directly affects this kind of commerce.

Be as definite as possible about the day and month first use occurs. Express any uncertainty with phrases such as "at least as early," "prior to," "before," and "on or about." The USPTO will accept the month and year or even just the year for the first use dates. However, the USPTO presumes the date to be the last day of the month when a month and year are given, and the last day of the year when only a year date is given.

If a composite mark is the subject of an application and part of it was first used before another component, the use statement can specify use dates for each component. Nonetheless, you must also give the use dates for the composite.

You do not have to specify separate first use dates for every item when the identification of goods (services) for a class lists more than one item. One set of dates can be used for the class.

Manner of Use

An application must specify how the mark is used on or in connection with an applicant's products or services. Ordinarily, the applicant indicates that the mark is used by applying it to labels, tags, containers, or whatever constitutes the specimens submitted to the USPTO. For services the applicant indicates that the mark is applied to advertising and/or promotional material referring to the services.

Drawing

The last page of an application usually is a sheet of paper that contains a "drawing" of the mark, although literally this word may not be an accurate description for the way a mark is shown on the page.

The purpose of the drawing is to show the mark that an applicant intends to register. It defines the mark covered by the registration. Any question as to what constitutes the mark to be registered is resolved by the drawing. Therefore, the drawing must substantially correspond to the mark that is actually used as shown by the specimens. The drawing should not include anything that does not constitute part of the mark.

When a mark shown on specimens consists of various integral components, the drawing should depict all of them. If it depicts only one element of a composite mark or the drawing is an incomplete representation of the mark, the USPTO is likely to require a new drawing depicting the composite.

The drawing can show a mark in two ways: It can be typewritten with all uppercase letters, or it can be drawn, in which case the drawing is referred to as being in "special form." A typewritten "drawing" can be used if a mark consists only of words, letters, numerals, or a combination of them and if it does not include any design or style of lettering features, color is not an element, and it does not contain unusual forms of punctuation or diacritical marks, such as the German umlaut, Spanish tilde, or French accent.

When a choice is possible, a typewritten drawing is recommended over a special form drawing. It permits use of the mark in a variety of formats without jeopardizing registration renewal if the format used at the time of renewal differs from what was registered. Perhaps more importantly, it avoids the possibility of another person's justifying use of a similar mark on the ground that the design elements are dissimilar or that the similar mark does not contain design elements.

For example, if your registered mark consists of "Penstemmon" combined with a coat of arms design and you discontinue use of the design element, renewing the registration based on "Penstemmon" alone may be difficult. The USPTO may conclude that the coat of arms design is a material part of the mark or a new applicant may be able to justify use of "Penstemmon" alone arguing that the coat of arms design is so dominant that when it is not used with "Penstemmon" the marks are distinguishable. In this hypothetical situation, you should show "Penstemmon" in a typewritten form for one application and separately register the design element with a special form drawing in another application.

You must submit a special form drawing when color is an element of the mark or the mark consists of pictorial features or designs. This kind of drawing also is appropriate when the mark includes special characteristics, is shown by a specific style of lettering or by a distinctive form, or includes unusual forms of punctuation or diacritical marks. A special form drawing is an exact representation of the mark as shown by the specimens.

A special form drawing cannot contain typewritten portions and the mark should not be drawn in color. The mark must be depicted in black and white. Every line and letter must be black, clear, clean and crisp, and all filled areas must be solid black. The use of gray to indicate shading is unacceptable. The mark can be drawn on the page with black india ink, or a photolithographic copy or printer's proof of the mark can be affixed to the page.

Color as element of the mark can be indicated by lining appropriate areas of the drawing in accordance with USPTO guidelines for color. Appendix C includes a copy of these guidelines.

When color is an element, a statement should be included in the application to the effect that the drawing is lined to designate specific colors, which are a feature of the mark. If an applicant lines the drawing to show color but does not wish to make color a feature of the mark, the application should include a statement that the drawing is lined for color but color is not a feature of the mark.

Stippling and lining can be used to indicate shading or to show design elements of a mark. In this case, a statement should be included that the stippling or lining is for purposes of indicating shading or design features of the mark.

Symbols such as "TM," ©, and similar notices should not appear in the drawing.

If a mark's position on products, containers, or labels is a feature of the mark (such as the Levi's pocket tab), a special form drawing must be used. A nonfunctional container or product configuration used as a mark also requires a special form drawing. The drawing should illustrate where the mark appears or the configuration. If position is a feature of the mark, an outline of the product, container, or label may be shown by dotted lines. A statement should be included that the dotted lines are not part of the mark but are used only to show the position of the mark.

The drawing page should be durable, white, smooth, good-quality paper 8 ½ inches wide by 11 inches long. Bond paper is suitable for typewritten drawings, and bristol board can be used for drawings in special form. The mark should appear centered on the page equidistant from the sides and approximately two-thirds from the top. The preferred size is 2 ½ by 2 ½ inches; it can be no larger than 4 inches by 4 inches.

If reducing the mark to the required size renders any of its details illegible, the applicant should insert a statement in the application that describes the mark and the details.

A heading must be placed at least an inch below and across the top of each drawing. It must contain the following information:

Applicant's complete name
Applicant's post office address
Date of first use
Date of first use in commerce
Description of the products and/or services

All drawings must be prepared to conform to USPTO rules. Otherwise, they will not be accepted.

Specimens

Specimens are submitted with an application to show the USPTO the mode or manner of use of a mark and to substantiate its actual use by or for the benefit of the owner. The USPTO maintains them in the application file and makes them available for inspection by the public. Therefore, the applicant must submit specimens that show the mark used in a format represented by the drawing, support the applicant's ownership of the mark, and indicate that the labeling, advertising and promotional material used on or in connection with the applicant's products or services are in compliance with applicable law.

If the products or services are the kind that suggest specimens should be in compliance with a particular law, the USPTO may inquire about an applicant's compliance to determine whether the mark is lawfully used. For example, if a mark is used for food products regulated by the federal Food and Drug Administration and the specimens do not feature an ingredient listing or net contents disclosure, the USPTO may ask the applicant if the product is lawfully distributed.

If color and/or design are important elements of the mark and registration is intended to include either or both, the submitted specimens should show the mark in color and/or with the design as a part of it.

The USPTO will inquire about any inconsistency between the mark shown on the specimens and the information given in the application. The mark depicted in the specimens will be compared to the mark represented in the drawing, and the name of a manufacturer, distributor, or other party shown on the speci-

Federal Registration

mens will be compared to the applicant's name. Furthermore, the products or services reflected by the specimens will be compared to those covered by the application.

Three specimens must be submitted for each class of products or services an application covers, but three different specimens are not necessary. They can all be the same. If an application covers more than one item in a class, submitting three specimens for every item is not necessary. You can submit three specimens for one of the items. For a multiple-class application, you must submit three specimens for each class, but they can be for only one of the items in the class. If fewer than three specimens are submitted, an application will be given a filing date, but the remaining number must be provided.

Articles submitted as specimens must be capable of being arranged flat, such as by being folded, and of material suitable for placement inside a manila folder. Their size cannot exceed 8 ½ inches by 13 inches. The USPTO may require that bulky specimens be replaced with specimens that meet these specifications.

Specimens should be duplicates of material an applicant actually uses on or in connection with the products or services covered by the application. For products, specimens can be labels; tags; containers; displays closely associated with products; or photographs of a product showing the mark affixed, stamped, stenciled, engraved, or otherwise applied to or used on or in connection with it.

To be acceptable specimens of use, displays must be directly associated with products. Usually they are point-of-sale material such as menus, shelf banners, and window displays. According to the USPTO, to be acceptable as specimens, displays must be so related to the sale of products that an association of the two is inevitable.

Drawings or printer's proofs are not acceptable specimens if they are not actually used on or in connection with an applicant's products or services but merely illustrate how the mark looks. In addition, advertising material, publicity releases, invoices, bills of lading, instruction sheets, price lists, catalog listings, circulars, and business cards featuring a mark and referring to the products it identifies may not be acceptable as specimens.

For services, specimens can be copies of advertising or promotional material, photographs of signage, or other material that features the mark and refers to the services.

How to Establish Distinctiveness

An application can include a claim of distinctiveness if an applicant anticipates the USPTO will initially refuse registration on the ground that the mark is merely descriptive, deceptively misdescriptive, primarily geographically descriptive, geographically deceptively misdescriptive, or primarily merely a surname. You can expedite registration by claiming distinctiveness before the application is filed. However, waiting to see how the USPTO views the mark and then making a claim of distinctiveness if registration is initially refused may be appropriate.

Section 2(f) of the Trademark Act indicates what kind of proof the USPTO may accept as prima facie evidence that a mark has become distinctive. It states that acceptable proof is evidence of substantially exclusive and continuous use of the mark in commerce by an applicant on or in connection with the applicant's products or services for five years before the date that a claim of distinctiveness is made. The evidence can be in a variety of forms. A statement should be made in the application itself that registration is being sought under the provisions of Section 2(f).

When an applicant owns an earlier granted registration for the same mark, a claim of distinctiveness that refers to the applicant's ownership of the earlier registration may be sufficient. The claim can be along the following lines:

Registration is requested under the provisions of Section 2(f). The mark sought to be registered is distinctive as evidenced by applicant's ownership of Registration No._____.

If no registration has been granted earlier, in many instances the USPTO will accept an applicant's affidavit or declaration for a claim of distinctiveness for a mark that is merely descriptive (but not highly descriptive), geographically descriptive (but not a well known location), or a surname. Such an affidavit would contain this kind of language:

> Applicant believes that the mark has become distinctive, as applied to applicant's products [services], by reason of substantially exclusive and continuous use thereof as a mark by the applicant in commerce for the five years next preceding the date of the filing of the application.

If this kind of affidavit is submitted, language claiming distinctiveness under this section can be as follows:

> Registration is requested under the provisions of Section 2(f). The mark has become distinctive as evidenced by the affidavit attached hereto.

When this kind of affidavit will not be sufficient to support a claim of distinctiveness, you can submit other evidence. This evidence can be affidavits, declarations, advertising and promotional material featuring the mark, information about expenditures incurred in connection with using the mark, statements from the public and trade, and other material referring to the nature and extent of use that show that the mark distinguishes the products or services with which it is used. If you take this approach, the following statement can be included in the application:

> Registration is requested under the provisions of Section 2(f). The mark has become distinctive of applicant's products [services] as evidenced by the showing separately submitted.

Disclaimer

An applicant who anticipates that the USPTO will not allow registration of a component in a composite mark can include disclaimer language in the application when it is filed. Alternatively, a disclaimer can be entered after the application is examined by the USPTO and entry of one is made a condition of registration.

A *disclaimer* is the applicant's statement that no exclusive rights are claimed in the disclaimed component standing alone but that rights are claimed in the composite mark. In effect, a disclaimer is an applicant's acknowledgment that others can use the disclaimed component except in combination with the rest of the applicant's mark.

The purpose of a disclaimer is to permit registration of a mark that is registrable as a whole without creating a false impression that the registrant possesses exclusive rights in the disclaimed component. A disclaimer is preferable over deletion of the component from the drawing if a deletion would materially alter the mark and create a different impression.

Registration is usually refused if a component is descriptive of the products or services covered by the application and can stand alone as a separable element of the mark. For example, the word *gate* is descriptive as found in the mark "Check Gate" shown on specimens for electronic walk-through metal detectors. Therefore, this word should be disclaimed.

The following language about disclaimed components is what the USPTO expects:

> No claim is made to the exclusive right to use [insert disclaimed matter], apart from the mark as shown.

It should appear in the application, usually below the manner of use clause.

A disclaimer ordinarily is not necessary for a mark that consists of either a descriptive word and a distinctive word combined to create one compound word that is not descriptive or two descriptive words combined to form a new word that is not descriptive, whether hyphenated or not in either case. For example, a disclaimer is not necessary with respect to the mark "Minitmix" for a cake mix, although it consists of the descriptive words *minute* and *mix*.

The Trademark Act states that a disclaimer will not prejudice or affect an applicant's rights in the disclaimed component, that exist at the time of the disclaimer or that may arise later. It also provides that a disclaimer will not prejudice or affect an applicant's right to register the disclaimed component in another application if it becomes distinctive.

Components of a mark that are registrable cannot be disclaimed. If a mark as a whole is unregistrable, disclaimer will not make it registrable unless something such as a design element remains after the disclaimer. Furthermore, disclaiming a component that is confusingly similar to another mark is not enough to overcome a refusal to register based on the other mark.

Ownership of Prior Registrations

An applicant who owns prior registrations for a mark that is the same as or similar to the mark to be registered can appropriately include this information in the application. Then the USPTO, having been advised of the applicant's ownership, will not cite the earlier registration(s) to refuse the mark to be registered.

STATE REGISTRATION

Required Information and Material

Applications for state registration require much of the same kind of information and material that is given in federal applications. You can compare a representative state application in Appendix C with a federal application in Appendix B to see the similarities.

The applicant must be the owner of the mark and identified by name and address. Also, the applicant's legal entity status as individual, partnership, or corporation must be indicated.

The verification portion of a state application should be signed by the applicant or by an authorized representative of an applicant who is a juristic person. In the latter case, give the title of the person who signs.

Some states require a list of the specific products or services with which the mark is used; others allow the use of classification headings as general descriptions for the products or services.

Most states use a classification system similar to that formerly used by the USPTO and require a designation of the class for the applicant's products or services. As with the USPTO, the classification system is used for the state's convenience in connection with administering the registration of marks. Appendix C includes a copy of the former USPTO classification system.

States do not seem to allow multiple-class applications. Consequently, to register products or services in more than one class, you will have to file separate applications.

The date the mark was first used anywhere must be given, as well as the date of first use in the state where you are applying for registration. Almost all states require that a mark be used in the state as a condition of registration by the state.

Most states require recitation of how the mark is used. Indicating that the mark is used on labeling or in advertising can fulfill this requirement.

Many states do not require a separate drawing of the mark, although you may have to describe in writing a mark that consists of a design or that has design components. Some states require tags, labeling, advertising, or photocopies of such material as specimens showing actual use of the mark. Other states accept typed, handwritten, or drawn representations of the mark as specimens.

States generally do not require a showing of distinctiveness to register a mark that is descriptive or a surname. They do not ordinarily require applicants to disclaim rights in nondistinctive matter forming part of a mark. Similarly, they do not usually require an applicant to claim ownership of a prior state or USPTO registration for the same or a similar mark.

Because application forms differ from state to state and because the law as well as state practices change from time to time, this information may not be accurate in all instances. To make sure that you provide all required information for a state application, you should contact the state agency responsible for mark registration to obtain its current requirements.

11

Filing and Prosecuting an Application

Ideally, you should file an application for registration as soon as possible after you have selected and searched a mark. Especially a mark that is to be federally registered on the Principal Register, whether the requisite use is made before filing or at a later date. As discussed in the Chapter 6 section "When Rights Come into Existence: Federal Registration," the federal application filing date can determine who has nationwide exclusive rights in a mark.

Promptly filing for federal registration is important for another reason. When two or more applications are pending for confusingly similar marks, the earliest application filed will be examined and moved toward registration first, without regard for the first use date for the mark it covers.

Although you do not gain the same legal advantages by filing an application for state registration, prompt filing after selection, searching, and use of the mark in the state have been achieved is still desirable. As is the case with federal registration, once a mark is registered by a state, ownership and use become a matter of public record, available procedural and legal advantages can be relied on, and the agency responsible for registration is likely to refuse registration to confusingly similar marks.

Ordinarily, filing an application does not involve more than mailing or delivering it to the USPTO or state. Then an applicant has nothing to do until the USPTO or state agency takes action. The USPTO or state may ask the applicant questions about specimens, compliance with laws, ownership, dates of use, or other matters affecting registrability of the mark. Registration may be refused because of a mark that is the subject of an existing registration or an earlier application filed by another person or the mark may be accepted for registration. The action the agency takes determines what an applicant must do next.

This chapter discusses what an applicant can expect from the USPTO and state examination of an application, possible responses to inquiries and/or refusal to register, and what happens when a mark is accepted for registration.

FEDERAL REGISTRATION

Filing an Application

When an application has been completed, it and all required accompanying material can be delivered or mailed to the USPTO. This material includes the filing fee, which is $175 per class as of 1990. If it is delivered, an application can be deposited in a box in the Department of Commerce Building, 14th Street, Washington, D.C., or a box in the lobby of the USPTO at 2021 Jefferson Davis Highway, Building 3, Crystal Plaza, Arlington, Virginia. A mailed application should be addressed to Commissioner of Patents and Trademarks, U.S. Patent and Trademark Office, Washington, D.C. 20231. Although the USPTO's offices are located at 2021 Jefferson Davis Highway, this address should not be used for mailing.

After the USPTO receives a fully and properly completed application, all required material, and the filing fee, the Correspondence and Mail Division assigns the application a filing date and serial number. The application, drawing, and specimens are placed in a three-fold manila jacket called the *file wrapper*. The Trademark Application Section designates on the file wrapper the class for the products or services identified by the mark. The class indicated by the applicant is typically used unless it is obviously incorrect. If it is incorrect or the applicant has not indicated a class, the Trademark Application Section selects what appears to be the correct class and notes it on the file wrapper. Also, the Trademark Application Section notes the law office within the USPTO to which the application has been assigned for examination. As of 1990, the USPTO had eight law offices, each consisting of approximately 15 examining attorneys.

Next, the Intelligent Key Entry Section mails a receipt to the applicant and delivers the file wrapper to the appropriate law office. The managing attorney of that law office assigns the file wrapper to an examining attorney in the law office. The receipt which contains the filing date, serial number, and class number, is mailed from one to two months after the application is received by the USPTO. Appendix C includes a copy of the form used by the USPTO for the filing receipt.

You can confirm the USPTO's receipt and learn this information within a few weeks after mailing an application. The USPTO will return to the applicant a self-addressed postpaid postcard with the filing date and serial number stamped on the back if the applicant submits the postcard with the application. If more than one application is mailed in the same envelope, a separate postcard should be clipped to each to obtain information about each application. The following statement or something similar should be written or typed on the back of the postcard:

This is to acknowledge receipt of an application seeking registration of [insert the mark] filed on behalf of [insert the applicant's name].

Only one serial number is assigned to an application regardless of the number of classes it may cover. This number is usually six digits. It identifies the application during the examination process and should always be used when communicating with the USPTO about the mark. When a mark is registered, a new number, which is called the *registration number*, is assigned to the mark.

If an application is incomplete when filed or the fee is not paid at the time of filing, the USPTO does not give it a filing date or serial number. The application and accompanying material, if any, are returned to the applicant with a statement indicating the defects that prevented acceptance for filing.

An application that has been returned to the applicant can be refiled at any time in the future by providing the required information, material, and fees. However, the filing date will be the date of refiling, not the date it was first submitted to the USPTO. If more than five weeks or so elapse from the date the verification was signed and the refiling date, you may need to have the verification reexecuted.

In the normal course, each examining attorney examines newly filed applications assigned to him or her, in the order of the dates on which they are filed. Accordingly, the application filed first is examined first.

An applicant who desires that an application be advanced out of its normal order of examination can petition the Commissioner of Patents and Trademarks for special treatment. The petition must explain why expedited examination is appropriate and justified. Ordinarily, this kind of petition is granted when actual or threatened infringement, pending litigation, or need for a registration as a basis for securing foreign registration is shown. If the petition is granted, the "special" application is given special treatment throughout the entire course of the registration process, including appeal. A fee must be paid with the petition.

An application can be examined out of the normal order of examination in a few other cases without petition at the time of filing or during the prosecution stage. The reasons for such treatment are given in the *Trademark Manual of Examining Procedure*. The major categories are:

1. New applications that are requests to register the same mark that was the subject of a previous registration inadvertently allowed to be cancelled or to become expired

2. New applications filed for the same mark in other classes as a result of a requirement to limit an application to one class of products or services
3. Applications of different parties that contain conflicting marks
4. Applications of the same party for the identical or virtually identical mark
5. Applications in which practice requires that action be taken within a specified time, such as an examining attorney's appeal brief and decisions on motions
6. Applications under suspension, as soon as they are removed from suspension
7. Applications that have been revived
8. Letters of express abandonment of the application
9. Petitions to the commissioner
10. Applications pending more than five years

Prosecuting an Application

An examining attorney examines each application to determine whether the mark it covers is entitled to registration. This examination is done in accordance with guidelines established by the *Trademark Rules of Practice* (37 Code of Federal Regulations) and *The Trademark Manual of Examining Procedure*, copies of which can be obtained from the USPTO to help an applicant understand the applicable procedures and standards.

Examination includes a search of the USPTO records for confusingly similar registered marks and those covered by pending applications. In addition, it includes an inspection of the specimens and drawing and consideration of whether the mark is used as a mark, the product or service description, classification, dates of use, manner of use, ownership, and the verification. For applications based on an intent to use, examination of specimens and dates of use is deferred until a statement of use is filed. For information about this statement, refer to the Chapter 9 section "Intent to Use Application."

Examination also involves an evaluation of the mark in terms of whether registration can be refused due to the nature of the mark itself, that is, because it is generic or within one of the categories of marks that should not be registered. Information about these categories is provided in the Chapter 8 section "Federally Registrable Marks: Principal Register."

After the examining attorney examines the application, the applicant is advised in writing of the results, which may or may not require the applicant's response. This examination happens four to six months or more from the date the application is filed.

The examining attorney's communication to an applicant is referred as an *action*. *Final action* refers to the last action an examining attorney takes concerning a refusal to register or request that an applicant satisfy a requirement.

In many cases, besides stating the basis for refusal and/or the requirements the applicant must satisfy, the action gives the applicant instructions to follow to prepare a response. If no instructions are provided, you can refer to the two USPTO publications for guidance or telephone the examining attorney to obtain assistance directly.

As a matter of form, the action identifies the application by serial number, mark, and applicant name and address. It contains a typed number in a space titled "Action No." to indicate that it is the examining attorney's first, second, third, or subsequent action on the application. The mailing date given marks the beginning of the six-month response period. The examining attorney's name, telephone number, and law office number appear at the end of the action. In addition, the action contains the mailing address for your response and the kind of identifying information that should be included in the response.

You have six months from the mailing date of an action to respond. A statement to this effect appears as a preprinted sentence at the bottom of the action. If you do not respond, do not respond on time, or do not respond completely within this six-month period, the application is deemed to be abandoned. The examining attorney cannot shorten or extend this time period because it is set by the Trademark Act.

When an application is abandoned, all examination and action by the USPTO concerning it ceases, and the applicant has no right to rely on anything regarding it. Consequently, the filing date is lost for constructive use purposes. However, abandonment does not prejudice or affect the applicant's rights in the mark or prevent the applicant from filing a new application. The applicant who has a continuing interest in registering the mark must begin anew by filing another application and paying another fee.

For one reason or another, an applicant may desire to abandon an application. It can be done by filing a letter in the form of a response with the USPTO that expressly abandons the application.

To be timely, a response must be received by the USPTO on or before the last day of the six-month period. If the last day falls on a Saturday, Sunday, or federal holiday in the District of Columbia, the next business day is treated as the last day.

Depending on the circumstances, an application abandoned for failure to respond may be revived by paying a fee and filing with the commissioner a petition to revive explaining why a delay in responding was unavoidable. The petition must be verified and accompanied by a proposed response.

If the application contains an obvious informality (such as incorrect classification), the examining attorney and the applicant are unlikely to disagree, and a verification signed by the applicant is not necessary, then the examining attorney can make a correction on his or her own initiative by an "examiner's amendment." Ordinarily the applicant's authorization is necessary and is obtained through a telephone conference with the applicant or the applicant's attorney. Then the examining attorney mails an action confirming the correction to the applicant, but no response is required. An examiner's amendment is used to expedite prosecution of an application.

Another way to expedite prosecution is a priority action, which can be issued when an informality requires an applicant's written response. Typically, the examining attorney telephones the applicant to request an appropriate response. Then a priority action, which indicates the kind of response required, is mailed to the applicant. If the USPTO receives a proper response within two months from the action mailing date, the application is given priority over other pending applications awaiting the examining attorney's reexamination. If the USPTO does not receive a response within this period, the response is accepted if it is filed within the six-month period, but the application is not given priority. Instead, it is reexamined in the regular course.

After the applicant files a response to a priority or regular action, the examining attorney reexamines the application. If it is not in condition for approval of the registration, another action is issued, and a response to it must be filed within six months from its mailing date unless the examining attorney indicates that the action is a final action. The USPTO policy is that second actions are final actions whenever possible.

Once a final action has been issued, an applicant's response is limited to an appeal to the Trademark Trial and Appeal Board, compliance with the requirement, or, if permitted, a petition to the Commissioner of Patents and Trademarks. During the period between a final action and the expiration of the time for filing an appeal, an applicant may request the examining attorney to reconsider the final action. However, such a request does not extend the time for filing an appeal or petitioning the commissioner. If an appeal is not filed in time or a petition is denied, the application becomes abandoned.

Under certain circumstances and for good and sufficient cause, USPTO activity on an application may be suspended for a reasonable time. This decison is within the examining attorney's discretion and may be initiated by the examining attorney or at the request of the applicant. If the applicant's response is due at the time suspension is considered, the response must be filed on time. Suspension does not relieve the applicant from responding or extend the response time. It only suspends action due to be taken by the examining attorney. When action is suspended, the applicant is notified in writing.

The examining attorney issues an action upon finding that additional information is required to facilitate examination, correction of the application is necessary, the search discloses a confusingly similar mark, the applied-for mark falls within one of the unregistrable mark categories, and/or another reason to refuse registration exists. The action contains information about the other mark and/or the statutory grounds, as well as reasons the examining attorney relied on to refuse registration. The action is also supposed to indicate all other grounds for refusal and informalities that should be corrected, and clearly advise the applicant of everything that is required to make the application acceptable for registration.

For example, if registration is refused on the basis of an existing registered mark and, in addition, the classification and identification of products or services are unacceptable, the action provides information about the registered mark, indicates the proper classification, and suggests an acceptable identification. If registration is refused because the examining attorney believes the applied-for mark is merely descriptive or a surname, the action contains a short statement giving the reasons for such a conclusion. Appendix C includes an example of an action that contains a refusal to register plus a request to correct informalities.

A response to an action must be signed by the applicant or the applicant's attorney of record. The response may request correction of informalities, provide information and/or material the examining attorney asks for, seek entry of a disclaimer, explain why a cited registered mark is not confusingly similar to the applicant's mark and/or why a mark is registrable, and make changes in the required information by amending the application itself in one way or another. Although no particular format must be used for a response, one is preferred. It is included in Appendix C.

To confirm the USPTO's receipt of a response, send with the filing a self-addressed postpaid postcard. It will be date-stamped by the USPTO and promptly returned to the applicant. If this procedure is not followed or the response is not delivered by hand or mailed certified and return receipt requested, the applicant has no way of knowing whether the USPTO has received it. The USPTO does not routinely confirm receipt of papers filed with it except for the filing receipt mentioned earlier. A statement along the following lines can be typed on the back of the postcard:

> Receipt is hereby acknowledged for a response to the Examiner's action dated [insert date] by [insert applicant's name] concerning serial no. [insert serial number].

Some responses must be accompanied by a verification of applicant-requested changes in the application. Verification is necessary for a change in the dates of use to confirm that they are accurate. It is also required when new specimens are submitted or products or services are listed in the identification of goods and services clause to confirm that they were used or identified by the mark at least as early as the application filing date. Appendix C includes a sample verification for such changes.

To the extent possible and appropriate, an applicant should follow the action's suggestions and instructions. When exactly what should be done is unclear, you may contact the examining attorney directly by telephone for an explanation.

A response must be as complete as possible. It should provide requested information and material, reply to each ground of refusal, make disclaimers and amendments mandated by the examining attorney, or provide reasons why they are not appropriate. When the USPTO receives a response on time, but it is incomplete or insufficient in its response to an action, abandonment of the application is the result.

If a response is incomplete but replies in part to the action, the examining attorney has the discretion either to determine whether the response is sufficient and to continue examination of the application or to rule that the application is abandoned for failure to respond completely. An inquiry about the action or other matters is not a proper response. However, a written disagreement with the examining attorney's refusal or requirement is a complete response.

In certain situations before the examining attorney makes an abandonment ruling, an applicant is given an opportunity to explain a failure to comply with a refusal to register or with a requirement for information from or action by the applicant. This is conditioned on the timely filing of a response that is a bona fide attempt to advance examination of the application and that substantially responds to the examiner's action.

When the examining attorney requires additional information and material, correction of the application, or entry of a disclaimer or other language in the application, the response should follow the examining attorney's instructions.

If a mark is refused registration because the examining attorney claims it is confusingly similar to a registered mark, you should file a response rebutting the refusal. If possible, the response should point out the differences between the marks themselves as well as the products or services covered by the application and those by the registration. In addition, it should note the difference in the trade channels through which they travel to reach ultimate purchasers. If you have search information showing similar registered marks, you should call them to the examining attorney's attention. Point out that they were registered notwithstanding the cited registration and indicate that it is not a strong mark that is entitled to a broad scope of protection.

When registration is refused because the examining attorney believes the mark is merely descriptive, deceptively misdescriptive, primarily geographically descriptive, or a surname, package, or product configuration, two kinds of response may overcome this ground of refusal. Depending on your timetable for obtaining a registration and using the mark, one kind of response can be tried first, and if it is not successful the other can be tried. For both kinds of response, the mark must be capable at the minimum of distinguishing your products or services.

The first response involves telling the examining attorney that the mark has become distinctive. Usually, this response involves amendment of the application to include a claim of distinctiveness. For information about distinctiveness and how this claim is made, refer to the Chapter 2 section "Distinctiveness" and the Chapter 10 section "How to Establish Distinctiveness."

If this approach does not work and the application is again refused registration, your next response should amend the application from the Principal Register to the Supplemental Register. Marks in the category mentioned earlier can be registered on the

Supplemental Register right after they are first used. See the Chapter 8 section "Federally Registrable Marks: Supplemental Register." This change is not possible for a generic word or symbol or for a mark that is in categories *a,b*, and *c* as noted in the Chapter 8 section "Federally Registrable Marks: Principal Register."

This change is also not possible for a mark refused registration because it is confusingly similar to a registered mark.

Approval for Registration

If the examining attorney determines that an application is in condition for approval for registration, a notice of publication is mailed to the applicant, and the mark is published in the *Official Gazette of the Patent and Trademark Office*. The same procedure is followed for applications based on use and those based on intent to use. For an intent to use application, the examining attorney must determine that the mark would be entitled to registration upon the USPTO's acceptance of the required statement of use.

The *Official Gazette* is published every Tuesday. It contains a list of and information about all marks determined to be entitled to registration as of the date of publication, all marks registered on that date, registrations for which affidavits have been accepted, and registrations that have been renewed. A copy of this publication or an annual subscription may be obtained from the Superintendent of Documents, Washington, D.C. Appendix C includes a sample page from the *Official Gazette* and a copy of a notice of publication.

Publication of a mark may be within a few months after the application is filed if the examining attorney's search does not disclose a confusingly similar mark, the mark is registrable, and the application meets all the requirements of the Trademark Act. However, it may not happen for a year or more if actions have been issued and responses received that result in satisfaction of all requirements.

The notice of publication gives the date the mark will be published. A mark that is to be registered on the Principal Register is published for opposition purposes. A Supplemental Register mark is published to give notice of its registration. Registration of marks on this register cannot be opposed; rather, it is challenged by filing and prosecuting a cancellation proceeding, as discussed in the Chapter 12 section "USPTO Opposition and Cancellation Proceedings."

If no one institues an opposition proceeding against a Principal Register application, the mark can be registered. For a period of 30 days after the *Official Gazette* publication date, anyone who desires to challenge registration of the mark may file an opposition proceeding with the USPTO. The Trademark Act provides

> Any person who believes he would be damaged by the registration of a mark on the principal register may, upon payment of the prescribed fee, file an opposition in the Patent and Trademark Office, stating the grounds therefor, within thirty days after publication ... of the mark sought to be registered.

If no opposition or a request for extension of time to file an opposition is filed within the 30 day period, the mark is registered or the applicant is notified that the mark can be registered. If an opposition is filed on time within that period or an extended period, however, an opposition proceeding is instituted. For information about opposition proceedings, refer to the Chapter 12 section "USPTO Opposition and Cancellation Proceedings."

A mark covered by an application based on use is automatically registrable at the expiration of the opposition period. However, the applicant is not given a notice to this effect. Rather, a registration certificate is mailed to the applicant approximately three months after the end of the opposition period, and notice of the registration is published in the *Official Gazette*. Appendix C includes a copy of a registration certificate.

The procedure differs for a mark covered by an intent to use application. A notice of allowance issued to the applicant after the opposition period ends indicates that the mark is registrable after a statement of use and specimens are filed, examined, and accepted by the USPTO. Information about filing the statement of use and specimens for an intent to use application are included in the Chapter 9 section "Intent To Use Application." Once this requirement has been satisfied, a registration certificate is mailed to the applicant and notice of the registration is published in the *Official Gazette*.

The initial period of registration is ten years measured from the date of registration. An affidavit of use must be filed in the USPTO between the fifth and sixth year after registration. Registration can be renewed for additional consecutive ten-year periods as long as bona fide use of the mark in commerce continues. For information about what is required to maintain a registration, see the section "Maintaining Registration" in this chapter.

Registration Notice

After a mark is registered, you should use a notice of registration with it. The notice can be one of three forms: ®, "Registered in U.S. Patent and Trademark Office," or "Reg. U.S. Pat. & Tm. Off."

Failure to use a notice of registration with a registered mark adversely affects the registrant's right to certain remedies in an infringement lawsuit. The Trademark Act provides that if a notice is not used no profits or damages shall be recovered under the Act by the registrant in an infringement suit, unless the defendant had actual notice of the registration.

Using a registration notice at least once at the most prominent appearance of a mark on labeling and in advertising is usually sufficient to avoid the loss of remedies.

Appeal of Refusal to Register

Every final action that refuses registration of a mark can be appealed. This is also the case for a second refusal on the same grounds. An applicant may consider it final for purposes of appeal.

The appeal is directed to the Trademark Trial and Appeal

Board (TTAB), an administrative hearing board within the USPTO. You initiate it by filing a Notice of Appeal and paying an appeal fee within six months from the date of the final refusal or date of action from which the appeal is taken.

In addition, you must file a brief giving the reasons and case law, if applicable, why the examining attorney's action should be overruled and the mark registered. The brief can accompany the notice of appeal or be filed within 60 days of the date of the appeal. If a brief is not filed within this period, the appeal may be dismissed.

The examining attorney has a right to file a response brief within 60 days after your brief is filed. A copy must be sent to you. Then you may file a reply to the examining attorney's brief within 20 days from the date the USPTO mails it.

If you want to present oral argument to the TTAB, you must make a separate written request for an oral hearing to the TTAB no later than ten days after the due date for the applicant's reply brief. If you do not request an oral hearing, the TTAB decides the appeal solely on the record and briefs.

If the TTAB decision agrees with the applicant and reverses the examining attorney, the application is published for opposition. Nothing further is required from you. The same procedure applies to an intent to use application.

If the TTAB decision affirms the examining attorney, you may request the TTAB to rehear, reconsider, or modify its decision. You must file the request within 30 days from the date of the decision. Alternatively, or after TTAB action on the request, an applicant can file an appeal to the U.S. Court of Appeals for the Federal Circuit, in Washington, D.C., or commence a civil action against the commissioner in a U.S. District Court. If you appeal to the U.S. Court of Appeals for the Federal Circuit, you cannot file a civil action in a U.S. District Court.

An appeal to the U.S. Court of Appeals for the Federal Circuit involves a court review of the TTAB decision based on the record before the TTAB. You have no right to introduce evidence or raise issues not before the TTAB. The TTAB decision will not be reversed without a showing that its ruling was clearly in error or that it abused its discretion. You initiate this kind of appeal by filing a Notice of Appeal in the USPTO directed to the commissioner within 60 days from the date of the TTAB decision or within 60 days after TTAB action on a request for rehearing, reconsideration, or modification.

A civil action involves a new trial, which gives you an opportunity to present evidence to the court that was not presented to the TTAB. Although a District Court gives due consideration to the TTAB decision, it also considers new evidence and is not limited to making a determination of whether the TTAB erred or abused its discretion. You commence a civil action by filing a complaint within the same period applicable to an appeal to the U.S. Court of Appeals for the Federal Circuit.

An unfavorable U.S. District Court decision can be appealed to the Court of Appeals for the circuit within which the District Court is located. A decision by the Court of Appeals can be appealed to the U.S. Supreme Court.

Obtaining Copies of Documents

You can obtain copies of the contents and file wrapper of an application, registration certificates, and other available material concerning marks through the mail by making a request to the Commissioner of Patents and Trademarks, Washington, D.C. 20231. Payment of the prescribed fee should be made with the request. You should contact the USPTO if you have a question about the availability of a document, the time involved to obtain a copy, or the applicable fee.

You can obtain access to and inspect the contents of a pending application file without showing good cause or obtaining permission from the applicant. To do so, you must make a written request to the examining attorney. You must inspect the file at the USPTO's offices. Nothing can be removed from the file without written authorization by the USPTO, although you can make copies.

Requests to inspect or obtain copies of registration files, abandoned files, and files for terminated inter partes proceedings should also be made in writing to the USPTO.

Amendment of Registration

A registration can be amended at the registrant's request under certain circumstances. A registration is most commonly amended when a registrant makes changes in the mark after registration. It can also be amended when certain products or services covered by the registration are no longer offered by the registrant or to modernize the terminology used to describe the products or services.

Amendment of the mark can be made only when the changes do not materially alter its character. It is accomplished by submitting a written request to the USPTO to amend the registration to cover the new version. Accompanying this request should be a verification supporting use of the new version as early as the amendment request date, specimens evidencing use of the new version, a drawing showing the new version, the original registration certificate, and the prescribed fee. If the original certificate is lost or destroyed, a certified copy must be ordered from the USPTO and submitted with the request. Appendix C includes a request for amendment.

To be acceptable for amendment, the new version must contain the essence of the mark as registered and create the impression of being essentially the same mark. For example, if the registered mark consists of a word combined with a surrounding design and the word is the essence of the mark with the design as background, removal or change of the design should not be a material alteration of the mark. If the design is integrated with the word and is a distinctive element of the mark, however, then a change will materially alter the mark. Usually no material alteration occurs in a mark that consists entirely of a word when change is only in the style of lettering, size, or other elements.

If an amendment is accepted by the USPTO, a printed certificate is attached to the original registration certificate, which is then returned to the registrant. The printed certificate sets forth the amendment. If the amendment is not accepted, the original registration is returned unchanged to the registrant. The registrant can petition the commissioner for review and then appeal to the courts if the commissioner does not favorably act on the review.

Correction of Mistakes

The Trademark Act provides for the correction of a mistake in a registration whether it occurred through the fault of the USPTO or through an applicant's fault. The USPTO does not itself initiate the applicable procedure but will make a correction if appropriate, when requested by a registrant.

If the mistake was the fault of the USPTO, a registrant should in writing note the mistake and request correction. The request must be accompanied by the original registration certificate or a certified copy. When the USPTO confirms that the mistake was material and its fault, it attaches a certificate of correction to the original registration certificate, records the correction in its records, and returns the certificates to the registrant at no charge.

The registrant can request correction of a mistake that occurred through an applicant's fault by submitting a written request that specifies the mistake and includes a statement indicating how the mistake arose and that it occurred in good faith. The request must be accompanied by the original registration certificate (or a certified copy if the original has been lost or destroyed), a verification referring to how the mistake arose and the applicant's good faith, and a prescribed fee. When a request is approved, a certificate of correction will be attached to the original registration certificate, recorded in the USPTO records, and returned to the registrant.

Maintaining Registration

Affidavit or Declaration of Use

The initial period of registration is ten years but only if an affidavit or declaration of use is filed in the USPTO. This affidavit or declaration is referred to as a "Section 8 Affidavit" because it is required under Section 8 of the Trademark Act. Appendix C includes a form for this kind of affidavit.

The affidavit must be executed and filed no later than six years but no earlier than five years from the registration date. It must be filed by the owner of the registration at that time, who may not be the person who registered the mark. If the owner is not the person who registered the mark, an assignment document providing transfer to the owner or a verified statement supporting the claim of ownership should be filed.

If the affidavit is not filed or not filed on time, the USPTO automatically cancels the registration. This period cannot be extended because it is set by the Trademark Act. Consequently, if the affidavit is filed one day late, the registration is cancelled.

Sending a self-addressed, postpaid postcard with the affidavit will confirm its timely receipt by the USPTO. Your statement on the back of the card can be along the following lines:

Receipt is hereby acknowledged of an Affidavit of Use in reference to Registration No. [insert the Registration No.], filed on behalf of [insert name of owner]

The USPTO does not send a notice to a registrant to indicate the affidavit is due or when it is due. The only notice a registrant receives is that given on the face of the registration certificate. Therefore, on receipt of the certificate, you must note the due date to avoid missing the affidavit due date five years later and losing the registration.

The affidavit must state that the mark is still in use in commerce regulated by Congress or state that nonuse of the mark is due to special circumstances that excuse nonuse and is not due to any intention to abandon the mark. If the USPTO believes the statement of nonuse is insufficient, it will ask for an explanation.

In particular, the affidavit must list those products or services recited in the registration on or in connection with which the mark is still in use. A specimen showing current use for each class must also be filed, along with a prescribed fee. The affidavit is refused if the mark in use as shown in the specimen is materially different than the registered version.

If the USPTO receives the affidavit within the six-year period unaccompanied by the specimen or fee, the USPTO notifies the registrant of this defect and sets a time by which the missing material must be received. If it is not received within this period, the registration is canceled.

At the time the affidavit is accepted, the USPTO sends the registrant a notice to this effect. If the USPTO finds the affidavit insufficient or defective, it gives the registrant written notice of the reasons and an opportunity to respond. The registrant has six months from the date of the notice to respond. If the six-year period expires before an affidavit that meets statutory requirements is filed, however, the registration is cancelled.

Incontestability Affidavit

When a mark registered on the Principal Register has been used in commerce for five consecutive years after the date of registration, an affidavit may be filed in the USPTO pursuant to the provisions of Section 15 of the Trademark Act. It is called a "Section 15 Affidavit."

Unlike a Section 8 Affidavit, the continuing existence of the registration does not depend on the filing of a Section 15 Affidavit. Filing it is entirely elective for a registrant. If it is filed and accepted by the USPTO, however, it gives the registrant a beneficial and desirable right, that is not available for a Supplemental Register mark.

The USPTO's acceptance of a Section 15 Affidavit gives the registrant an incontestable right to use the mark in commerce. This right applies to the products or services on or in connection with which the mark has been used for five consecutive years. The effect is that no person can challenge the registration on the ground that the mark is merely descriptive, primarily geographically descriptive, deceptively misdescriptive, or a surname. Nevertheless, a registration can be canceled if the mark becomes the generic name for the products or services, has been abandoned, or for a few other reasons. For information about canceling a registration, refer to the Chapter 12 section "USPTO Opposition and Cancellation Proceedings."

The owner of a registration must file a Section 15 Affidavit during the one year period immediately following any five consecutive years of use of the registered mark in commerce. It is frequently filed at the same time a Section 8 Affidavit is filed. In this case, it is combined with that affidavit and the combination is referred to as a "Combined Section 8 & 15 Affidavit." Appendix C includes a Section 15 Affidavit form and a form for a Combined Section 8 & 15 Affidavit.

The Section 15 Affidavit must list the products or services recited in the registration that have been offered under the mark for five consecutive years. Also, it must state that no final decision adverse to the registrant's claim of ownership of the mark for the products or services or to the registrant's right to register the mark or to keep it registered has been made. In addition, it must state that no proceeding is pending in the USPTO or in a court that involves the registrant's rights. The USPTO provides written notice to a registrant that the Section 15 Affidavit has been accepted.

Renewal

A registration has a life of ten years if the Section 8 Affidavit is filed on time and accepted. Thereafter, the registration may be renewed for additional ten year periods by filing a timely renewal application with the USPTO around the time of expiration of each renewal period.

Ordinarily, the USPTO does not send a notice to a registrant that a renewal application is due or when it is due. The only notice given is the one on the face of the registration certificate. Accordingly, you ought to note the renewal date when you first receive the registration certificate.

The application should be filed during the six calendar month period immediately prior to the expiration of each ten year period, or it can be filed within the three calendar month period immediately following expiration of the ten years. The date used to measure expiration is the month and day the registration was first issued.

If a renewal application is not filed on time, the USPTO cancels the registration. Like the Section 8 Affidavit filing period, the time for filing a renewal application cannot be extended because it is set by the Trademark Act.

To confirm the USPTO's receipt of the renewal application,

send a stamped, self-addressed, postcard with it for date-stamping and return to you. The statement on the back can be along the following lines:

> Receipt is hereby acknowledged for a Renewal Application in reference to Registration No. [insert the Registration No.], filed on behalf of [insert name of owner].

The application must be signed and filed by the owner of the registration at the time renewal is due. The signature date must be within the filing time period. If the owner is not the person who registered the mark, a document reflecting ownership transfer should be recorded with the USPTO. If the owner is not domiciled in the United States, the renewal application must include the appointment of a domestic representative.

The application must state that the mark is still in use in commerce regulated by Congress or that nonuse of the mark is due to special circumstances that excuse such nonuse and is not due to any intention to abandon the mark. A foreign registrant must state that the mark is in use between the United States and a particular foreign country (if it is not used in interstate commerce). As is the case with a Section 8 Affidavit, if the USPTO believes a statement of nonuse is insufficient, it will ask for an explanation.

In addition to the use statement, the application must list only those products or services given in the registration on or in connection with which the mark is still in use at the time of renewal. Use the description of products or services in the registration to set forth those currently offered. If the descriptions do not substantially correspond, the USPTO may refuse to accept the application. When fewer products or services are set forth in the application than are given in the registration, the renewal registration certificate reflects this change by lines drawn through the products or services not being offered. Appendix C includes a renewal application.

A specimen showing current use for products or services in each class must also be filed, along with the prescribed fee. The application is refused if the mark in use at the time of filing, as shown in the specimen(s), is materially different than the registered version.

A registration is not cancelled if the specimen(s) or fee is filed after expiration of the renewal period as long as the specimen(s) or fee is filed within the time set by the USPTO in its notice that the specimen(s) or fee was not filed with the application or was insufficient.

On acceptance of a renewal application, a renewal certificate is issued and mailed to the registrant and notice of the renewal is published in the *Official Gazette*. If the application is unacceptable to the USPTO, the registrant is sent a notice giving the reasons for refusal. On receipt of this notice, the registrant has six months to make the application acceptable. Otherwise, the registration is cancelled.

STATE REGISTRATION

Because forms and practices vary from state to state and laws change, you must contact the state agency responsible for mark registration before filing an application for registration in that state. The information that follows is a general guide that may not be completely accurate in all instances.

Filing and Prosecuting an Application

The procedure to follow in filing an application for state registration is similar to the procedure for filing a federal application. After you complete the prescribed form, file it, along with the applicable fee and specimens showing the mark, with the appropriate state agency.

Unlike the USPTO, most states do not send the applicant a filing receipt. Thus, the only way you know whether the application has been received is by sending it by certified mail with return receipt requested or by enclosing a stamped, self-addressed, postcard. The state will confirm its receipt of the application if asked to date and return the postcard to the applicant. The back of the card should include language of the kind suggested for filing a federal application.

Typically, state examination of an application involves many of the same considerations as federal examination. However, the degree of examination is not the same. The mark shown on specimens is usually compared to the mark in the application, and the application is reviewed to make sure it was correctly and fully completed and signed. Ordinarily, however, a state-conducted search of its record is not comprehensive. Often, the search looks only for names and/or marks that are identical to the applied-for mark, even though most state statutes prohibit registration of confusingly or deceptively similar marks. A state may register a mark in a state that would not be allowed federal registration.

Although most state statutes also prohibit registration of the same kind of marks that are federally unregistrable, such marks usually can be registered in states. For one reason or another, states do not strictly apply the law. As a result, in many cases you may obtain state registration of marks that cannot be federally registered. Deceptive, scandalous, merely descriptive, primarily geographically descriptive, deceptively misdescriptive marks, surnames, and similar kinds of marks can be registered. Furthermore, obtaining a state registration for a generic word is not impossible.

Generally, states do not have many of the procedures the USPTO uses with application examination. For example, most do not have procedures for expedited examination of an application out of order, state-initiated application amendment, a time period for responding to state action on the application, priority action, or suspension of action on an application.

Registration, Appeal of Refusal, Opposition

If the state finds a mark to be registrable, the state notifies the applicant by sending the registration certificate. Marks are not published for opposition.

No uniform or state-prescribed notice indicates that a mark is registered by a state. The ® symbol and other forms of notice that indicate federal registration of a mark should not be used in connection with a mark that is not federally registered, even if it is state registered.

If registration is refused, states ordinarily have no appeal mechanism. Normally no mechanism provides for the right to oppose or cancel a registration by a person who may be damaged by or objects to it. In addition, usually amending or correcting a mistake in a registration is not possible.

Maintaining Registration

States do not have a procedure for filing affidavits of use to maintain registrations. However, they do provide for registration renewal.

Generally, a state registration has a life of ten years and can be renewed for a similar term by filing a renewal application prior to expiration of the current term and paying a renewal fee. In many states, the renewal application is the same as an application initially used to register a mark; some states have a specific form for registration renewal.

12

Conflicts Between Marks

Use of the same or a similar mark by two or more persons does not necessarily create a conflict. Being the first user and/or registrant of a mark does not necessarily guarantee favorable results when a claim of confusion is asserted against another user in a court or USPTO action. If you contemplate action against someone else's use of a confusingly similar mark, therefore, you usually should not forgo investigating that person's use before sending a cease and desist letter, initiating an opposition or cancellation proceeding in the USPTO, or filing an infringement suit.

When you believe another person's use of a confusingly similar mark should be challenged, you are prudent to learn as much as possible about that use prior to asserting a claim of confusion and to consider when and how the challenge should be made as well as where it should be made in terms of a tribunal. You should weigh the advantages of making a challenge against the risk of losing an adjudication. Also, do not overlook the kind of relief you desire. If you give little thought to these preliminary matters, the outcome of the challenge may be unfavorable.

If your use of a mark has been challenged, you must also study the situation. Among other things, defending a challenge requires learning about use of the mark by the person alleging confusion and developing a plan for rebuttal. Filing a declaratory judgment action may be appropriate if you have been sent a cease and desist letter by the person alleging confusion.

STEPS PRELIMINARY TO A CHALLENGE

The first thing to do in deciding whether another mark creates a conflict and should be challenged is to evaluate it with the likelihood of confusion standard. As mentioned in the Chapter 5 section "Standard to Apply When Searching," the courts and the USPTO use this standard.

A *likelihood of confusion* exists when a mark used by one person on or in connection with products or services so resembles a mark previously used in the United States by another person as to be likely to cause confusion or mistake, or to deceive.

The evaluation involves a comparison of the marks in the same way that a mark is evaluated to determine its availability for use and registration. Most of the steps in that evaluation process are followed, as described in the Chapter 5 section "How to Evaluate Search Information."

The conflict evaluation process involves consideration of whether the marks are similar in terms of sound, appearance, and meaning; the identity or similarity of the products or services offered or intended to be offered; the likelihood of an expansion of product lines or services; the trade channels through which the products or services are or may be offered; the conditions under which the products or services are offered; where the products or services are offered geographically; the dates of first use for each mark; the number and nature of similar marks used by third parties; the length of time during and conditions under which the marks in question have been concurrently used without evidence of actual confusion; and the fame or notoriety of the mark that is the basis for the challenge.

In addition, this process involves considering whether the other mark prevents registration of the challenger's mark; whether use of the other mark is causing damage, injury, or lost profits to the challenger's mark; how much it costs to assert a challenge; and the chances of obtaining a successful result.

To make this kind of evaluation, you need as much information as possible about the other mark and third party uses of similar marks. Therefore, you ought to undertake a thorough investigation.

Among other things, conduct a search to obtain information and material that refers to the other mark. It may be generally available to the public or otherwise accessible without substantial effort. If possible, it should include information and material that is primarily known and circulated to employees and/or customers of the other user.

You may find information in material such as annual reports; trade directories; computer data bases similar to the kind used for searching; newspaper, magazine, and/or trade publication articles or reports about the other user; federal and state Securities and Exchange Commission and other governmental agency filings; license applications; state and USPTO applications for registration; credit and/or financial reports such as those issued by Dun & Bradstreet; yellow page and directory advertising; franchise-offering brochures and agreements; business merger documents, assignments, deeds, and other publicly recorded documents; labeling and packaging; invoices and shipping documents; print, radio, and/or television advertising; and promotional brochures, flyers, and circulars. You may also obtain information from others who have it, such as competitors, trade associations, and former employees of the other user. In some cases, the only way to get it is through the services of a private investigator.

When possible, obtaining actual evidence of confusion is beneficial. Evidence can include copies of misdirected mail, orders, supplier invoices, and customer complaints, telephone inquiries from people trying to reach the other user and incorrect directory listings and advertisements by third persons mistakenly referring to the other user's products or services.

This information must be accurate and current, especially with respect to the other user's date of first use. If it is not, the other might posses superior rights in the mark, will agree that confusion exists, and assert a confusion counterclaim.

When an evaluation supports making a challenge and indicates reasonably good chances of successfully prosecuting an action in the USPTO or a court, you can do a number of things. A protest letter can be filed with the USPTO if the other mark is the subject of a pending application, a cease and desist letter can be sent to the other user, or an action can be initiated against the other user in the USPTO or a court.

Filing a protest letter and/or sending a cease and desist letter before initiating action in the USPTO court has some advantages. Sometimes this approach achieves the desired result without substantial effort or cost. The USPTO may refuse registration on the basis of information provided in the protest letter, and/or the other user may agree to withdraw the application and/or discontinue using the mark on receipt of a cease and desist letter.

PROTEST LETTER TO USPTO

A protest letter is directed to the Office of the Director of the Trademark Examining Operation and requests the USPTO to refuse registration to the other mark. It must list facts and make a persuasive argument why the applicant is not entitled to registration. If it recites facts that clearly affect or prevent registration, it will be given to the examining attorney for consideration with all other facts available to him or her. The examining attorney then communicates the facts and argument to the applicant for response. Should it not be given to the examining attorney, nothing is done with it.

The likelihood of favorable USPTO action on a protest letter is greater when it objects to registration on the ground that a mark is generic, descriptive, or otherwise unregistrable than when it argues only that the applied-for mark is confusingly similar to a registered mark. Consequently, a protest letter that contains no more than an adversary-style argument to the effect that registration should be refused is not likely to be given to the examining attorney. The USPTO believes objections of this kind should be made by means of an opposition or cancellation proceeding.

CEASE AND DESIST LETTER

A cease and desist letter demands that use of the recipient's mark be discontinued and, if appropriate, that an application for registration be withdrawn or a registration be surrendered for cancellation by the USPTO. In some instances, it may demand that use of the recipient's mark be limited in a specified way. It should set a date by which the sender expects a response. Appendix D includes an example of a cease and desist letter.

The purpose of sending this kind of letter is to give notice of the sender's superior rights in the mark, indicate that the recipient's continuing use of a confusingly similar mark infringes the sender's rights, and warn that if the recipient does not discontinue use the sender will take legal action against the recipient.

Whether a cease and desist letter contains more than statements of the type just mentioned depends on the facts of each conflict. In some instances, providing additional information and material is appropriate; in others, doing so may not be in the sender's interest. Therefore, give careful consideration to what is said in the letter and what material, if any, accompanies it. For example, if you do not possess exclusive rights throughout the country, initially telling the recipient where you use it may not be a good idea. Such information may make the recipient consider asserting concurrent use rights for areas where the recipient and not the sender is using the mark.

If you feel strongly about rights claimed in the mark and comfortable that you can prevail if a USPTO proceeding or court action is filed, make the letter persuasive. The objective is to get the recipient to comply promptly with your demand. The letter should provide as much relevant information as possible about the mark claimed to be infringed, evidence some familiarity with the recipient's mark, and be accompanied by meaningful documentation supporting the sender's claim of rights. In other words, it should disclose enough information to allow the recipient to make an informed decision about the demand.

If you own a state or federal registration, refer to it and enclose photocopies of registration certificates with the letter. You can also send photocopies of labels, advertising, or other items evidencing your usage, as well as photocopies of material supporting your first use date, such as invoices, shipping documents, and customer orders referring to your mark.

If your position is good, usually you do not harm yourself by providing all of this kind of information and material at the same time. It can expedite resolution of a challenge. If a USPTO proceeding or court action were filed, you would have to provide it at that time. By making it available at this stage, there is a possibility it will convince the recipient to comply with the demand and thereby avoid a time-consuming and costly USPTO proceeding or court action. Giving it to the recipient piecemeal in response to requests for it merely delays bringing the matter to a conclusion and allows the recipient to continue using the confusingly similar mark while discussions are ongoing.

If the letter makes a demand with little to support the sender's claim of rights, a number of things may happen. The recipient may ignore it, no matter how threatening, because it seems to be a bluff, the recipient may ask for substantiation of the sender's claim to evaluate it on an informed basis, or the recipient may respond with a letter denying the sender's claim. The recipient may also respond by filing a declaratory judgment action asking a court to declare that the recipient's mark does not infringe the sender's rights.

FAILURE TO TAKE ACTION OR TIMELY ACTION

Failing to take any action or timely action concerning another person's use of a confusingly similar mark can be dangerous. The law recognizes a number of affirmative defenses to inaction and late action. Both can result in an inability to obtain legal relief, even though use of the other mark causes confusion and damage to the owner of the mark with superior rights.

The defenses are referred to as *estoppel*, *laches*, and *acquiescence*. They are based on the principle that a person should not be entitled to legal relief against another when that first person's acts lead the other to rely on them in a way that will be harmful to the other. This is generally referred to as *estoppel*. The loss of

legal relief under such circumstances occurs if intentional acts
or failure to exercise care induces another to do something.

Laches occurs with one person's inexcusable delay in asserting rights or taking action concerning the known use of a confusingly similar mark by another person. The first person's
knowledge may be actual or by reason of constructive notice. No
generally accepted period of delay makes this defense applicable. It can be as short as six months and as long as 20 years.

Acquiescence occurs when the acts of a person explicitly or
implicitly indicate that nothing will be done about the known
use of a confusingly similar mark by another person.

Keep these defenses in mind when you consider whether a
cease and desist letter should be sent or a USPTO proceeding or
court action instituted on learning about another's use of a confusingly similar mark. You also have to consider how much time
should pass before you take action and what should be done if
a cease and desist letter does not generate a response or results
in an unfavorable response.

Delay in taking action may foreclose the possibility of challenging federal registration of a mark. If you do not file to object
to registration of a mark or to cancel a mark within the applicable period, you may not be able to challenge USPTO registration. For information about these time periods, see the section
"USPTO Opposition and Cancellation Proceedings" in this
chapter.

Delay in taking action also may foreclose the possibility of
obtaining certain kinds of legal relief in an infringement lawsuit.
If sufficient time passes between first use of a confusingly similar
mark and the filing of an infringement lawsuit, a court may find
that preliminary injunctive relief is not available. For information about this kind of relief, refer to the section "Court Actions"
in this chapter.

NEGOTIATING CESSATION OF USE

You can take a number of approaches to encourage the recipient
of a cease and desist letter, defendant, applicant, or registrant

voluntarily to discontinue use of a confusingly similar mark and, if appropriate, withdraw an application or cancel a registration. Similarly, different approaches can be taken to confirm discontinuance.

In response to such a letter, lawsuit, or initiation of a USPTO proceeding, some people promptly comply with the demand or action sought, automatically discontinue use, and, where appropriate, withdraw an application or cancel a registration. In this case, all you need to do is confirm in some way that use will not resume or that a new application will not be filed. In contrast, some people need to be encouraged to settle conflicts. In such cases, you should give careful consideration to whether doing so is practical and the kind of encouragement that is likely to obtain results. Some alternatives that seem to work are the following:

1. Allow a phaseout or changeover time during which the confusingly similar mark may be used and after which all use must cease. All applications and/or registrations should be withdrawn or canceled before expiration of this period. The time allowed can be determined by the amount of labeling, advertising, or other kinds of material inventory featuring the mark. Setting a specific date is better than allowing exhaustion of inventory which may take a long time depending on the rate of usage.

   When you take this approach, the other user does not lose the investment in this inventory, which may be a controlling reason for resisting cessation of use. The disadvantage that usage of the mark continues may be acceptable because you know it will end on a specific date.

2. Agree to pay the costs of changeover up to a specific dollar amount, with the understanding usage will cease immediately on receipt of new labeling, advertising, or other material featuring a different mark. All applications and/or registrations must be withdrawn or canceled. An outside date by which use must cease should be specified.

   Prompt cessation of usage is the advantage of this approach. Payment of money is a disadvantage. However,

weighed against the cost of prosecuting a USPTO proceeding or court action (which is difficult to control), it makes
sense because the cost is fixed and a certain result is
obtained.

3. Agree to a limited use of the other mark in terms of products or services, trade channels through which the products or services are offered, geographic area where it can
occur, and/or use of a disclaimer or additional wording
with the mark. Again, specifying a date by when the limitation will be effective is important. Amending pending
applications or existing registrations to concurrent use
applications or concurrent use registrations may be
appropriate.

An advantage of this approach is that it may not involve
the payment of money yet may avoid likelihood of confusion in the mind of the customers for the products or
services.

Because oral agreements can be difficult to enforce or are
unenforceable, confirming all agreements in writing is very
important. Among other things, an agreement should clearly set
forth all obligations of the parties, timetables for action, representations and warranties that use will be discontinued and not
resumed, and liabilities that may be imposed if a party fails to
comply with the terms of the agreement, such as payment of the
nonbreaching party's attorneys fees if that party takes action to
enforce or defend an action concerning the agreement. Appendix D includes a sample settlement agreement.

When settlement of a legal proceeding is negotiated, the terms
should be made part of a final order by the USPTO or a court or
of an order of dismissal. Alternatively, or a separate written
agreement can be signed and generally referred to in the order.
A final order can be in the form of a consent judgment and an
order of dismissal may be in the form of a consent order of dismissal. Appendix D includes a sample for each kind of order.

USPTO OPPOSITION AND CANCELLATION PROCEEDINGS

When a conflict involving a federal application or registration cannot be settled by agreement, you have to institute a USPTO proceeding to challenge the application or registration. Alternatively, a court action may be instituted to cancel a registration, but a ruling on such a challenge concerns only the right to register a mark and not the right to use it. If registration is denied or canceled but use of the confusingly similar mark is not voluntarily discontinued, you must institute an infringement action in a court to force cessation of use. For information about this topic, see the section "Court Actions" in this chapter.

States do not appear to have a mechanism that allows the agency responsible for registration to conduct proceedings that involve challenges to applications or registrations. To determine the possibilities in a particular situation, contact the proper state agency.

Two types of USPTO proceedings are available to challenge federal registration of a mark. The primary difference between them is the time when each can be instituted. An opposition proceeding concerns a mark that is the subject of a pending application, before registration is granted. The person filing it is referred to as the *opposer* and the owner of the mark is the *applicant*. A cancellation proceeding concerns a registered mark. The person filing it is referred to as the *petitioner* and the owner of the registration is the *respondent*.

Both proceedings are prosecuted before and administered by the TTAB in substantially the same way. They are governed by the Trademark Act as well as the Trademark Rules of Practice, which provide that the Federal Rules of Civil Procedure are followed, except as otherwise noted.

These proceedings require an understanding and knowledge of these rules, case law, and approaches to take with respect to litigating a controversy. Although individuals may represent themselves, you ought to retain the services of a trademark attorney.

The legal documents that initiate these proceedings can be

likened to a complaint that is filed in a court action. They are called *notice of opposition* in an opposition proceeding and *petition to cancel* in a cancellation proceeding. They are similar in format and in terms of the kind of allegations they make. Each contains statements that give the grounds for challenging registration, allege how the person filing it is or will be damaged, and specify the relief sought. Appendix D includes copies of these documents.

The USPTO must receive a notice of opposition within the 30 day opposition period or extension discussed in the Chapter 11 section "Approval for Registration." It must be accompanied by a filing fee. If it is not filed on time, the mark is registered but you can challenge the registration by filing a cancellation proceeding.

A cancellation proceeding can be instituted at any time after a mark is registered. It is initiated by filing a petition to cancel and paying a filing fee to the USPTO. However, registration cannot be challenged by cancellation after five years from the date of registration except under certain circumstances as provided by the Trademark Act.

The Trademark Act states that registration can be canceled at any time if

1. The registered mark becomes the generic name for the products or services, or a portion of them, for which the mark is registered.
2. The registered mark becomes abandoned.
3. Registration was obtained fraudulently.
4. The registered mark is being used by, or with the permission of, the registrant so as to misrepresent the source of the products or services on or in connection with which the mark is used.

After the USPTO receives a notice of opposition or petition to cancel, the TTAB mails a copy to the applicant or registrant, who has 40 days to answer, assert affirmative defenses, and make a counterclaim, if any. A copy must be served on the opposer or petitioner. If an answer or a request for an extension of time to file one is not filed on time, a default judgment may be entered in favor of the opposer or petitioner.

When an answer is filed, the TTAB issues an order setting a trial schedule for the proceeding without input by the parties. The schedule sets cutoff dates for discovery and taking testimony by each party, for rebuttal testimony, and for filing briefs. A date for oral argument to the TTAB is set if an oral hearing is requested. A request must be made in a separate notice filed no later than ten days after the due date for filing the last reply brief in the proceeding.

At a minimum, prosecuting an opposition or cancellation proceeding takes more than one year from the time it is filed to the time the TTAB renders a decision. If extensions of time are granted, which usually occurs, two or three years and more may pass.

In certain ways, the conduct of these proceedings differs from other kinds of litigation. The principal difference is the way in which evidence is introduced and considered by the TTAB. No trial before the TTAB takes place. Evidence is not introduced through the live examination of witnesses and introduction of exhibits in the presence of the TTAB. Instead, evidence is presented in the form of deposition transcripts of testimony given by witnesses called by the parties during their respective testimony periods. Exhibits identified by witnesses and offered as evidence, if any, accompany the deposition transcripts. Also, evidence may be in the form of stipulations by the parties and copies of official records, as well as printed publications available to the general public in libraries or in general circulation.

Each party files its evidence with the TTAB within 30 days after expiration of the respective testimony periods. Copies must be served on the other party. When additional time is needed to take testimony or introduce evidence, a motion requesting an extension of the testimony period must be filed before the particular period expires. If the motion is granted, all previously scheduled trial dates are usually changed.

If the notice of opposition is sustained, the challenged mark will not be registered. Similarly, when a petition to cancel is granted, the challenged registration is canceled. However, a decision of this kind in either case cannot require the applicant or registrant to discontinue or modify use of the challenged mark. You must obtain a court order for that.

A decision of the TTAB can be appealed as outlined in the Chapter 11 section "Appeal of Refusal to Register."

COURT ACTIONS

As is the case with USPTO proceedings, prosecution of a court action requires an understanding and knowledge of the law as well as ability to obtain and present evidence. Therefore, you are recommended to retain the services of a trademark attorney to provide counsel and representation if you contemplate a court action. Most courts do not allow a corporation to represent itself.

Depending on the particular facts in a given situation, federal registration and use of a confusingly similar mark can be challenged by filing a lawsuit in a state or federal court. Ordinarily, state registration is challenged by means of a lawsuit filed in a state court. To learn whether this action is possible, you have to review the law of the state where the mark is registered.

In the absence of a basis for federal court jurisdiction, you must assert a challenge in a state court lawsuit, even if the challenging party owns a pending federal application and when the mark being challenged is federally registered.

Federal jurisdiction does not exist if the person filing the lawsuit does not own a federal registration, if the challenger cannot satisfy the jurisdictional requirements of diversity of citizenship and the required amount in controversy, or if no basis for federal jurisdiction under a federal statute exists. As noted in the Chapter 8 section "Procedural and Legal Advantages," the Trademark Act states that federal courts have jurisdiction of actions based on the Act.

After you reach a decision to file a lawsuit in a state or federal court, you need to determine where it can be filed from a geographic standpoint. If it is not filed in the correct court, the lawsuit may be dismissed.

The proper court has authority over the parties. Usually,

authority is determined by statute, although it may be determined by agreement of the parties. The person who files a lawsuit is referred to as *plaintiff* and the person who defends is referred to as *defendant*.

For a federal court lawsuit about a mark, a federal statute provides guidance for determining proper *venue*, which is the location where a lawsuit may be filed. It instructs that this kind of lawsuit, if based only on diversity of the parties' citizenship, can be filed only in the judicial district where all plaintiffs reside, or where all defendants reside, or where the claim arose. If it is based on rights under the Trademark Act and not solely on diversity, it may be filed only in the judicial district where all defendants reside or the claim arose. A lawsuit involving a corporate defendant may be filed in any judicial district in which it is incorporated or licensed to do business or is doing business.

In determining proper venue in an infringement lawsuit, a claim could be said to arise everywhere a likelihood of confusion occurs, ordinarily, wherever products or services are offered under the infringing mark. However, the extent of usage in a particular area sufficient to support venue is not absolutely clear. Some courts say a substantial amount must occur, but others say that more than a small amount is enough.

State law should be reviewed to find the proper venue for a lawsuit to be filed in a state court. It states the factors used to determine the county or other state subdivision where the lawsuit can be filed.

Once you select the proper court, you initiate the lawsuit filing a complaint. It sets forth the basis for the plaintiff's belief that the defendant should be prohibited from using a confusingly similar mark, requests a court order that the USPTO or a state should deny or cancel a federal registration and asks for injunctive relief plus money damages. The defendant's response is referred to as an *answer*. It denies or admits the plaintiff's allegations and may include affirmative defenses such as estoppel, laches, acquiescense, abandonment, fair use, and/or fraud.

Specifically, the Trademark Act states that the following defenses are applicable to a federal registrant's exclusive right to use a mark:

1. The registration was obtained fraudulently.
2. The mark has been abandoned.
3. The mark is being used, by or with the permission of the registrant or a person in privity with the registrant, so as to misrepresent the source of the products or services on or in connection with which the mark is used.
4. The name, term, or device charged to be an infringement is a use, otherwise than as a mark, of the person's individual name in his own business, or of the individual name of anyone in privity with such person, or of a term or device which is descriptive of and used fairly and in good faith only to describe the products or services of such person, or their geographic origin.
5. The mark whose use is charged as an infringement was adopted without knowledge of the registrant's prior use and has been continuously used by such person or those in privity with such person from a date prior to (a) the date of constructive use of the mark established under the Trademark Act, (b) the registration of the mark under the Trademark Act if the application for registration is filed before the November 16, 1989, or (c) the publication of a mark registered under an earlier federal trademark statute; provided, however, that this defense shall apply only for the area in which such continuous prior use is proved.
6. The mark whose use is charged as an infringement was registered and used prior to registration of the registered mark, and not abandoned; provided, however that this defense shall apply only for the areas in which the mark was used prior to registration of the registrant's mark.
7. The mark has been or is being used to violate the antitrust laws of the United States.
8. That equitable principles, including laches, estoppel, and acquiescence, are applicable.

An answer may include any of these defenses, if applicable, plus a counterclaim that the plaintiff's mark violates the defendant's rights, and/or seek cancellation of plaintiff's registered mark, if appropriate.

After the answer is filed, a trial date is set and both parties are entitled to proceed with discovery. Depending on the court's docket the matter may be concluded in as little as six months or it can take years.

Frequently, a plaintiff is primarily interested in stopping another person's use of a confusingly similar mark. Therefore, a plaintiff seeks injunctive relief in the form of a permanent injunction. Until a court renders a decision on the evidence presented, however, the plaintiff does not know whether this relief will be granted. In the meantime, the defendant is entitled to continue using the confusingly similar mark. This use may be for a long time after the lawsuit is filed and may damage the plaintiff. Accordingly, if the defendant's continuing use will have a substantial adverse impact on the plaintiff, the plaintiff should consider asking the court for entry of a preliminary injunction.

Because a preliminary injunction is an extraordinary remedy, a plaintiff must convince the court that early relief is warranted. To do this, the plaintiff must show that the defendant's use or intended use is causing or will cause the plaintiff immediate, irreparable damage and injury with no adequate money remedy; that the plaintiff is likely to be successful at a trial; and that the plaintiff will be injured more if the defendant is allowed to continue use than the defendant will be injured if use is ordered to cease at this stage of the lawsuit.

From a practical standpoint, a plaintiff should not seek a preliminary injunction without being certain of being able to make this kind of showing and to put on the best case possible at this early stage of the lawsuit. In effect, the kind of evidence required is substantially the same that will be presented at a trial.

One factor, among others, that can indicate that preliminary relief should not be granted is the plaintiff's delay in filing suit after first learning about an infringing use. A court may reason that a plaintiff being injured should not be dilatory in seeking relief. A delay in filing a lawsuit can suggest an absence of immediate, irreparable injury.

The granting of a preliminary injunction often ends a lawsuit.

A defendant who is required to discontinue use of a mark until a trial is held is likely to adopt and use a new mark. Consequently, if the lawsuit is not a matter of principle and the mark is not important to the operation of the defendant's business, pursuing the lawsuit may not be practical.

Nevertheless, failure to obtain a preliminary injunction does not mean the lawsuit is over. In effect, the plaintiff has a second chance to convince the court that an injunction should be granted. However, it does indicate that the court does not find the evidence presented to that point sufficient to establish the plaintiff's claims.

The granting or denial of a preliminary injunction can be appealed as is the case with a permanent injunction.

Without a request for a preliminary injunction, a lawsuit proceeds in the normal course. If a permanent injunction is granted, the defendant may be immediately required to cease all use of the confusingly similar mark or to modify its usage in some way. Also, the court may order the destruction of all labels, signs, packages, advertisements, and the like that bear the confusingly similar mark.

Money damages may be awarded to a plaintiff based on the defendant's profits that are attributable to the infringement plus the plaintiff's damages caused by it. When a defendant has not made profits and the plaintiff cannot show damages, a money damage award is not likely unless the plaintiff can base it on other factors. In such situations, case law suggests that the amount of money a defendant spent on advertising and promoting the confusingly similar mark should be used as a basis for a money award to the plaintiff.

The Trademark Act provides that attorney fees may also be awarded to a successful plaintiff but only in exceptional cases. Most cases are not exceptional. Many state trademark laws also provide that attorney fees may be awarded but do not seem to require an exceptional case finding.

COUNTERFEITING

The federal Trademark Counterfeiting Act of 1984 was enacted to establish criminal penalties and strengthen civil remedies for the use of counterfeit marks on or in connection with products or services. The civil remedy elements of this law are incorporated in the Trademark Act, whereas the criminal penalty elements are part of Title 18 of the U.S. Code.

The definition of *counterfeit mark* in each statute is substantially the same. Generally, it means a spurious mark used in connection with trafficking in products or services that is identical with or substantially indistinguishable from a mark registered by the USPTO on the Principal Register for those products or services. It does not include a mark that the producer, at the time of production, was authorized to use by the owner of the mark. For example, the unauthorized use of "Levis" on or in connection with blue jeans constitutes use of a counterfeit mark. When "Coca-Cola" is used by a licensee in connection with carbonated beverages produced under license but sold after termination of the license, however, the mark is not counterfeit.

The owner of a federally registered mark who learns about its counterfeit use should give careful consideration to taking action under the applicable section of the Trademark Act. This section gives an owner the ability to stop the counterfeiting promptly. It authorizes the immediate entry of a temporary restraining order without notice to the other party. In addition, it permits the owner to seize and place in the court's custody counterfeit products, the means of making the counterfeit mark, and records documenting the manufacture, sale, or receipt of things involved in the counterfeiting activity. Unless a court finds extenuating circumstances, the Act mandates a judgment in the owner's favor for three times the owner's damages or counterfeiter's profits, whichever is greater, plus reasonable attorney fees.

Because these remedies are extraordinary, the person seeking them must make a convincing showing to the court that counterfeiting has occurred, establish that an order other than a seizure order is not adequate, provide enough security for the payment of damages if a seizure is wrongful, and strictly adhere to the procedures for seizure. After a seizure, the owner must be prepared to present evidence at a hearing, unless waived by all parties, scheduled no later than 15 days after the seizure order is entered.

13

Transferring and Licensing Rights

Rights in a mark can be obtained in two ways besides being the first user. Both can result in rights that are the same as or less than those possessed by the first user, and both allow for use of the mark without infringing or adversely affecting the first user's rights.

When the first user or a subsequent owner voluntarily or involuntarily conveys ownership of all or some of the rights in a mark, the conveyance is referred to as a *transfer of rights*. Frequently the conveyance is also called an *assignment*. The person transferring rights may be referred to as the *transferor* or *assignor* and the person obtaining rights the *transferee* or *assignee*.

When an agreement between the first user or subsequent owner and another person permits use of the mark on an exclusive or nonexclusive basis, the transaction is a *license*. The owner of rights may be referred to as the *licensor* and the person obtaining permission to use the mark the *licensee*.

Whether a particular transaction is an assignment or a license, you should take care to do everything necessary to make it valid. An ineffective assignment can prevent the assignee from taking advantage of the assignor's first use or priority date, and a defective license can impair the licensor's rights in the licensed mark.

Sometimes, the right to use a mark without objection by a

prior user can be obtained other than by a transfer or license. This objective may be accomplished by securing a "consent to use" from the prior user.

TRANSFERS

An owner's exclusive right to use a mark can be voluntarily or involuntarily transferred. When a transfer occurs, the transferee acquires the right subject to any limitations on it while owned by the transferor. In effect, the transferee assumes the transferor's position in ownership of the mark. As a consequence of a transfer, the transferor no longer has a right to use the mark to identify the products or services it identifies, to determine the quality of products or services identified by the mark, or to control or challenge its use by others. These rights, among others, belong to the transferee.

To be valid, the transfer must include a conveyance of the goodwill of the transferor's business that is represented by the mark. To avoid misunderstandings or challenges concerning its enforceability, the transfer should be referred to in and evidenced by a written document signed by the tranferor. To prevent the possibility of voiding the transfer of rights in a federally registered or applied-for mark, the document should be recorded in the USPTO. Appendix E includes a copy of the kind of document that can be used to transfer rights.

A transfer may involve all the marks of a business or only those that are associated with a particular portion. It may be nationwide in scope or limited to a particular geographic area. Whether one mark or more is transferred and regardless of the area covered, however, the transfer must involve a conveyance of the business associated with the mark, which is referred to as the *goodwill* of the business connected with the use of and symbolized by the mark. Without a conveyance of the goodwill, the transfer is invalid.

Rights in a mark exist only when and as long as it is used on or in connection with the products or services it identifies, that is, when it is used in connection with a going business. If no such business exists and nonuse of the mark is not due to special circumstances that excuse nonuse, no one has rights in the mark.

A valid transfer of a mark requires two things: At the time of the transfer, the mark must be in use or at least nonuse must be excusable, and the goodwill or the portion of it associated with the products or services identified by the mark must be conveyed.

The goodwill transferred may be manifested in the form of customer lists and supplier sources, product inventory, labeling, and equipment used to produce products or facilities involved in the offering of services, among other things. If the mark being transferred is used only in connection with a portion of the transferor's business, only that portion and the kinds of things that represent that portion must be conveyed.

When a valid transfer occurs, the transferee acquires all the transferor's rights in the mark covered by the transfer, including the right to rely on the transferor's priority date, which can be very important in the event of a dispute with a later user of the mark. If the transfer is invalid, however, the transferee is not entitled to take advantage of any of the transferor's rights and usually gets nothing more than an agreement that the transferor will not challenge the transferee's use of the mark. One such instance is a business that goes bankrupt and ceases its activities. A person who acquires the mark from the bankruptcy trustee cannot rely on the bankrupt's rights.

An invalid transfer occurs if an abandoned mark is transferred or if the goodwill associated with an active mark is not conveyed. It is invalid regardless of language in an agreement that says the mark is not abandoned or that the goodwill is conveyed. The facts in existence at the time of the transfer control the situation, not the language of the parties.

Although every valid transfer requires a conveyance of the goodwill associated with a mark, every conveyance of a business does not necessarily include a transfer of the marks associated with it. An agreement can expressly except the marks from the conveyance. In this case, however, the transferor may lose rights in the reserved marks if use is not resumed in connection with a similar business of the transferor.

When a business is conveyed without an agreement that refers to the marks associated with it, they are automatically transferred with the other business assets. The transfer is valid despite the absence of a written document that expressly refers to the marks.

Nevertheless, a mark that is covered by a federal application or registration must be transferred by means of a written document signed by the transferor. The name and address of the transferor and transferee should be given, and the application serial number or registration number must be noted. Furthermore, the transferor's signature should be acknowledged by a notary public.

The Trademark Act provides that the transfer of a registered or applied-for mark may be void if it is not recorded on time. If, after transferring a mark to one person the transferor subsequently transfers it to another person for consideration, the earlier transfer will be void if it is not recorded in the USPTO within three months from the transfer date or before the mark is transferred to the later transferee. For example, a transfer of the registered mark "Penstemmon" is void when it is tranferred to one person on April 5, 1990, and to another person on September 18, 1990, if the first transferee does not record it before September 18.

Another reason exists for promptly recording a transfer covering a mark that is the subject of a federal application. If the transfer is recorded before the mark is registered, the registration certificate is issued in the transferee's name as registrant rather than in the transferor's name. For this to happen, the document must be recorded in the USPTO Assignment Division before the notice of publication is mailed to the applicant.

The original of the transfer document or a legible certified copy should be recorded. A document that is not in English cannot be recorded without an accompanying translation signed by the translator. If the transferee is not domiciled in the United States, a domestic representative for the transferee must be appointed in writing on a separate document.

A transfer document can be recorded by mailing the original along with the prescribed fee to the Assignment Division of the

USPTO. A stamped, self-addressed postcard for acknowledgment of receipt and a letter requesting recording should accompany the document. The USPTO acknowledges receipt of the document by returning the postcard and records it in the normal course of business, which may take three or four months. When the document has been recorded, the original is returned to the sender. The reel and frame number where it is recorded in the USPTO records is stamped on it, as well as the date of recording, which is the date the USPTO receives the document in proper form with the fee.

Many states have procedures for recording transfers of state registrations. To learn what is involved for a particular state, contact the agency responsible for mark registration.

LICENSES

An owner's exclusive right to use a mark gives that person the authority to prevent or permit other's use of a confusingly similar mark. When an owner permits and retains control over another person's use of such a mark, the agreement is a license. Although it can be oral or in writing, an oral license may be unenforceable or difficult to enforce, and therefore a license ought to be in writing. The parties' signatures do not have to be notarized for the license to be enforceable.

Unlike a transfer, a license does not convey ownership of rights in a mark or stop the owner from determining the nature and quality of the products or services offered under the mark. The owner keeps all rights, can continue using the mark on or in connection with the products or services it identifies, has the power to control its use by others, and can challenge its unauthorized use.

Like a transfer, a license can result in the owner's loss of the right to use the mark. Also like a transfer, a license can give another person the right to assert infringement claims against unauthorized users of the mark. Whether these or other things can happen depends on the license's terms and conditions for use of the mark. Appendix E includes a license agreement.

At a minimum, a license must reserve to the licensor the right to control the nature and quality of the products or services offered by a licensee under the licensed mark. Furthermore, the licensor must actually exercise such control; recitation of it in an agreement is not enough. If you do not reserve and exercise this right, your rights in the mark may be challenged on the ground that the mark has been abandoned because it has lost its significance as a mark. A mark can be said to lose significance as a mark when it ceases to function as a quality indicator, regardless of whether the quality is good or bad. Without control over quality, the mark cannot function as a quality indicator because the quality may vary.

Quality control can be exercised in many ways. For example, the production of products or the provision of services can be supervised, production facilities can be inspected, or specifications can be set for products and services, with licensor approval required as a condition of distribution.

A licensor's reservation of control over quality is a two-edged sword. It prevents loss of the licensor's rights, yet it also exposes the licensor to liability claims. If a product or service is defective, the licensor may be liable for the injury and damages it causes, even though the licensor did not make or provide it. Liability may be imposed solely because of the licensor's right to control quality.

Regardless of the liability exposure a license creates, licensing can be an attractive business practice for many reasons. The licensor does not have to produce, inventory, market, advertise, or offer the products or services covered by the license, yet the licensor can earn money attributable to these activities through the fees or royalties it charges for permission to use a licensed mark. Companies such as Universal Studios ("Star Wars"), Vail Associates, Inc. ("Vail"), Ralph Lauren ("Polo"), CTW Products ("Sesame Street"), and Weight Watchers International, Inc. ("Weight Watchers") have been paid large amounts of money for the right to use their marks. National Football League Properties, Inc., generates significant revenues from royalty obligations imposed on licensees of National Football League team marks. Individuals like the Rolling Stones, Reggie Jackson, Gloria Vanderbilt, Johnny Carson, and Christian Dior have licensed their names as marks for a variety of products.

To a certain extent, the terms and conditions of a license are limited by the creativity of the parties. They can be for any length of time and cover the entire geographic area throughout which the licensor owns rights or only a portion of that area. Also, a licensee may be given permission to use the mark on or in connection with all the products or services offered by the licensor or only some of them. When a license authorizes a licensee to use the mark on or in connection with products or services beyond those offered by the licensor under the mark, the rights of the licensor can be expanded to include the additional products or services because controlled use of a mark inures to the licensor's benefit.

In addition, a license can require the licensee to place a notice on labeling for products and on promotional material for services to the effect that the mark is used under license from the licensor. However, such notices are not legally required and the licensor's rights are not materially affected by their absence.

Also, a license can require the licensee to pay money to the licensor on a flat-fee or royalty basis, or it may be royalty free. It can prohibit or authorize sublicensing and/or transfer by the licensee, and it may be exclusive or nonexclusive.

A license that gives a licensee the exclusive right to use a licensed mark is called an *exclusive license*. During the term of this kind of license, the owner cannot use the mark in a way that conflicts with the licensee's rights or grant anyone else permission to use the mark in such a way. For example, if "Penstemmon" is the subject of an exclusive license that gives the licensee the right to use it to identify cassette tapes embodying music for distribution in Colorado, California, Utah, and Nevada, the licensor cannot itself distribute or authorize others to distribute such tapes in those states under the mark during the term of the license.

A license can be exclusive in a number of ways and for any period of time. For example, it can cover a particular geographic area or particular products or services. A franchise agreement typically contains an exclusive license to use a mark throughout a particular geographic area and for specific products or services.

An exclusive licensee has a right to institute an infringement suit concerning the licensed mark but only with respect to the rights covered by the license. This right is not exclusive in the sense that the owner of the mark cannot also institute such a lawsuit.

A nonexclusive license grants a licensee permission to use a licensed mark but does not limit the owner's right to use it concurrently in the same way. Thus, two or more persons can be nonexclusive licensees of the same mark for the same products or services in the same area during the same period of time, and nonexclusive licensees may compete with each other. For this reason, a nonexclusive licensee's fee is usually less than an exclusive licensee's fee.

Unlike an exclusive licensee, a nonexclusive licensee cannot institute an infringement action concerning the mark and rights covered by the license. Instead, the nonexclusive licensee must rely on the licensor to take action against infringers.

Whether a license is exclusive or nonexclusive, the licensee acquires no rights in the licensed mark other than those provided by the license. Furthermore, a licensee who is not the owner of a mark cannot federally register it. A nonexclusive licensee is not the owner of a mark. However, an exclusive licensee may be an owner for registration purposes.

Ordinarily, when a person uses a mark that is confusingly similar to one owned by an earlier user, that person must obtain a license to avoid infringing the earlier user's rights.

A license is not necessary to distribute or buy and resell products or services identified by another person's mark unless the distributor or reseller changes the product or service. If changes are made, the product or service can be said to be no longer the same as that offered by the owner of the mark and thus should not be identified by it without the owner's permission. For example, resellers of "Dr. Pepper" beverages, "IBM" computers, or "Michelin" tires can use these marks to advertise and promote their sale as long as the products are not modified.

The license in Appendix E shows the kind of language used to grant a licensee permission to use a mark.

CONSENT TO USE

A *consent to use* is an agreement by the owner of a mark to its use by another person. In effect, it says that the owner will not challenge that person's use of the mark.

A consent to use is distinguishable from a transfer and a license. It does not convey all or any portion of the owner's rights, nor does it give the owner the right to control the recipient's use of the mark.

From an owner's standpoint, a consent to use may be attractive because the rights are not transferred and the owner has no obligation to monitor the other person's use, as required by a license. Because it results in uncontrolled third-party use of the same mark, however, it may make the owner's mark less distinctive and thereby weaken it.

A consent to use is attractive to the recipient for a number of reasons. It does not allow the person who gives consent to control the recipient's use of the mark and, unlike a license, it is not subject to termination.

Appendix E includes a sample consent to use agreement.

14

Foreign Protection

If products or services identified by a mark will or may be marketed in a foreign country, you must promptly determine whether the mark can be used and/ or registered there. This determination is especially important if you intend to use the same mark in each country where the products or services will be offered. Its use and federal registration in the United States does not guarantee its availability everywhere, although this standing may be the basis for obtaining protection in a foreign country if it is available there.

In making this determination, keep in mind that each country that grants protection has its own law governing the subject and that applicable law varies from country to country. Despite the differences in applicable laws, the similarities can help you approach using, registering, and protecting a mark in many countries in the same way you would in the United States, especially where rights and registration depend on a mark's distinctiveness and the absence of an earlier registration of the same or a similar mark.

A mark should be evaluated in terms of whether it is distinctive based on the foreign-language meaning of the mark. It should also be evaluated based on the results of a search conducted in the country.

Evaluations of this kind can be done best by a trademark

attorney in each country where you seek rights. It can also be done by a U.S. trademark attorney who is knowledgeable about the applicable law of the foreign country and local practices there for obtaining and protecting rights in a mark.

Rights are not acquired in the same way in every country. They may be based on use or on registration only or acquired under the provisions of a treaty the United States has signed.

TREATY RIGHTS

The United States is a party to the International Convention for the Protection of Industrial Property of 1883, which is a treaty concerning the registration and protection of marks. Referred to as the Paris Convention, it is the treaty most often relied on by U. S. nationals to register their marks in foreign countries.

By reason of this treaty, U.S. nationals have a right to obtain registrations for their marks in approximately 100 signatory countries, subject to certain limitations. The limitations typically concern the registrability of a mark and whether it is confusingly similar to an existing registered mark.

Similarly, nationals of countries that have also signed this treaty are entitled to federal registration of their marks in the United States. However, their marks must be registrable and cannot be confusingly similar to USPTO registered marks. For more information on registering foreign marks, refer to the Chapter 9 section "Foreign Application and Registration-Based Application."

People relying on this treaty have a right to obtain protection for their marks in a signatory foreign country to the same extent that country grants protection to its own nationals. This relationship is referred to as *reciprocity*. However, this protection is not necessarily the same as the kind the U.S. national might receive in the United States.

For example, a U.S. national can register a mark in Japan by applicable Japanese law and receive protection for it the same as a Japanese national receives protection for a mark registered in Japan. However, this protection may not be the same as the kind that the United States grants to marks registered in the United States.

This treaty offers another benefit to a U.S. national: the right to obtain a priority date in a foreign country for a mark that is to be registered there. The U.S. national who files a federal application for the mark in the United States and within six months from that date also files an application for registration of the mark in a signatory foreign country has as a priority date in the foreign country the date the USPTO application is filed.

For example, if a USPTO application is filed for "Penstemmon" on May 19, 1990, and one is also filed for it in Japan before November 19, 1990, claiming rights under the Paris Convention, the priority date for the Japanese application will be May 19, 1990. This date holds even though the Japanese application is filed on September 18, 1990.

Obtaining a priority date earlier than the application filing date in the foreign country is an advantage. Rights in most countries are based on it. Therefore, in the event of a conflict with another user or registrant of the mark, the priority date may decide who has superior rights.

The United States has signed other treaties that provide benefits to owners of marks. Information about them may be obtained from a trademark attorney whose practice encompasses foreign registration or from such books as *Trademarks Throughout the World* (Clark Boardman Co., Ltd., New York).

ACQUIRING RIGHTS

As is the case in the United States, in many countries rights in a mark are primarily based on use. In these countries generally the first user is entitled to register a mark but may assert exclusive rights without owning a registration. These countries include the United Kingdom, Canada, Australia, New Zealand, and other countries that were or are British Commonwealth countries.

Most countries in this group permit filing an application for registration based on an intent to use the applied-for mark. Like

U.S. law, if the mark is not used within a prescribed time after it is accepted for registration, a registration is not granted. Also, if registration is granted before use occurs, it is subject to cancellation if no use occurs within a prescribed time after registration.

In a different group of countries, rights in a mark are based solely on ownership of a registration. Use of a mark without registration does not result in rights. In these countries the first person to register acquires superior rights against others. As a consequence, a registrant possesses exclusive rights in the registered mark despite earlier use by a person who did not register or, where registration is based on intent to use, despite the absence of use by the registrant at the time of registration. The more than 65 countries in this group include France, Germany, and Japan.

Because registration determines rights in the latter group, promptly filing for registration is important in each country where products or services will or may be offered. A delay may result in the loss of rights in that country due to someone else's registration, and then nothing can be done to use the mark in that country unless the registrant fails to use it within a prescribed time after registration.

Most countries require use of a mark after it is registered as a condition of maintaining the registration. These countries include those where rights are based on use as well as those countries where rights are based only on registration.

Like the United States, many countries require filing documents to renew registrations after prescribed time periods and have mechanisms for challenging the registration and/or use of marks in proceedings in courts and before the governmental agency responsible for registration.

Unlike the United States, many countries impose restrictions and/or taxes on royalty payments made under licenses covering marks. Many require licenses covering marks to be recorded with a governmental agency, either the agency responsible for registration of marks or another agency, depending on the country. In these countries a licensee is often referred to as a *registered user.*

To gain a fuller understanding of what is required to obtain rights in a particular country, their scope, and how they can be protected as well as maintained, you should consult a trademark attorney who is knowledgeable about that country's law.

Glossary

Abandonment: When use of a mark has been discontinued with intent not to resume use; intent not to resume may be inferred from circumstances; nonuse for two consecutive years shall be prima facie evidence of abandonment; any course of conduct of the owner of a mark, including acts of omission as well as commission, that causes a mark to become the generic name for the goods or services on or in connection with which it is used or otherwise to lose significance as a mark.

Acquiescence: Action by a person explicitly or implicitly indicating that nothing will be done about another person's activities.

Action: A written communication to a federal applicant by a U.S. Patent and Trademark Office examining attorney concerning the application.

Amendment: Amendment of an application or registration.

Arbitrary mark: A mark whose meaning bears no relationship to the products or services with which it is used.

Assignee: A person who acquires ownership of rights.

Assignment: A transfer of an ownership interest in property, whether tangible or intangible.

Assignor: A person who transfers rights.

Assumed name: A trade name.

Brand name: A trademark.

©: A form of notice used to indicate a work is protected by copyright.

Cancellation proceeding: A U.S. Patent and Trademark Office adversary proceeding in which one person (petitioner) seeks to cancel a federal registration owned by another person (registrant), based on a claim that the petitioner is or will be damaged by registration of the mark.

Cease and desist letter: A letter by the owner of a mark to an unauthorized user advising that such use is infringing and demanding that it cease.

Certification mark: Any word, name, symbol, device, or combination thereof used by a person other than its owner, or that its owner has a bona fide intention to permit a person other than the owner to use in commerce, to certify regional or other origin, material, mode of manufacture, quality, accuracy, other characteristics of such person's goods or services, or that the work or labor on the goods or services was performed by members of a union or other organization.

Clearing a name or mark: A search.

Coined mark: A mark that has no meaning and is created solely for use as a mark.

Collective mark: A trademark or service mark used in commerce by the members of a cooperative, an association, or other collective group or organization, or that such a cooperative, association, or other collective group or organization has a bona fide intention to use in commerce; and it includes marks indicating membership in a union, an association, or other organization.

Combined application: A multiple class application.

Combined Section 8 & 15 affidavit: An affidavit containing all the requisite allegations of both a Section 8 affidavit and a Section 15 affidavit.

Commissioner: The Commissioner of Patents and Trademarks.

Common law: Law based on court decisions and developed through precedent.

Compu-Mark On-Line Searching: A data base containing information about common law, state, and federally registered names and marks.

Concurrent use: Simultaneous use of the same mark by two or more persons on or in connection with the same or similar products or services in different geographic areas or in different trade channels in the same geographic area.

Concurrent use application: An application seeking federal registration of a mark based on concurrent use rights.

Concurrent use proceeding: A U.S. Patent & Trademark Office proceeding to determine whether two or more persons are entitled to simultaneous registration of the same or similar mark.

Concurrent use registration: A federal registration recognizing concurrent use of a mark.

Confusing similarity: Similarity between two marks that creates a likelihood of confusion.

Consent judgment: A judgment by consent of the parties.

Consent to use: Agreement by the owner of a mark to its use by another person to identify products or services originating from the other person.

Constructive notice: A presumption of the law, making it impossible for a person to deny the matter concerning which notice is given, even though the person has no actual knowledge of the matter.

Constructive use: Use of a mark created by statute without regard to whether use actually occurs; it has the same legal effect as actual use.

Co-owner: A person who, with one or more other persons, owns the same rights in a mark.

Copyright: The exclusive right to reproduce, vary, as well as publicly perform, display, and distribute a work entitled to copyright protection under the Copyright Act of 1976.

Copyright Act of 1976: The federal statute concerning copyright protection.

Copyright Office: The federal agency, within the Library of Congress, that has jurisdiction over the registration of ownership claims in works under copyright law.

Copyright protection: The kind of protection available for literary, dramatic, pictorial, graphic, sculptural, and audiovisual works, as well as for motion pictures, sound recordings, pantomimes, choreography, and musical compositions; it is in the nature of the five rights denoted by copyright.

Corporate name: The name of a corporation under which a state grants a corporate charter.

Counterfeit: A spurious mark that is identical with, or substantially indistinguishable from, a federally registered mark.

Date of first use: The date a mark is first used.

Date of first use in commerce: The first use of a mark in commerce regulated by Congress.

Descriptive mark: A mark that immediately communicates information about the qualities, features, functions, purpose, use, components, ingredients, or characteristics of a product or service.

Disclaimer: A disclaimer of exclusive rights in a word or symbol constituting a portion of a federally registered mark.

Distinctive mark: A mark that can be associated by relevant members of the public and trade with one source.

Domestic representative: A person in the United States who may be served notices or process in proceedings affecting a mark covered by a federal application or registration.

Drawing: A depiction of the mark covered by a federal application or registration; a drawing may be typewritten or drawn, depending on the makeup of the mark as shown on specimens.

Drawing page: The page in a federal application that depicts the mark to be registered.

Estoppel: Action by a person that leads another person to rely on it in a way that will be harmful to the person who relies on it.

Examiner's amendment: Amendment of a federal application made by a U.S. Patent and Trademark Office examining attorney.

Exclusive license: Permission given by one person to another to do a thing and agreement not to give anyone else permission to do the same thing.

Exclusive licensee: A person given the exclusive right and license to do a thing.

Exclusive ownership: Ownership free from any kind of legal or equitable interest by anyone else.

Exclusive rights: A right that only the owner thereof can exercise and from which all other persons are prohibited.

Federal Patent Act: The federal statute that exclusively governs all rights in and to patented inventions and patent grants by the U.S. Patent and Trademark Office.

Fictitious name: A trade name.

File wrapper: A three-fold manila jacket in which the U.S. Patent and Trademark Office places all material, actions, and responses concerning a particular federal application.

Final action: The last action a U.S. Patent and Trademark Office examining attorney will take concerning a refusal to register a mark or request that a requirement be satisfied by an applicant.

First use: The first use of a mark.

First use date: The date a mark is first used.

Generic word: The common descriptive name for a product or service.

Incontestable mark: A federally registered mark that cannot be contested unless it becomes abandoned, registration was fraudulently obtained, it misrepresents the source of goods or services, it becomes the generic name of the goods or services on or in connection with which it is used, or for other specific reasons set forth in the Trademark Act.

Infringement: The exercise of an exclusive right without permission by its owner.

Intent to use: An intention to make a bona fide use of a mark in the ordinary course of trade and not merely to reserve a right in a mark.

Intent to use application: An application for federal registration of a mark filed prior to actual use of the mark but based on an intent to use it.

International class: A class in which a mark is categorized based on the products or services it identifies.

International classification: Classification of a mark using the International Classification System relied on by the U.S. Patent and Trademark Office in connection with federally registering marks.

Interstate use: Use of a mark on or in connection with products or services that are sold, transported, or offered in more than one state; use of a mark in a way that affects interstate commerce.

Intrastate use: Use of a mark on or in connection with products or services that are sold, transported, or offered in one state only.

Invention: The act of devising something not previously known or existing; a new and useful process, machine, or composition of matter.

Joint ownership: Co-ownership of the same rights in a mark by two or more persons.

Laches: Inexcusable delay in asserting rights or taking action.

Lanham Act: The Trademark Act of 1946.

License: Authority or permission to do something that, without such authority or permission, would violate a right.

Licensed right: A right that is the subject of a license.

Licensee: A person who holds a license.

Licensor: A person who grants a license.

Likelihood of confusion: Confusion caused when the same or a similar mark is used by two or more persons to identify the same or closely related products or services with the likely result that the relevant public and/or trade will be mistaken or deceived concerning the source of the products or services.

Manner of use: The way a mark is used on or in connection with products or services.

Mark: Any trademark, service mark, collective mark, or certification mark.

Multiple-class application: A federal application seeking registration of a mark in two or more international classes.

Nameholder corporation: A corporation formed for the purpose of reserving a corporate name.

Name reservation: Reserving a name in a state for registration as a corporate or trade name.

Natural expansion: The extension of exclusive rights in a mark in areas beyond where it is actually used based on the concept that a business will naturally expand into such areas.

Nonexclusive license: Permission given by a person to one or more others to do the same thing at the same time in the same geographic area and elsewhere.

Nonexclusive licensee: A person who holds a nonexclusive license to do a thing that others also can do.

Notice of allowance: A notice issued to an intent to use applicant by the U.S. Patent and Trademark Office to the effect that a mark is acceptable for federal registration, conditioned on the filing and acceptance of a Statement of Use.

Notice of Publication: A notice issued to an applicant by the U.S. Patent and Trademark Office to the effect that a mark has been accepted for federal registration and indicating the *Official Gazette* publication date.

Official Gazette: The *Official Gazette of the United States Patent and Trademark Office*: a weekly publication that contains information about marks accepted for federal registration, registration of marks, affidavits filed to maintain federal registration, and renewal of registration.

Opposer: A person who opposes federal registration of a mark.

Opposition proceeding: A U.S. Patent and Trademark Office adversary proceeding in which one person (opposer) opposes federal registration of a mark sought to be registered by another person (applicant), based on a claim that the opposer is or will be damaged by registration of the mark.

Paris Convention: The International Convention for the Protection of Industrial Property of 1881 providing for the right of nationals of member countries to register their marks in signatory countries.

Patent: A monopoly given by the federal government entitling the owner of a patented invention the right to preclude others from making, selling, or using the invention throughout the area covered by the patent; it can last up to 17 years.

Patented invention: An invention that is the subject of a patent; generally it can be a new and useful industrial or technical process, machine, article of manufacture, or composition of matter, a new, original, and ornamental design for an article of manufacture, or a distinct and new asexually reproduced variety of plant.

Patent protection: The limited monopoly given under the Federal Patent Act to a patented invention.

Petitioner: A person who seeks to cancel federal registration of a mark.

Principal Register: The principal register provided for by the Trademark Act for federal registration of marks that identify and distinguish products and services.

Priority action: An action by a U.S. Patent and Trademark Office examining attorney giving priority to an application for examination purposes by acting on it ahead of other pending applications in the examining attorney's docket.

Priority date: The date used to determine who has exclusive use rights when a conflict arises concerning use of confusingly similar marks.

Protest letter: A letter to the U.S. Patent and Trademark Office protesting registration of a mark covered by a pending application.

Publication of a mark: Publication of a mark in the *Official Gazette* to advise the public of its acceptance for federal registration or its federal registration.

®: A form of notice used to indicate a mark is federally registered.

Registered mark: A mark registered in the U.S. Patent and Trademark Office and/or by a state.

Registered U.S. Patent & Trademark Office: A form of notice used to indicate that a mark is federally registered.

Registration notice: A notice used on or in connection with a mark that is federally registered.

Related company: Any person whose use of a mark is controlled by the owner of the mark with respect to the nature and quality of the goods or services on or in connecion with which the mark is used.

Renewal application: An application to renew a mark registered by the U.S. Patent and Trademark Office or a state.

Renewal of a registration: Renewing a state or federal registration for an additional period of time.

Reserving a name: Reserving a name in a state by filing a request to reserve it for use as a corporate or trade name.

Right of priority: A right to exclusive use of a mark based on a first or constructive use date.

Right of publicity: A right to control the use of a person's name, likeness, and personality characteristics.

Search: An investigation to determine whether a word or symbol is available for use and registration without infringing the rights of another person; also referred to as *clearing* a name or mark.

Secondary meaning: The meaning a word takes on as a result of becoming distinctive through its use as a mark to identify products or services, which is different than its primary meaning; a primary meaning of *ivory* is a particular color, but when it is used as a mark to identify a soap product it has a secondary meaning.

Section 2(f): A section of the Trademark Act allowing federal registration of a mark based on a claim of distinctiveness.

Section 2(f) claim: A claim that a mark is distinctive by reason of long and continuous use and/or by widespread use and promotion.

Section 8 affidavit: An affidavit of use required to be filed with the U.S. Patent and Trademark Office between the fifth and sixth year after the federal registration date, stating that the mark is in use at that time or reasons that excuse its nonuse.

Section 15 affidavit: An affidavit that may be filed with the U.S. Patent and Trademark Office at any time after a mark on the Principal Register has been continuously used for five consecutive years after the federal registration date, stating such continuous use; on acceptance of this affidavit, a registration becomes incontestable.

Service mark: Any word, name, symbol, device, or combination thereof used by a person, or that a person has a bona fide intention to use, in commerce to identify and distinguish the services of one person, including a unique service, from the services of others and to indicate the source of the services, even if that source is unknown.

Special application: An application that is given special expedited treatment during the examination process by being advanced from its normal order of examination.

Special form drawing: A drawing of a mark depicting its special characteristics, pictorial features, or design elements; a special form drawing is required to show color as an element of a mark.

Specimens: Material evidencing use of a mark; they can be tags, labels, photographs, advertising, and promotional material, among other things.

Statement of use: A statement required to be filed in connection with an intent to use application to the effect that a mark has been used in commerce regulated by Congress.

Suggestive mark: A mark that requires imagination, thought, and perception to reach a conclusion about the nature of the products or services with which it is used.

Supplemental Register: The supplemental or secondary register provided for by the Trademark Act for federal registration of marks that are capable of identifying and distinguishing products and services.

TM: A form of notice used to indicate that a word, name, symbol, or device, or combination thereof is a mark.

Token use: Use of a mark made merely to reserve rights in it.

Trade dress: A product's overall design or appearance.

Trademark: Any word, name, symbol, device, or combination thereof used by a person, or that a person has a bona fide intention to use, to identify and distinguish his or her goods, including a unique product, from those manufactured or sold by others and to indicate the source of the goods, even if that source is unknown.

Trademark Act: The Trademark Act of 1946 (Lanham Act).

Trademark Act of 1946: The federal statute governing the registration and maintenance of marks as well as actions for unfair competition.

Trademark Manual of Examining Procedure: A manual referred to by U.S. Patent and Trademark Office examining attorneys and applicants concerning guidelines and rules applicable to the registration of marks and the maintenance of registrations.

Trademark notice: A notice used adjacent to or in association with a mark to indicate that it is federally registered (®), or that common law rights are claimed in it (TM).

Trademark Rules of Practice: The rules applicable to the federal registration of marks and their maintenance; also referred to as 37 Code of Federal Regulations.

TRADEMARKSCAN: A data base containing information about common law, state, and federally registered marks and names.

Trademark Trial and Appeal Board: An U.S. Patent and Trademark Office administrative hearing board that considers matters affecting federal registration of a mark and the cancellation of federal registrations.

Trade name: Any name used by a person to identify his or her business or vocation.

Transferee: A person who acquires rights.

Transfer of rights: A conveyance of the ownership of all or some of the rights in a mark.

Transferor: A person who conveys ownership of rights.

Typewritten drawing: A drawing depicting a mark in a typewritten format in all uppercase letters.

United States Patent and Trademark Office: The federal agency which has jurisdiction over the issuance of patent grants and federal registration of marks.

Use in commerce: The bona fide use of a mark in the ordinary course of trade and not made merely to reserve a right in a mark; use on goods occurs when a mark is placed in any manner on the goods, or their containers, or the displays associated therewith, or on the tags or labels affixed thereto, or if the nature of the goods makes such placement impracticable, then on documents associated with the goods or their sale; use on services occurs when a mark is used or displayed in the sale or advertising of services, and the services are rendered in commerce.

Verification: An affidavit or declaration verifying the truth and accuracy of statements.

Zone of natural expansion: The geographic area beyond where actual use of a mark occurs but where the user of a mark possesses rights because use is likely to occur in the future due to a natural expansion of that person's business.

Appendix A

Search Report

THE FOLLOWING SEARCH REPORT IS NOT TO BE CONSTRUED AS A LEGAL OPINION AS TO THE REGISTRABILITY OF THE TRADEMARK.

NAME

DAVID A. WEINSTEIN, Esq.

ADDRESS

4100 East Mississippi Avenue
Denver, Co. 80222

DATE

THE FOLLOWING SEARCH REPORT IS BASED UPON THE UNITED STATES PATENT AND TRADEMARK OFFICE RECORDS OF REGISTERED,
PUBLISHED, AND PENDING TRADEMARKS, INCLUDING RECORDS OF CANCELLATIONS, ASSIGNMENTS, ABANDONMENTS AND
OPPOSITIONS; REGISTRATIONS IN THE FIFTY STATES; MARKS LISTED IN TRADE DIRECTORIES AND OTHER ADVERTISING MEDIA;
AND BUSINESS NAMES LISTED IN TRADE DIRECTORIES AND IN MAJOR CITY TELEPHONE DIRECTORIES.

MARK SEARCHED

CENTENNIAL PRESS

APPLIED TO: Books and publications.

CLASSES SEARCHED: Prior U. S. Classes 38,37,100,101.
International Classes 16,35,42.

APPLICATIONS FILED IN THE UNITED STATES PATENT AND TRADEMARK OFFICE THROUGH ____Jan. 11, 1989____ HAVE
BEEN EXAMINED IN PREPARATION OF THIS REPORT, except those few not released by the PTO.

SHEPARD'S CITATIONS

CENTENNIAL
11-FC-697
17-FC-370
  Cir. 2
1-FS-430
1873-CD-24
1875-CD-103
1876-CD-158
1878-CD-310
1881-CD-25
TEX
96-SW-685

230

SN 511,319. ARAPAHOE COUNTY PUBLIC AIRPORT AU-
THORITY, ENGLEWOOD, CO. FILED 11-30-1984.

4-23-85

CENTENNIAL APPROACH

FOR MAGAZINE DEALING WITH ISSUES PERTAIN-
ING TO AIRPORTS (U.S. CL. 38).
FIRST USE 10-23-1984; IN COMMERCE 10-23-1984.

TM. 1,346,121
Reg. July 2, 1985

SN 703,668. BOARD OF REGENTS OF THE UNIVERSITY
OF OKLAHOMA, THE, NORMAN, OK. FILED
12-30-1987.

12-6-88

OWNER OF U.S. REG. NOS. 1,342,617, 1,401,611 AND
OTHERS.
NO CLAIM IS MADE TO THE EXCLUSIVE RIGHT TO
USE "CENTENNIAL", "1890" AND "1990", APART FROM
THE MARK AS SHOWN.
THE MARK CONSISTS OF THE WORD "CENTENNI-
AL" WITH THE DESIGN INCLUDING THE WORDS
"THE UNIVERSITY OF OKLAHOMA" AND THE YEAR
"1890" AND "1990".
FOR PAPER GOODS AND PRINTED MATERIALS,
NAMELY, BROCHURES, CATALOGUES, STATIONERY,
ENVELOPES, NOTE PADS, AND DECALS (U.S. CLS. 37
AND 38).
FIRST USE 8-24-1987; IN COMMERCE 8-24-1987.

Int. 9, 16, 21, 25, 24, 35

THE GREAT MONTANA
CENTENNIAL CATTLE DRIVE
& Design

SER # 747,290
FILED 8-19-88
USE 2-1-88

9,16,21 — Advertising Centennial Coin,
25,24,35 +— Shirts, hats, Scarves, Flags,
printed Materials, bumper Stickers,
glasses.
Latigo Corporation
Red Lodge, MT

INT 16

SN 680,919. INDUSTRIAL COATINGS GROUP, INC., CHICAGO, IL. FILED 8-27-1987. **APR.** 1 2 1988

CENTENNIAL

FOR BOOK CLOTH (U.S. CL. 37).
FIRST USE 5-1-1972; IN COMMERCE 5-1-1972.

37

37

Ser. No. 517,957. BYRON WESTON COMPANY, Dalton, Mass. Filed Feb. 24, 1947.

Dec 16 1947

CENTENNIAL

FOR WRITING PAPER.
Claims use since Jan. 11, 1926.

TM 432,343
Reg 3-16-48
Ren 3-16-68
No7 Ren 9/0 2-21-89

INT 16

SN 695,905. 1989 WASHINGTON CENTENNIAL COMMISSION, OLYMPIA, WA. FILED 11-16-1987.

12-6-88

FOR PAPER ARTICLES, NAMELY NAPKINS, STICKER LABELS AND POSTER BOARDS (U.S. CL. 38).
FIRST USE 11-11-1985; IN COMMERCE 11-11-1985.

INT 16

10-14-86

SN 604,493. ALLIED CORPORATION, MORRISTOWN, NJ. FILED 6-16-1986.

LINOTYPE CENTENNIAL

OWNER OF U.S. REG. NOS. 74,289, 1,256,739 AND OTHERS.
FOR TYPEFACE RECORDED ON A DATA MEDIUM FOR USE IN TYPESETTING AND PRINTING (U.S. CL. 14).
FIRST USE 5-12-1986; IN COMMERCE 5-12-1986.

BYTE .01-CENTENNIAL ISSUE   A MAGAZINE
_____ _____
TRADE MARK   PRODUCT

BYTE PUBLICATIONS, INC.   ---   .
70 MAIN STREET
Peterborough, N. H.
_____
REGISTRANT
(NAME & ADDRESS)

9/7/76   NEW HAMPSHIRE
_____ _____
DATE OF REG.   STATE

BI-CENTENNIAL   Prints and publication
_____ _____
TRADE MARK   PRODUCT

CHARLES TOWNE TOURS
Charleston, S. C.

_____
REGISTRANT
(NAME & ADDRESS)

6-11-73   SOUTH CAROLINA
_____ _____
DATE OF REG.   STATE

T10442

CENTENNIAL TIMES   #38 Prints & Publ.
_____ _____
TRADE MARK   PRODUCT

The Centennial Times Publishing Company
P. O. Box 8
Fairplay, Colorado
_____
REGISTRANT
(NAME & ADDRESS)

February 23, 1973   COLORADO
_____ _____
DATE OF REG.   STATE

#21465
CENTENNIAL CLARION   Prints and publications
                                    Cl. 38
_____ _____
TRADE MARK   PRODUCT

OKLAHOMA CITY ECONOMIC DEVELOPMENT FOUNDATION, INC.
Four Santa Fe Plaza
Oklahoma City, Ok. 73102
_____
REGISTRANT
(NAME & ADDRESS)

Sept. 21, 1987   OKLAHOMA
_____ _____
DATE OF REG.   STATE

MARK: PRODUCT: COMPANY:

CENTENNIAL   books   Cliffs Notes, Inc.
PRESS   Box 80728
                                        Lincoln, Nb.
                                        (1988 General Directory #8)

LAWRENCE, ERNEST O. CENTENNIAL OF THE SHEFFIELD SCIENTIFIC SCHOOL.
FACSIMILE ED. BAITSELL, GEORGE A., EDITOR. LC 70-107681.
(ESSAY INDEX REPRINT SER.). 1959. $21.50. (ISBN
0-8369-1544-5). AYER COMPANY PUBLISHERS, INCORPORATED.
NAME: AYER COMPANY PUBLISHERS, INCORPORATED
STREET: 382 MAIN ST., P.O. BOX 958
CITY: SALEM
STATE: NH
ZIP: 03079

CENTENNIAL OF LIFE & FAITH IN DEL NORTE COUNTRY (CAL.): 1854-1954.
(ILLUS.). 1954. PAPER. $3.00. (ISBN 0-918634-25-3). CHASE,
DON M.
NAME: CHASE, DON M.
STREET: 8569 LAWRENCE LN.
CITY: SEBASTOPOL
STATE: CA
ZIP: 95472

BAITSELL, GEORGE A., EDITOR. THE CENTENNIAL OF THE SHEFFIELD
SCIENTIFIC SCHOOL (YALE UNIVERSITY). 1950. $19.5CX. (ISBN
0-686-51350-9). ELLIOT'S BOOKS.
NAME: ELLIOT'S BOOKS
STREET: P.O. BOX 6
CITY: NORTHFORD
STATE: CT
ZIP: 06472

UNITED EMPIRE LOYALISTS CENTENNIAL COMMITTEE. THE CENTENNIAL OF
THE SETTLEMENT OF UPPER CANADA BY THE UNITED EMPIRE
LOYALISTS, 1784-1884. BILLIAS, GEORGE, EDITOR. LC 72-8670.
(AMERICAN REVOLUTIONARY SER.). REPR. OF 1885 ED. LIBRARY
BINDING - ADULT. $49.50X. (ISBN 0-8398-2000-3). IRVINGTON
PUBLISHERS.
NAME: IRVINGTON PUBLISHERS
STREET: 740 BROADWAY, SUITE 905
CITY: NEW YORK
STATE: NY
ZIP: 10003

Appendix B

Trademark/Service Mark Application

Certification Mark Application

Collective Mark Application

Multiple Class Application

Declaration

Appointment of Domestic Representative

TRADEMARK OR SERVICE MARK APPLICATION
PRINCIPAL OR SUPPLEMENTAL REGISTER
USE/INTENT TO USE/FOREIGN APPLICATION OR REGISTRATION

IN THE UNITED STATES PATENT AND TRADEMARK OFFICE

Mark   : (<u>insert mark to be registered</u>)
International Class : (<u>insert international class</u>)

TO THE COMMISSIONER OF PATENTS & TRADEMARKS:

(1) (insert name and address of applicant)
(2)

Applicant requests registration of the above-identified mark shown in the accompanying drawing in the United States Patent & Trademark Office on the (3) Register established by the Act of July 5, 1946, as amended, for the following goods (services): (<u>insert products or services to be covered by the application</u>).

(4) Applicant is using the mark in commerce on or in connection with the above identified goods (services). Three specimens showing the mark as used in commerce are submitted with this application.

> Date of first use of the mark anywhere: (<u>insert date</u>)
> Date of first use of the mark in commerce which the U.S. Congress may regulate: (<u>insert date</u>)
> The mark has been used in the following kind of commerce: (<u>insert kind of commerce – e.g., interstate, between the U.S. and a specified foreign country</u>)

(5) The mark has been used on or in connection with the goods (services) by applying it to (<u>insert the manner or method of using the mark, i.e., "the goods," "containers for the goods," "displays associated with the goods," "tags or labels affixed to the goods," "advertising and promotional material for the services," or other manner or mode of use</u>).

(6) **NOTE**: If the applicant is not domiciled in the U.S., a domestic representative must be designated on a separate page.

1

DECLARATION

The undersigned being hereby warned that willful false statements and the like so made are punishable by fine or imprisonment, or both, under 18 U.S.C. 1001, and that such willful false statements may jeopardize the validity of this application or any registration resulting therefrom declares: that the undersigned is properly authorized to execute this application on behalf of the applicant; the undersigned believes the applicant to be the owner of the mark sought to be registered, or, if the application is being filed under 15 U.S.C. 1051(b), the undersigned believes applicant to be entitled to use such mark in commerce; to the best of the undersigned's knowledge and belief no other person, firm, corporation or association has the right to use said mark in commerce, either in the identical form or in such near resemblance thereto as may be likely, when applied to the goods/services of such other person, to cause confusion, or to cause mistake, or to deceive; and that all statements made of the undersigned's own knowledge are true and all statements made on information and belief are believed to be true.

(insert name of applicant)

(7)_____(Signature)_____
(insert title of person who signs)
Date: (insert date signed)

(8) **NOTE**: If the applicant is represented by an attorney who will file and prosecute the application, a Power of Attorney should be inserted here.

2

DRAWING

Applicant : (insert applicant's name and address)

Date of First Use : (insert first use date if application based on use)

Date of First Use
in Commerce : (insert first use date if application based on use in commerce)

Goods (Services) : (insert product or service description)

(insert typed or special form drawing)

3

INSERT NOTES

(1)   Insert: For a partnership applicant, the names of all partners, the partnership address, and the phrase "doing business as _____;" For joint applicants, the name of each joint applicant.

(2)   Insert: For an individual, that person's citizenship. For a partnership, each partner's citizenship. For joint applicants, each joint applicant's citizenship. For a corporation or association, the state or country of incorporation or formation.

(3)   Insert: The word "Principal" or "Supplemental" depending on which register the mark is to be registered.

(4)   Insert: For an Intent to Use Application based on use -

    Applicant has a bona fide intention to use the mark in commerce on or in connection with the above identified goods (services).

    Insert: For an Intent to Use Application based on a foreign application -

    Applicant has a bona fide intention to use the mark in commerce on or in connection with the above identified goods (services), and asserts a claim of priority based upon a foreign application in (insert name of foreign country) on (insert foreign application filing date) in accordance with 15 U.S.C. 1126(d), as amended.

    Insert: For an Intent to Use Application based on a foreign registration -

    Applicant has a bona fide intention to use the mark in commerce on or in connection with the above identified goods (services) and, accompanying this application, submits a certification or certified copy of a foreign registration issued by (insert name of foreign country) under (insert foreign registration number) in accordance with 15 U.S.C. 1126(e), as amended.

(5)   Insert: For an Intent to Use Application based on use -

    The mark will be used on or in connection with the goods (services) by (insert the intended manner or method of using the mark, e.g., "the mark will be applied to labeling for the goods," or "the mark will be used in advertising material for the services.")

    Delete: For an Intent to Use Application based on a foreign application/registration.

4

(6)

APPOINTMENT OF DOMESTIC REPRESENTATIVE

(<u>insert name and address of domestic representative</u>), is hereby designated applicant's representative upon whom may be served notice or process ain proceedings affecting the mark.

(7) Only the following person may sign the Declaration for the application, depending on the status of the applicant: (a) the individual applicant; (b) an officer of a corporate applicant or an applicant that is an association; (c) one general partner of a partnership applicant; (d) all joint applicants.

(8)

POWER OF ATTORNEY

Applicant hereby appoints (insert name and address of attorney), an attorney at law, to prosecute this application to register, to transact all business in the Patent and Trademark Office in connection therewith, and to receive the certificate of registration.

5

FIRST PAGE OF APPLICATION

CERTIFICATION MARK APPLICATION
PRINCIPAL OR SUPPLEMENTAL REGISTER
USE/INTENT TO USE/FOREIGN APPLICATION OR REGISTRATION

IN THE UNITED STATES PATENT AND TRADEMARK OFFICE

Mark   : (insert mark to be registered)
International Class : (insert international class)

TO THE COMMISSIONER OF PATENTS & TRADEMARKS:

(1) (insert name and address of applicant)
(2)

Applicant requests registration of the above-identified certification mark shown in the accompanying drawing in the United States Patent & Trademark Office on the (3) Register established by the Act of July 5, 1946, as amended, for the following goods (services): (insert products or services to be covered by the application). The certification mark, as used by persons authorized by applicant certifies: (insert statement describing what the mark certifies).

(4) Applicant has adopted and is exercising legitimate control over the use of the certification mark in commerce on or in connection with the above identified goods (services). Three specimens showing the mark as used in commerce are submitted with this application.
      Date of first use of the mark anywhere under the
      authority of applicant: (insert date)
      Date of first use of the mark in commerce which the U.S.
      Congress may regulate, under the authority of applicant:
      (insert date)
      The mark has been used in the following kind of commerce:
      (insert kind of commerce - e.g., interstate, between the
      U.S. and a specified foreign country)

(5) The mark has been used on or in connection with the goods (services) by applying it to (insert the manner or method of using the mark, i.e., "the goods," "containers for the goods," "displays associated with the goods," "tags or labels affixed to the goods," "advertising and promotional material for the services," or other manner or mode of use).

(6) **NOTE:** If the applicant is not domiciled in the U.S., a domestic representative must be designated on a separate page.

THE SECOND AND THIRD PAGES OF THIS APPLICATION
SUBSTANTAILLY CORRESPOND TO THE SECOND AND THIRD PAGES
OF THE TRADEMARK/SERVICE MARK APPLICATION

1

<u>FIRST PAGE OF APPLICATION</u>

COLLECTIVE TRADEMARK OR SERVICE MARK APPLICATION
PRINCIPAL OR SUPPLEMENTAL REGISTER
USE/INTENT TO USE/FOREIGN APPLICATION OR REGISTRATION

IN THE UNITED STATES PATENT AND TRADEMARK OFFICE

Mark   : (<u>insert mark to be registered</u>)
International Class : (<u>insert international class</u>)

TO THE COMMISSIONER OF PATENTS & TRADEMARKS:

(1) (insert name and address of applicant)
(2)

Applicant requests registration of the above-identified collective mark shown in the accompanying drawing in the United States Patent & Trademark Office on the **(3)** Register established by the Act of July 5, 1946, as amended, for the following goods (services): (<u>insert products or services to be covered by the application</u>).

(4) Applicant has adopted and is exercising legitimate control over the use of the collective mark in commerce on or in connection with the above identified goods (services). Three specimens showing the mark as used in commerce are submitted with this application.

> Date of first use of the mark anywhere by members of applicant: (<u>insert date</u>)
> Date of first use of the mark in commerce which the U.S. Congress may regulate, by members of applicant: (<u>insert date</u>)
> The mark has been used in the following kind of commerce: (<u>insert kind of commerce - e.g., interstate, between the U.S. and a specified foreign country</u>)

(5) The mark has been used on or in connection with the goods (services) by applying it to (<u>insert the manner or method of using the mark, i.e., "the goods," "containers for the goods," "displays associated with the goods," "tags or labels affixed to the goods," "advertising and promotional material for the services," or other manner or mode of use</u>).

(6) **NOTE:** If the applicant is not domiciled in the U.S., a domestic representative must be designated on a separate page.

<u>THE SECOND AND THIRD PAGES OF THIS APPLICATION</u>
<u>SUBSTANTAILLY CORRESPOND TO THE SECOND AND THIRD PAGES</u>
<u>OF THE TRADEMARK/SERVICE MARK APPLICATION</u>

1

<u>FIRST PAGE OF APPLICATION</u>

COLLECTIVE MEMBERSHIP MARK APPLICATION
PRINCIPAL OR SUPPLEMENTAL REGISTER
USE/INTENT TO USE/FOREIGN APPLICATION OR REGISTRATION

IN THE UNITED STATES PATENT AND TRADEMARK OFFICE

Mark   : (<u>insert mark to be registered</u>)
International Class : (<u>insert international class</u>)

TO THE COMMISSIONER OF PATENTS & TRADEMARKS:

(1) (insert name and address of applicant)
(2)

Applicant requests registration of the above-identified collective membership mark shown in the accompanying drawing in the United States Patent & Trademark Office on the (3) Register established by the Act of July 5, 1946, as amended, for the following kind of organization: (<u>insert kind of organization</u>).

(4) Applicant has adopted and is exercising legitimate control over the use of the collective membership mark in commerce on or in connection with the above identified kind of organization. Three specimens showing the mark as used in commerce are submitted with this application.

    Date of first use of the mark anywhere by a member of
    applicant: (<u>insert date</u>)
    Date of first use of the mark in commerce which the U.S.
    Congress may regulate, by a member of applicant: (<u>insert</u>
    <u>date</u>)
    The mark has been used in the following kind of commerce:
    (<u>insert kind of commerce - e.g., interstate, between the</u>
    <u>U.S. and a specified foreign country</u>)

(5) The mark has been used by applying it to (<u>insert the manner or</u>
<u>method of using the mark, i.e., "membership cards," "wall plaques,"</u>
<u>or other manner or mode of use</u>).

(6) **NOTE:** If the applicant is not domiciled in the U.S., a domestic representative must be designated on a separate page.

THE SECOND AND THIRD PAGES OF THIS APPLICATION
SUBSTANTIALLY CORRESPOND TO THE SECOND AND THIRD PAGES
OF THE TRADEMARK/SERVICE MARK APPLICATION

1

MULTIPLE CLASS APPLICATION
PRINCIPAL OR SUPPLEMENTAL REGISTER
USE/INTENT TO USE/FOREIGN APPLICATION OR REGISTRATION

IN THE UNITED STATES PATENT AND TRADEMARK OFFICE

Mark   : (insert mark to be registered)
International Class : (insert international class)

TO THE COMMISSIONER OF PATENTS & TRADEMARKS:

(1) (insert name and address of applicant)
(2)

Applicant requests registration of the above-identified mark shown
in the accompanying drawing in the United States Patent & Trademark
Office on the (3) Register established by the Act of July 5, 1946,
as amended, for the following goods (services): (a separate
paragraph should be used for each class of products/services in
ascending order and the International Class number should be noted
at the end of the description, i.e., "in International Class   ")

(4) Applicant is using the mark in commerce on or in connection
with the above identified goods (services). For each class, three
specimens showing the mark as used in commerce are submitted with
this application.

NOTE: (a separate use dates paragraph should be used for each class
when the use dates differ for each class. If the use dates are the
same for all classes, the following paragraph can be used by
indicating the mark was used in all classes for the dates noted)

      Date of first use of the mark anywhere: (insert date)
      Date of first use of the mark in commerce which the U.S.
         Congress may regulate: (insert date)
      The mark has been used in the following kind of commerce:
      (insert kind of commerce - e.g., interstate, between the
      U.S. and a specified foreign country)

(5) The mark has been used on or in connection with the goods
(services) by applying it to (insert the manner or method of using
the mark, i.e., "the goods," "containers for the goods," "displays
associated with the goods," "tags or labels affixed to the goods,"
"advertising and promotional material for the services," or other
manner or mode of use).

NOTE: (a separate manner of use paragraph should be used for each
class when the manner of use differs for each class. If the manner
of use is the same for all classes the preceding paragraph should
indicate that the manner of use is applicable to all classes.

1

(6) **NOTE**: If the applicant is not domiciled in the U.S., a domestic representative must be designated on a separate page.

**THE SECOND AND THIRD PAGES OF THIS APPLICATION
SUBSTANTAILLY CORRESPOND TO THE SECOND AND THIRD PAGES
OF THE TRADEMARK/SERVICE MARK APPLICATION**

2

DECLARATION

(*Name of person signing below) being hereby warned that willful false statements and the like so made are punishable by fine or imprisonment, or both, under Section 1001 of Title 18 of the United States Code and that such willful false statements may jeopardize the validity of the registration resulting therefrom, declares:

APPOINTMENT OF DOMESTIC REPRESENTATIVE

LISA SHAWN, whose postal address is 4100 East Mississippi Avenue, Suite 1000, Denver, CO 80222, is hereby designated applicant's representative upon whom notice or process in proceedings affecting the mark may be served.

THE SHERETH GROUP, INC.

By_____

Appendix C

APPLICATION FOR REGISTRATION OF TRADEMARK

STATE OF COLORADO

INSTRUCTIONS

1. MUST BE TYPEWRITTEN
2. COMPLETE ALL SECTIONS AND HAVE NOTARIZED
3. SEND TO: CORPORATIONS SECTION
   Colorado Secretary of State
   State Social Services Building
   1575 Sherman St., Room 200
   Denver, CO 80203

FEE: $11.00
Make check payable to "Secretary of State"

SUBMIT ONE COPY

1 | NAME OF OWNER/APPLICANT (person, corporation, partnership, association, etc.)

STATE OF INCORPORATION _____(complete only if a corporation)

2 | BUSINESS ADDRESS OF OWNER/APPLICANT (principal place of business)

NUMBER	STREET	SUITE OR APT.

CITY	STATE	ZIP CODE

DO NOT WRITE IN THIS BOX · OFFICE USE ONLY

The above-named, being desirous of complying with the provisions of Article 70, Chapter 7, Colorado Revised Statutes 1973, as amended, has adopted and is using in the State of Colorado the following TRADEMARK:

3 | DESCRIPTION OF TRADEMARK — Complete A or B, but not both

A

WORDS _____

CHECK ONE:

☐ WORDS ONLY   ☐ WORDS WITH STYLIZED LETTERING (3 FACSIMILES REQUIRED)   ☐ WORDS & DESIGN (3 FACSIMILES REQUIRED)

B

DESIGN ONLY — NO WORDS IN TRADEMARK (3 FACSIMILES REQUIRED)

DESCRIBE BRIEFLY _____

4 | CLASSIFICATION — Choose ONE ONLY from list on back of form

CLASS NUMBER   CLASS TITLE

(   )

5 | DATE FIRST USED by applicant or his predecessor in the same business — Complete both A & B

FIRST USED ANYWHERE (DAY/MO/YR)   FIRST USED IN COLORADO

A ____ / ____ / ____   ◄— THIS DATE MUST BE BEFORE OR SAME AS THIS DATE —►   B ____ / ____ / ____

6 | MANNER IN WHICH TRADEMARK IS USED — Be Brief!

7 | DECLARATION — SIGNATURE — NOTARIZATION

STATE OF _____ ⎫ SS
COUNTY OF _____ ⎭

I, _____being duly sworn, declare that I am the
(FULL NAME OF PERSON EXECUTING APPLICATION)
owner/applicant named above, or am the authorized agent or officer of said owner/applicant; that I verily believe the applicant is the owner of the trademark and that no other person or organization has the right to use such trademark in this State either in the identical form thereof or in such near resemblance thereto as might be calculated to deceive or be mistaken therefor; that the statements set forth above are true; that the accompanying specimens or facsimiles, and/or description above truly represent the mark as used; and that the applicant hereby appoints the Secretary of State as agent for service of process in any action relating to the registration which may be issued, if the applicant be or shall become a nonresident or foreign corporation not licensed to do business in this State, or cannot be found in this State.

INDICATE SIGNER'S RELATIONSHIP
TO OWNER/APPLICANT BELOW

APPLICANT'S _____SIGNED _____
(Self, President, Vice-President, etc.)

Subscribed and sworn to before me this_____day of _____19_____.

(SEAL) My commission expires_____

_____
(NOTARY PUBLIC)

FORM SS: TM-1 (Rev. 9/79)

Goods

1. Chemicals products used in industry, science, photography, agriculture, horticulture, forestry; artificial and synthetic resins; plastics in the form of powders, liquids or pastes, for industrial use; manures (natural and artificial); fire extinguishing compositions; tempering substances and chemical preparations for soldering; chemical substances for preserving foodstuffs; tanning substances; adhesive substances used in industry.

2. Paints, varnishes, lacquers; preservatives against rust and against deterioration of wood; colouring matters, dyestuffs; mordants; natural resins; metals in foil and powder form for painters and decorators.

3. Bleaching preparations and other substances for laundry use; cleaning, polishing, scouring and abrasive preparations; soaps; perfumery, essential oils, cosmetics, hair lotions; dentifrices.

4. Industrial oils and greases (other than oils and fats and essential oils); lubricants; dust laying and absorbing compositions; fuels (including motor spirit) and illuminants; candles, tapers, night lights and wicks.

5. Pharmaceutical, veterinary, and sanitary substances; infants' and invalids' foods; plasters, material for bandaging; material for stopping teeth, dental wax, disinfectants; preparations for killing weeds and destroying vermin.

6. Unwrought and partly wrought common metals and their alloys; anchors, anvils, bells, rolled and cast building materials; rails and other metallic materials for railway tracks; chains (except driving chains for vehicles); cables and wires (nonelectric); locksmiths' work; metallic pipes and tubes; safes and cash boxes; steel balls; horseshoes; nails and screws; other goods in nonprecious metal not included in other classes; ores.

7. Machines and machine tools; motors (except for land vehicles); machine couplings and belting (except for land vehicles); large size agricultural implements; incubators.

8. Hand tools and instruments; cutlery, forks, and spoons; side arms.

9. Scientific, nautical, surveying and electrical apparatus and instruments (including wireless), photographic, cinematographic, optical, weighing, measuring, signalling, checking (supervision), life-saving and teaching apparatus and instruments; coin or counterfreed apparatus; talking machines; cash registers; calculating machines; fire extinguishing apparatus.

10. Surgical, medical, dental, and veterinary instruments and apparatus (including artificial limbs, eyes and teeth).

11. Installations for lighting, heating, steam generating, cooking, refrigerating, drying, ventilating, water supply, and sanitary purposes.

12. Vehicles; apparatus for locomotion by land, air or water.

13. Firearms; ammunition and projectiles; explosive substances; fireworks.

14. Precious metals and their alloys and goods in precious metals or coated therewith (except cutlery, forks and spoons); jewelry, precious stones, horological and other chronometric instruments.

15. Musical instruments (other than talking machines and wireless apparatus).

16. Paper and paper articles, cardboard and cardboard articles; printed matter, newspaper and periodicals, books; bookbinding material; photographs; stationery, adhesive materials (stationery); artists' materials; paint brushes; typewriters and office requisites (other than furniture); instructional and teaching material (other than apparatus); playing cards; printers' type and cliches (stereotype).

17. Gutta percha, india rubber, balata and substitutes, articles made from these substances and not included in other classes; plastics in the form of sheets, blocks and rods, being for use in manufacture; materials for packing, stopping or insulating; asbestos, mica and their products; hose pipes (nonmetallic).

18. Leather and imitations of leather, and articles made from these materials and not included in other classes; skins, hides; trunks and travelling bags; umbrellas, parasols and walking sticks; whips, harness and saddlery.

19. Building materials, natural and artificial stone, cement, lime, mortar, plaster and gravel; pipes of earthenware or cement; roadmaking materials; asphalt, pitch and bitumen; portable buildings; stone monuments; chimney pots.

20. Furniture, mirrors, picture frames; articles (not included in other classes) of wood, cork, reeds, cane, wicker, horn, bone, ivory, whalebone, shell, amber, mother-of-pearl, meerschaum, celluloid, substitutes for all these materials, or of plastics.

21. Small domestic utensils and containers (not of precious metals, or coated therewith); combs and sponges; brushes (other than paint brushes); brushmaking materials; instruments and material for cleaning purposes, steel wool; unworked or semi-worked glass (excluding glass used in building); glassware, porcelain and earthenware, not included in other classes.

22. Ropes, string, nets, tents, awnings, tarpaulins, sails, sacks; padding and stuffing materials (hair, kapok, feathers, seaweed, etc.); raw fibrous textile materials.

23. Yarns, threads.

24. Tissues (piece goods); bed and table covers; textile articles not included in other classes.

25. Clothing, including boots, shoes and slippers.

26. Lace and embroidery, ribands and braid; buttons, press buttons, hooks and eyes, pins and needles; artificial flowers.

27. Carpets, rugs, mats and matting; linoleums and other materials for covering existing floors; wall hangings (nontextile).

28. Games and playthings; gymnastic and sporting articles (except clothing); ornaments and decorations for Christmas trees.

29. Meats, fish, poultry and game; meat extracts; preserved, dried and cooked fruits and vegetables; jellies, jams; eggs, milk and other dairy products; edible oils and fats; preserves, pickles.

30. Coffee, tea, cocoa, sugar, rice, tapioca, sago, coffee substitutes; flour, and preparations made from cereals; bread, biscuits, cakes, pastry and confectionery, ices; honey, treacle; yeast, baking powder; salt, mustard, pepper, vinegar, sauces, spices; ice.

31. Agricultural, horticultural and forestry products and grains not included in other classes; living animals; fresh fruits and vegetables; seeds; live plants and flowers; foodstuffs for animals, malt.

32. Beer, ale and porter; mineral and aerated waters and other nonalcoholic drinks; syrups and other preparations for making beverages.

33. Wines, spirits and liqueurs.

34. Tobacco, raw or manufactured; smokers' articles; matches.

Services

35. Advertising and business.

36. Insurance and financial.

37. Construction and repair.

38. Communication.

39. Transportation and storage.

40. Material treatment.

41. Education and entertainment.

42. Miscellaneous.

BOX 4 – CLASSIFICATION OF TRADEMARKS

GOODS

CLASS NO.	CLASS TITLE
(1)	Raw or partly prepared materials
(2)	Receptacles
(3)	Baggage, animal equipments, portfolios, and pocketbooks
(4)	Abrasives and polishing materials
(5)	Adhesives
(6)	Chemicals and chemical compositions
(7)	Cordage
(8)	Smokers' articles, not including tobacco products
(9)	Explosives, firearms, equipments, and projectiles
(10)	Fertilizers
(11)	Inks and inking materials
(12)	Construction materials
(13)	Hardware and plumbing and steam-fitting supplies
(14)	Metals and metal castings and forgings
(15)	Oils and greases
(16)	Protective and decorative coatings
(17)	Tobacco products
(18)	Medicines and pharmaceutical preparations
(19)	Vehicles
(20)	Linoleum and oiled cloth
(21)	Electrical apparatus, machines, and supplies
(22)	Games, toys, and sporting goods
(23)	Cutlery, machinery, tools, and parts thereof
(24)	Laundry appliances and machines
(25)	Locks and safes
(26)	Measuring and scientific appliances
(27)	Horological instruments
(28)	Jewelry and precious-metal ware
(29)	Brooms, brushes, and dusters
(30)	Crockery, earthenware, and porcelain
(31)	Filters and refrigerators
(32)	Furniture and upholstery
(33)	Glassware
(34)	Heating, lighting, and ventilating apparatus
(35)	Belting, hose, machinery packing, and nonmetallic tires
(36)	Musical instruments and supplies
(37)	Paper and stationery
(38)	Prints and publications
(39)	Clothing
(40)	Fancy goods, furnishings, and notions
(41)	Canes, parasols, and umbrellas
(42)	Knitted, netted, and textile fabrics, and substitutes therefor
(43)	Thread and yarn
(44)	Dental, medical, and surgical appliances
(45)	Soft drinks and carbonated waters
(46)	Foods and ingredients of foods
(47)	Wines
(48)	Malt beverages and liquors
(49)	Distilled alcoholic liquors
(50)	Merchandise not otherwise classified
(51)	Cosmetics and toilet preparations
(52)	Detergents and soaps

SERVICES

CLASS NO.	CLASS TITLE
(100)	Miscellaneous
(101)	Advertising and business
(102)	Insurance and financial
(103)	Construction and repair
(104)	Communication
(105)	Transportation and storage
(106)	Material treatment
(107)	Education and entertainment
(200)	Collective membership

UNITED STATES PATENT & TRADEMARK OFFICE
COLOR LINING CHART

Linings for color. Where color is a feature of a mark, the color or colors employed may be designated by means of conventional linings as shown in the following color chart:

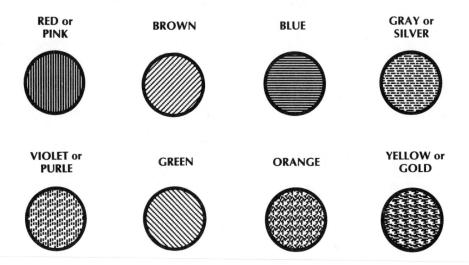

RED or PINK

BROWN

BLUE

GRAY or SILVER

VIOLET or PURLE

GREEN

ORANGE

YELLOW or GOLD

FILING RECEIPT FOR TRADEMARK APPLICATION

Receipt is acknowledged of the application and filing fee for the registration of the MARK identified below. Your application will be considered in order and you will be notified as to the examination thereof. When inquiring about this application, include the SERIAL NUMBER, DATE OF FILING, NAME OF APPLICANT, and IDENTIFICATION OF MARK. Fees transmitted by check or draft are subject to collection.

Please review the accuracy of the Filing Receipt data. Corrections should be submitted within 30 days of receipt of this notice. The Office will review requests for correction and make corrections when appropriate. Submit request for correction of filing receipt to:

COMMISSIONER OF PATENTS AND TRADEMARKS
Box 5 Crystal Plaza 2 -- Room 4C16
Washington, DC 20231

No correspondence on this application should be expected before approximately 03 months from the filing date.

SERIAL NO.: 73/756664   FILING DATE: 1988/10/11

MARK: AMERICAN SKIER

MARK TYPE: SERVICEMARK

ATTORNEY: DAVID A. WEINSTEIN

OWNER NAME   : INNOVATIVE PRODUCTIONS, INC.
OWNER ADDRESS: SUITE 345
               2302 PARKLAKE DRIVE, N.E.
               ATLANTA
               GEORGIA   30345

CITIZENSHIP/INCORPORATION: GEORGIA

ENTITY: CORPORATION

INTERNATIONAL CLASS: 041   U.S. CLASS: 107

DATES OF 1ST USE: 1988/06/00   DATES 1ST USE COMMERCE: 1988/06/00

GOODS/SERVICES: 041-ENTERTAINMENT SERVICES IN THE NATURE OF
A WEEKLY TELEVISION PROGRAM

SPACE LIMITATIONS DEMAND THE SIZE OF INFORMATION FIELDS BE LIMITED. AN * DENOTES ADDITIONAL INFORMATION PRESENT IN PTO RECORDS.

U.S. DEPARTMENT OF COMMERCE – Patent and Trademark Office

IN REPLY REFER TO THE FOLLOWING AND THE FILING DATE: RECEIVED

Paper No.

SERIAL NO.	APPLICANT	ADDRESS:

73/775166 TRAVEL AND TOURISM RESEARCH ASSOCIATION

Commissioner of Patents and Trademarks

MARK

TTRA

ADDRESS

DAVID A. WEINSTEIN
BOURKE AND JACOBS, P.C.
4100 EAST MISSISSIPPI AVENUE
SUITE 1000
DENVER, CO 80222

ACTION NO.

01

MAILING DATE

04/12/89

Washington, DC 20231

The address of all correspondence not containing fee payments should include the word "Box 5."

FORM PTO-1525 (2-84)   U.S. DEPT. OF COMM. PAT. & TM OFFICE

Also furnish: (1) Serial number of application, (2) The mark, (3) Examining Attorney's name and Law Office number, (4) Mailing date of this action, and (5) Applicant's name (or applicant's attorney), telephone number and zip code.

A PROPER RESPONSE TO THIS OFFICE ACTION MUST BE RECEIVED WITHIN 6 MONTHS FROM THE DATE OF THIS ACTION IN ORDER TO AVOID ABANDONMENT.

775166

NOTE: For your information, effective April 17, 1989, filing fees are reduced from $200.00 to $175.00 per class. If filed prior to April 17, 1989, new applications or amendments to add classes to pending applications must be accompanied by the fee of $200.00 per class. If filed on or after April 17, 1989, new applications or amendments to add classes must be accompanied by the reduced fee of $175.00 per class.

In addition, effective April 17, 1989, the fee for recording assignments and agreements, or other papers relating to a registration or application, is $8.00 for each registration or application against which the document is to be referenced.

NOTE: Please note that the Office will deny a filing date to application papers submitted on or after July 3, 1989 which display the mark in a special form drawing in an area which exceeds the specified size limitations. Trademark Rule 2.21(a)(3), 37 C.F.R. Section 2.21(a)(3), requires, as one of the elements for receiving a filing date, a drawing of the mark "substantially meeting all the requirements of Section 2.52." Trademark Rule 2.52(c), 37 C.F.R. Section 2.52(c), states that in no case may the drawing be larger than 4 inches (10.3 cm.) high and 4 inches (10.3 cm). wide.

The Examining Attorney has searched the Office records and has found no similar registered or pending mark which would bar registration under Trademark Act Section 2(d), 15 U.S.C. Section 1052(d) (1986). TMEP section 1105.01.

The Applicant must indicate whether the individual who signed the application is an officer of the Applicant corporation. If not, then the Applicant must submit a substitute affidavit or declaration under 37 C.F.R. Section 2.20 signed by an officer. Trademark Act Section 1, 15 U.S.C. Section 1051 (1986); TMEP sections 803.09, 803.10 and 803.11.

The Trademark Act requires that a corporate officer sign an application for a corporation. Trademark Act Section 1, 15 U.S.C. Section 1051 (1986). The Examining Attorney cannot waive this requirement. An officer is a person who holds an office established in the articles of incorporation or the corporate by-laws. Officers may not delegate this authority to non-officers.

HF:ji1   Hannah Fisher
                                    Trademark Attorney/Law Office 4
                                    (703) 557-9304

IN THE UNITED STATES PATENT AND TRADEMARK OFFICE

Mark	:	SHERETH MUSIC
Application Serial No.	:	74/889,199
Examiner	:	John Demos
Division	:	4

Box 5
COMMISSIONER OF PATENTS AND TRADEMARKS
Washington, D.C. 20231

This paper is filed in response to the Examiner's action mailed April 19, 1990.

AMENDMENT

Applicant requests the examiner to enter the following disclaimer in the application

> No claim is made to exclusive use of
> "music" apart from the mark shown
> in the drawing.

RESPONSE

In response to the examiner's disclaimer request, applicant asks that the application be amended as noted above.

The individual who signed the application is president of applicant.

In light of the foregoing, the application is now in order for publication. Accordingly, Applicant respectfully requests the Examiner to publish the instant mark for opposition.

In the event the Examiner has any further questions referring to this application which may be answered by Applicant's attorney through a telephone conversation, the Examiner is hereby authorized to contact Applicant's attorney of record at the telephone number noted below.

Dated: April 17, 1990

Respectfully submitted,

David A. Weinstein
4100 East Mississippi Avenue
Suite 1000
Denver, Colorado 80222
Telephone: (303) 759-3000

VERIFICATION

STACY ERRIN, being hereby warned that willful, false statements and the like so made are punishable by fine or imprisonment, or both, under Section 101 of Title 18 of the United States Code and that such willful false statements may jeopardize the validity of the application or any registration resulting therefrom, declares: That she is Vice President of applicant and is authorized to execute this Declaration on behalf of said corporation; that the label evidencing use of the mark SHERETH, submitted at the time the application was filed, is a photocopy of an actual label used by applicant in connection with the goods covered by the application.

THE SHERETH GROUP, INC.

By_____
    Stacy Errin

Class 40 —(Continued).

SN 332,307. Power Cutting, Inc., Lake Bluff, Ill. Filed Oct. 13, 1981.

PCI

For Machining and Welding Services for Others (U.S. Cl. 106). First use Feb. 1, 1979; in commerce Feb. 1, 1979.

SN 350,414. North American Photo, Inc., Livonia, Mich. Filed Feb. 16, 1982.

Applicant disclaims the words "Photo Inc." apart from the mark as shown.

The mark comprises a fanciful representation of the letters "NAP".

For Photographic Services—Namely, Film Processing and Printing (U.S. Cl. 106).

First use Nov. 1, 1981; in commerce Nov. 1, 1981.

Class 41—Education and Entertainment

SN 205,051. Snowmen, Sciota Village, Corry, Pa. Filed Feb. 26, 1979.

SNOWMEN

For Entertainment Services—Namely, Rendering Musical Performances (U.S. Cl. 107).

First use Jan. 1, 1978; in commerce Jan. 1, 1978.

SN 248,257. Dick Clark Teleshows, Inc., Burbank, Calif. Filed Jan. 31, 1980.

THE AMERICAN MUSIC AWARDS

Sec. 2(f).

For Entertainment Services—Namely, a Musical Variety Television Program (U.S. Cl. 107).

First use Jul. 1973; in commerce Feb. 19, 1974.

Class 41 —(Continued).

SN 254,111. Automation Industries, Inc., Greenwich, Conn. Filed Mar. 17, 1980.

SPERRY

Owner of U.S. Reg. Nos. 806,035, 812,493 and 812,968.

Sec. 2(f).

For Educational Services—Namely, Providing Instruction in Methods of Testing for Welding Defects and in Methods of Nuclear Auditing; and Providing Instruction in Non-Destructive Methods of Testing the Mechanical and Structural Integrity of Materials, Semi-Finished Products, and Finished Products, Said Non-Destructive Testing Methods Utilizing Visual, Acoustic Emission, Ultrasonic, Liquid Penetrant, Radiographic, Electromagnetic and Leak Testing Techniques (U.S. Cl. 107).

First use Dec. 1975; in commerce Dec. 1975.

SN 277,442. Charlotte Sports Promotions, Charlotte, N.C. Filed Sep. 10, 1980.

No claim is made to exclusive use of "Charlotte" apart from the mark as shown in the drawing, but the applicant waives none of its common law rights in the mark as shown in the drawing or any feature thereof.

The lining is for purposes of shading to represent the fur-type outer surface of the three-dimensional dog design.

For Entertainment Services—Namely, the Live Performance of Cheerleading Services at Baseball Games (U.S. Cl. 107).

First use Jul. 4, 1980; in commerce Jul. 4, 1980.

SN 285,209. Donna Weihofen, d.b.a. The Nutrition Magician, Verona, Wis. Filed Jan. 23, 1981.

THE NUTRITION MAGICIAN

For Educational Services—Namely, Teaching Nutrition Concepts to Children Through the Use of Magic Tricks (U.S. Cl. 107).

First use Feb. 15, 1980; in commerce May 22, 1980.

UNITED STATES DEPARTMENT OF COMMERCE
Patent and Trade k Office

ASSISTANT SECRETARY AND COMMISSIONER
OF PATENTS AND TRADEMARKS
Washington, D.C. 20231

NOTICE OF PUBLICATION UNDER 12(a)

1. Serial No.:
   73/776,072

2. Mark:
   VOLANT
   (Stylized)

3. Applicant:
   VARION LTD.

4. Publication Date:
   JUN. 27, 1989

The mark of the application above identified appears to be entitled to registration. The mark will, in accordance with Section 12(a) of the Trademark Act of 1946, be published in the Official Gazette on the date indicated above for the purpose of opposition by any person who believes he will be damaged by the registration of the mark. If no opposition is filed within the time specified by Section 13 of the Statute or by rules 2.101 and 2.102 of the Trademark Rules, the Commissioner of Patents and Trademarks may issue a certificate of registration.

Copies of the trademark portion of the Official Gazette containing the publication of the mark may be obtained at $9.50 each for domestic orders, or at $11.88each for foreign orders from:

The Superintendent of Documents
U.S. Government Printing Office
Washington,D.C. 20402

By direction of the Commissioner.

Int. Cl.: 28

Prior U.S. Cl.: 22

Reg. No. 1,556,989
United States Patent and Trademark Office Registered Sep. 19, 1989

TRADEMARK
PRINCIPAL REGISTER

VARION LTD. (COLORADO LIMITED PART-
NERSHIP)
P.O. BOX 936
BOULDER, CO 80306

FOR: SNOW SKIS, IN CLASS 28 (U.S. CL. 22).

FIRST USE 12-0-1988; IN COMMERCE
12-0-1988.

SER. NO. 776,072, FILED 1-23-1989.

W. A. CONN, EXAMINING ATTORNEY

UNITED STATES PATENT AND TRADEMARK OFFICE

Registrant   :
Mark   :
Registration No.   :
Registration Date   :
Class No.   :

COMMISSIONER OF PATENTS AND TRADEMARKS
Washington, D.C. 20231

REQUEST TO AMEND REGISTRATION

Registrant hereby requests that the above-identified registration be amended in part to reflect the mark as shown in the drawing attached hereto.

The mark as shown in the drawing has been and is currently used in interstate commerce on and in connection with the services covered by the registration as reflected by the attached specimen. The requested amendment does not materially alter the character of the mark.

Respectfully submitted,

_____

Date:

DECLARATION

(*Name of person signing below) being hereby warned that willful false statements and the like so made are punishable by fine or imprisonment, or both, under Section 1001 of Title 18 of the United States Code and that such willful false statements may jeopardize the validity of the registration resulting therefrom, declares:

That he/she is (*title of person signing below) of registrant and is authorized to execute this Declaration on behalf of registrant; that to the best of his/her knowledge and belief the facts set forth in the Request to Amend Registration are true; and, further, that all statements made herein of his/her own knowledge are true and that all statements made on information and belief are believed to be true.

(*insert registrant's name)

By_____
                  Date:

SECTION 8 AFFIDAVIT

UNITED STATES PATENT AND TRADEMARK OFFICE

```
Registrant          :
Mark                :
Registration No.    :
Registration Date   :
Class No.           :
```

STATE OF_____)
COUNTY OF_____)

(*Name of person who signs affidavit), being sworn states that
(*name of registrant who owns registration at time affidavit is
filed) owns the above-identified registration issued (*registration
date), as shown by records in the Patent and Trademark Office; and
that the mark shown therein is still in use (*if the mark is not
in use at the time of filing this affidavit, but there is no
intention to abandon the mark, facts must be recited to show that
the nonuse is due to special circumstances) as evidenced by the
specimen included showing the mark as currently used.

<u>(*Signature)</u>_____
(*Title, of person who signs)
Date:

Subscribed and sworn to before me, this _____ day of _____,
_____.

_____
Notary public

(If the registrant is not domiciled in the United States, a
domestic representative must be designated. If a designation is
not submitted with this form, a prior unrevoked designation will
meet the requirement if it is already in the registration file)

SECTION 15 AFFIDAVIT

UNITED STATES PATENT AND TRADEMARK OFFICE

Registrant   :
Mark   :
Registration No.   :
Registration Date   :
Class No.   :

STATE OF_____   )
COUNTY OF_____   )

(*Name of person who signs affidavit), being sworn states that (*name of registrant who owns registration at time affidavit is filed) owns the above-identified registration issued (*registration date), as shown by records in the Patent and Trademark Office; and that the mark shown therein has been in continuous use in (*type of commerce should be specified as "interstate," "foreign," "territorial," or other commerce which may lawfully be regulated by Congress) commerce for five consecutive years from (*the date should be the beginning of a five year period of continuous use, all of which five year perod falls after the date of registration) to the present on each of the following goods (*if a service mark registration, state "in connection with each of the following services") recited in the registration:

(*list products or services)

that such mark is still in use in (*type of commerce should be specified as "interstate," "foreign," "territorial," or other commerce which may lawfully be regulated by Congress) commerce; that there has been no final decision adverse to registrant's right to register the same or to keep the same on the register, and that there is no proceeding involving said rights pending and not disposed of either in the Patent and Trademark Office or in the courts.

(*Signature)_____
(*Title, of person who signs)
Date:

Subscribed and sworn to before me, this _____ day of _____, _____.

_____
Notary public

COMBINED SECTION 8 & 15 AFFIDAVIT

UNITED STATES PATENT AND TRADEMARK OFFICE

```
Registrant           :
Mark                 :
Registration No.     :
Registration Date    :
Class No.            :
```

STATE OF_____)
COUNTY OF_____)

(*Name of person who signs affidavit), being sworn states that (*name of registrant who owns registration at time affidavit is filed) owns the above-identified registration issued (*registration date), as shown by records in the Patent and Trademark Office; and that the mark shown therein has been in continuous use in (*type of commerce should be specified as "interstate," "foreign," "territorial," or other commerce which may lawfully be regulated by Congress) commerce for five consecutive years from the date of the registration to the present, on each of the following goods (*if a service mark registration, state "in connection with each of the following services") recited in the registration:

(*list products or services)

that such mark is still in use in (*type of commerce should be specified as "interstate," "foreign," "territorial," or other commerce which may lawfully be regulated by Congress) commerce; that such mark is still in use as evidenced by the specimen included showing the mark as currently used; that there has been no final decision adverse to registrant's right to register the same or to keep the same on the register, and that there is no proceeding involving said rights pending and not disposed of either in the Patent and Trademark Office or in the courts.

```
                            (*Signature)_____
                            (*Title, of person who signs)
                            Date:
```

Subscribed and sworn to before me, this ____ day of _____, _____.

```
                            _____
                            Notary public
```

(If the registrant is not domiciled in the United States, a domestic representative must be designated. If a designation is not submitted with this form, a prior unrevoked designation will meet the requirement if it is already in the registration file)

RENEWAL APPLICATION

UNITED STATES PATENT AND TRADEMARK OFFICE

```
Registrant          :
Mark                :
Registration No.    :
Registration Date   :
```

Commissioner of Patents & Trademarks
Washington, D.C. 20231

The above-identified applicant for renewal requests that the above-identified registration, granted to (*name of original registrant) on (*date of issuance), which applicant for renewal now owns, as shown by records in the Patent and Trademark Office, be renewed in accordance with the provisions of section 9 of the Act of July 5, 1946.

The mark shown in said registration is still in use (*type of commerce should be specified as "interstate," "foreign," "territorial," or other commerce which may lawfully be regulated by Congress) commerce on each of the following goods (*if a service mark registration, state "in connection with each of the following services") recited in the registration:

(*list products or services)

The attached specimen shows the mark as currently used (*if the mark is not in use in commerce at the time of filing the application for renewal, but there is no intention to abandon the mark, facts must be recited to show that the nonuse is due to special circumstances).

(*Name of person signing below) being hereby warned that willful false statements and the like so made are punishable by fine or imprisonment, or both, under Section 1001 of Title 18 of the United States Code and that such willful false statements may jeopardize the validity of this application, delcares that all statements made in this application of his/her knowledge are true and all statements made on information believe are believed to be true.

(*Signature)_____
(*Title, of person who signs)
Date:

(If the renewal applicant is not domiciled in the United States, a domestic representative must be designated. If a designation is not submitted with this form, a prior unrevoked designation will meet the requirement if it is already in the registration file)

Appendix D

Cease and Desist Letter

Settlement Agreement

Consent Judgement

Consent Order of Dismissal

Notice of Opposition

Petition to Cancel

CEASE AND DESIST LETTER

(*name and address)

     Re: (*infringing mark)

Dear

     I am writing to you in reference to your unauthorized use of (*insert infringing mark) on or in connection with (*insert products or services). On the basis of information available to me, it appears you first used your mark on _____. Your use of this mark recently came to my attention and presents a matter of concern to me.

     For your information, I am the owner of the mark (*insert sender's mark) used to identify (*insert sender's products or services). This mark was first used at least as early as (*insert first use date) and is the subject of U.S. Patent & Trademark Office (or state) Registration No. _____ (if applicable). A copy of my registration is enclosed as well as copies of material featuring my mark.

     It is my opinion your mark is confusingly similar to mine. Therefore, I feel your use of (*insert infringing mark) constitutes an infringement of my proprietary rights in (*insert sender's mark). It is likely to lead others to believe they are purchasing products (or services) which are offered or sponsored by, or in some way connected with me and meet my high quality standards. Since this is not the case I request that you immediately cease all use of (*insert infringing mark).

     Now that my rights have been called to your attention, I trust you will respect them. To enable me to close my file on this matter I request that you send me a copy of this letter signed by you in the space for your signature. It is not unreasonable to expect you to do this no later than one month from the date of this letter.

1

In the event I do not receive a favorable response, as requested, I will take appropriate action to enforce my rights concerning your use of (*insert infringing mark). I trust this will not be necessary as it will result in the expenditure of time, effort and money by you as well as me.

Sincerely,

In consideration for your agreement to refrain from instituting an infringement action against me concerning use of (*insert infringing mark), I hereby agree to immediately cease all use of (*insert infringing mark) and/or variations or colorable imitations thereof, no later than (*insert date use should cease).

Title: _____
Date:

2

SETTLEMENT AGREEMENT

THIS AGREEMENT is entered into this _____ day of _____, _____, by and between (*insert name and address as well as state of incorporation, if applicable), hereafter called "___A___" and (*insert name and address as well as state of incorporation, if applicable), hereafter called "___B___."

WHEREAS, A adopted, is the owner of, and currently uses the mark _____ on or in connection with (*insert products or services), which was first used at least as early as _____ and is the subject of U.S. Patent & Trademark Office (or state) Registration No. _____, hereafter "A's Mark;"

WHEREAS, B adopted and first used the mark _____ on or in connection with (*insert products or services) on _____;

WHEREAS, A asserted infringement claims against and requested B to cease use of (*insert B's mark) and B is agreeable to comply with A's request;

WHEREAS, the parties hereto desire to resolve A's infringement claims against B concerning B's use of (*insert B's mark).

NOW, THEREFORE, in consideration of the promises, covenants, and understandings of the parties recited below, it is agreed:

1. B and B's directors, officers, employees, agents, and all persons in active concert and participation with B shall:

    (a) not use or cause to be used as a mark, corporate name, trade name, or in any manner whatsoever (*insert B's mark) and/or variations thereof or any other mark or notation that is confusingly similar or a colorable imitation of (*insert A's mark);

    (b) not produce, print, distribute, ship, sell, promote, or advertise any services or products bearing a mark, name, or notation confusingly similar to, or which is a colorable imitation of (*insert A's mark);

    (c) destroy all material in their possession or under their control that contains (*insert B's mark) and/or variations thereof or any other mark or notation that is confusingly similar or a colorable imitation of (*insert A's mark).

2. In the event B fails to fully comply with all the provisions of this Agreement and A institutes action against B for failure to comply and obtains a ruling by a Court or administrative body in A's favor, B shall pay all costs and expenses incurred by A, including reasonable attorney fees.

269

3. B agrees not to contest, administratively or judicially, in the United States or elsewhere, the right of A to use, register, maintain, and/or enforce rights in A's mark (*insert A's mark).

4. A hereby releases and forever discharges B of and from any and all claims A has or may have arising from B's use of (*insert B's mark) prior to the date of this Agreement. B hereby releases and forever discharges A of and from any and all claims B has or may have arising from or attributable to the subject matter of this Agreement.

5. This Agreement is binding on the legal representatives, successors, and assigns of the parties.

6. The individuals who sign this Agreement on behalf of the respective parties hereby represent and warrant they have the legal capacity, requisite power and authority, and power to sign this Agreement on behalf of the party for whom they sign.

A

By_____
    Title:
    Date:

B

By_____
    Title:
    Date:

IN THE UNITED STATES DISTRICT COURT
FOR THE DISTRICT OF _____

Civil Action No. _____

_____

_____)
)
                 Plaintiff,)
)
        vs.   )
)
_____)
)
_____)
)
              Defendants.   )

CONSENT JUDGMENT

Plaintiff, _____and defendant
_____having settled the above
entitled action, hereby agree to entry of a final judgment herein
as follows:

1. Defendant hereby acknowledges service of the Summons and Complaint herein as well as jurisdiction of this Court over the parties and subject matter pleaded in the Complaint.

2. Plaintiff is the owner of all right, title, and interest in and to the trademarks registered in the United States Patent & Trademark Office under Registration Nos. _____ which are attached hereto as Exhibit A and incorporated herein by reference ("Plaintiff's Marks").

3. Subsequent to plaintiff's first use of the Plaintiff's Marks, defendant did adopt and use the mark _____ ("Infringing Mark") on and in connection with _____ products (or services) ("Defendant's Products or Services").

4. Plaintiff requested and demanded that defendant cease and desist from defendant's use of the Infringing Mark on the basis that said use constitutes an infringement of plaintiff's proprietary rights in Plaintiff's Marks.

5. Defendant acknowledges that the aforesaid acts of defendant were and are an infringement of plaintiff's proprietary rights in Plaintiff's Marks.

6. Defendant acknowledges that use of the Infringing Mark

1

was and is without permission by plaintiff.

7. Defendant acknowledges the validity and enforceability of plaintiff's federal registrations and proprietary rights in Plaintiff's Marks.

8. Defendant and defendant's agents, employees, servants and all persons in active concert and participation with them, except as may be otherwise provided for herein, are hereby permanently enjoined from the date of entry of this Final Consent Judgment from using or causing to be used as a trademark, service mark, tradename, corporate name or in any manner whatsoever Plaintiff's Marks and/or variations thereof or any other mark or notation confusingly similar to or any colorable imitation of Plaintiff's Marks.

9. In the event defendant fails to fully comply with all of the provisions of this Consent Judgment, and plaintiff institutes action against defendant for failure to so comply and obtains a ruling by the Court in its favor, defendant shall be liable for and pay all costs and expenses, including reasonable attorneys' fees, incurred by plaintiff in this regard.

10. In consideration of the foregoing, plaintiff does hereby release, remise and discharge defendant of any and all liabilities, actions, damages (including but not limited to actual, direct, consequential and punitive damages), claims or demands whatsoever, in law or in equity, which plaintiff now has against defendant, arising from use of the Infringing Mark prior to the date of the entry of this order.

11. In consideration of the foregoing, defendant does hereby release, remise and discharge plaintiff, its directors, officers, employees and agents of any and all liabilities, actions, damages (including but not limited to actual, direct, consequential and punitive damages), claims or demands whatsoever, in law or in equity, which defendant now has or may have against plaintiff arising from the claims asserted by plaintiff in this action.

12. This Court shall retain jurisdiction over the parties for purposes of enforcing any rights of plaintiff specified herein.

13. This Consent Judgment is to be entered without the taxation of costs, damages, or attorneys' fees and shall be binding upon and inure to the benefit of plaintiff and defendant, their successors, parent companies, subsidiaries, affiliates, legal representatives, and assigns.

Dated: _____.

_____
United States District Judge

IN THE UNITED STATES DISTRCT COURT
FOR THE DISTRICT OF _____

Civil Action No. _____

_____   )
_____   )
                  Plaintiff,   )
)
        vs.   )
)
_____   )
_____   )
                  Defendants.   )

CONSENT ORDER OF DISMISSAL

The Court hereby enters this Order as agreed to by the parties:

1.   Plaintiff agrees to dismiss the above-entitled action without prejudice and by stipulation pursuant to F.R.C.P. 41(a)(1)(ii) based on the undertakings of defendant as set forth below.

2.   Defendant acknowledges that plaintiff is the owner of all right, title, and interest in and to the trademarks registered in the United States Patent & Trademark Office under Registration Nos. _____ which are attached hereto as Exhibit A and incorporated herein by reference ("Plaintiff's Marks"); that subsequent to plaintiff's first use of the Plaintiff's Marks, defendant did adopt and use the mark _____ ("Infringing Mark") on and in connection with _____ products (or services) ("Defendant's Products or Services"); that plaintiff requested and demanded that defendant cease and desist from defendant's use of the Infringing Mark on the basis that said use constitutes an infringement of plaintiff's proprietary rights in Plaintiff's Marks; that the aforesaid acts of defendant were and are an infringement of plaintiff's proprietary rights in Plaintiff's Marks; that use of the Infringing Mark was and is without permission by plaintiff; the validity and enforceability of plaintiff's federal registrations and proprietary rights in Plaintiff's Marks.

3.   Defendant agrees that defendant and defendant's agents, employees, servants and all persons in active concert and participation with them, except as may be otherwise provided for herein, shall not use or cause to be used as a trademark, service mark, tradename, corporate name or in any manner whatsoever

Plaintiff's Marks and/or variations thereof or any other mark or notation confusingly similar to or any colorable imitation of Plaintiff's Marks.

4. In the event defendant fails to fully comply with all of the provisions of this Consent Judgment, and plaintiff institutes action against defendant for failure to so comply and obtains a ruling by the Court in its favor, defendant shall be liable for and pay all costs and expenses, including reasonable attorneys' fees, incurred by plaintiff in this regard.

5. In consideration of the foregoing, plaintiff does hereby release, remise and discharge defendant of any and all liabilities, actions, damages (including but not limited to actual, direct, consequential and punitive damages), claims or demands whatsoever, in law or in equity, which plaintiff now has against defendant, arising from use of the Infringing Mark prior to the date of the entry of this order.

6. In consideration of the foregoing, defendant does hereby release, remise and discharge plaintiff, its directors, officers, employees and agents of any and all liabilities, actions, damages (including but not limited to actual, direct, consequential and punitive damages), claims or demands whatsoever, in law or in equity, which defendant now has or may have against plaintiff arising from the claims asserted by plaintiff in this action.

7. This Consent Dismissal is to be entered without prejudice and without the taxation of costs, damages, or attorneys' fees and shall be binding upon and inure to the benefit of plaintiff and defendant, their successors, parent companies, subsidiaries, affiliates, legal representatives, and assigns.

Dated: _____.

_____
United States District Judge

We stipulate to entry of the foregoing Order.

Plaintiff: Defendant:

By_____   By_____
    Title: Title:
    Date: Date:

IN THE UNITED STATES PATENT AND TRADEMARK OFFICE
BEFORE THE TRADEMARK TRIAL AND APPEAL BOARD

In the matter of Application:
Serial No.:
Filed   :
Applicant :
Mark   :
For   :
Class   :
Published in the Official Gazette on:

(*insert opposer's name)   )
Opposer,   )
)
v.   )   Opposition No._____
)
(*insert name of applicant),   )
Applicant.   )

Commissioner of Patents & Trademarks
Washington, D.C. 20231

NOTICE OPPOSITION

     (*insert name and address of opposer, and state of
incorporation if applicable), believes that he/she/it will be
damaged by registration of the mark shown in the above-identified
application, and hereby opposes the same.

The grounds for opposition are as follows:

1. Application Serial No._____ seeks registration of (*insert
applicant's mark) on the Principal Register as a mark for (*insert
applicant's products or services), alleging a date of first use on
(*insert applicant's first use date) and a date of first use in
commerce on (*insert applicant's date of first use in commerce).

2. Opposer uses the mark (*insert opposer's mark) on and in
connection with (*insert products or services identified by
opposer's mark) and first used said mark prior to (*insert date of
applicant's first use), the date of applicant's first use.

3. Opposer owns the following registration (if applicable) for
(*insert opposer's registration by indicating the mark,
registration number, and registration date). Said registration is
currently valid and in force. Opposer also owns pending
Application Serial No. (if applicable) for (*insert the application

serial no. for opposer's mark, the mark covered by it, and the filing date). Two copies of opposer's registration are attached hereto as Exhibit A, pursuant to Trademark Rule 2.122(b).

4. Opposer has extensively and continuously used (*insert opposer's mark) on and in connection with (*insert opposer's products or services) since opposer's aforesaid first use date. By reason of such use, advertising, and distribution of opposer's products (or services) under said mark the public has come to recognize it as signifying opposer and opposer's products (or services), resulting in opposer's acquisition and ownership of valuable goodwill in said mark.

4. Applicant's mark (*insert applicant's mark), as applied to (*insert applicant's products or services), so resembles Opposer's earlier used and registered mark (*insert opposer's mark), as applied to opposer's products (or services) as to be likely to cause confusion, or cause mistake, or to deceive.

5. Based on the foregoing, registration of the mark shown in Application Serial No. (*insert applicant's serial no.) will cause injury and damage to opposer.

WHEREFORE, opposer requests that registration of applicant's mark (*insert applicant's mark) be denied.

(*insert opposer's name)

By_____
    Title:
    Date:

DECLARATION

(*Name of person signing below) being hereby warned that willful false statements and the like so made are punishable by fine or imprisonment, or both, under Section 1001 of Title 18 of the United States Code and that such willful false statements may jeopardize the validity of the registration resulting therefrom, declares:

He/she is authorized to execute this Declaration for opposer named in the Notice of Opposition; that he/she has read the Notice of Opposition and knows the contents thereof; and that the allegations are true, except as to the matters stated therein to be upon information and belief, and as to those matters he/she believes them to be true.

(*signature)_____
    Title:
    Date:

IN THE UNITED STATES PATENT AND TRADEMARK OFFICE
BEFORE THE TRADEMARK TRIAL AND APPEAL BOARD

In the matter of Registration:
Registration No.   :
Registered   :
Registrant   :
Mark   :
For   :
Class   :

```
(*insert name of petitioner)   )
Petitioner,                    )
                               )
v.                             )     Cancellation No._____
                               )
(*insert name of registrant),  )
Registrant.                    )
```

Commissioner of Patents & Trademarks
Washington, D.C. 20231

PETITION TO CANCEL

(*insert name and address of petitioner, and state of incorporation if applicable), believes that he/she/it will be damaged by the above-identified registration and hereby petitions for cancellation of the same.

The grounds for cancellation are as follows:

1. Registration No._____ covers the mark (*insert registrant's mark) for (*insert registrant's products or services), alleging a date of first use on (*insert registrant's first use date) and a date of first use in commerce on (*insert registrant's date of first use in commerce).

2. Petitioner uses the mark (*insert petitioner's mark) on and in connection with (*insert products or services identified by petitioner's mark) and first used said mark prior to (*insert date of registrant's first use), the date of registrant's first use.

3. Petitioner owns the following registration (if applicable) for (*insert petitioner's registration by indicating the mark, registration number, and registration date). Said registration is currently valid and in force. Two copies of said registration showing status and titled are attached hereto as petitioner's Exhibit A, pursuant to Trademark Rule 2.122(b).

4. Petitioner has extensively and continuously used (*insert

277

petitioner's mark) on and in connection with (*insert petitioner's products or services) since petitioner's aforesaid first use date. By reason of such use, advertising, and distribution of petitioner's products (or services) under said mark the public has come to recognize it as signifying petitioner and petitioner's products (or services), resulting in petitioner's acquisition and ownership of valuable goodwill in said mark.

4.   Registrant's mark (*insert registrant's mark), as applied to (*insert registrant's products or services), so resembles petitioner's earlier used and registered mark (*insert petitioner's mark), as applied to petitioner's products (or services) as to be likely to cause confusion, or cause mistake, or to deceive.

5.   Based on the foregoing, registration of the mark shown in Registration No. (*insert registrant's registration no.) will cause injury and damage to petitioner.

WHEREFORE, petitioner requests that Registration No. (*insert registrant's registration no.) be cancelled.

(*insert petitioner's name)

By_____
    Title:
    Date:

DECLARATION

(*Name of person signing below) being hereby warned that willful false statements and the like so made are punishable by fine or imprisonment, or both, under Section 1001 of Title 18 of the United States Code and that such willful false statements may jeopardize the validity of the registration resulting therefrom, declares:

He/she is authorized to execute this Declaration for petitioner named in the Petition to Cancel; that he/she has read the Petition to Cancel and knows the contents thereof; and that the allegations are true, except as to the matters stated therein to be upon information and belief, and as to those matters he/she believes them to be true.

(*signature)_____
    Title:
    Date:

Appendix E

Assignment with Acknowledgement

Trademark License

Consent to Use

TRADEMARK ASSIGNMENT

WHEREAS, The Shereth Group, Ltd., a Colorado corporation having a mailing address at 4100 East Mississippi Avenue, Suite 1000, Denver, CO 80222 (hereafter "Assignor") is the owner of the entire right, title, and interest in and to the trademark PENSTEMMON and U.S. Patent & Trademark Office Registration No. 0,000,000 therefor.

WHEREAS, Morris, Inc., a Colorado corporation having a mailing address at P.O. Box 6492, Denver, CO 80206 (hereafter "Assignee") desires to acquire the entire right, title, and interest in and to said trademark and all of the rights and privileges appertaining thereto, together with the entire goodwill of the business in connection with which said trademark is used.

NOW, THEREFORE, TO ALL WHOM IT MAY CONCERN, BE IT KNOWN that for good and valuable consideration, the receipt and sufficiency of which is hereby acknowledged, Assignor has sold, assigned, and transferred to said Assignee, its successors, assigns, and legal representatives the trademark hereinabove designated, including the entire right, title, and interest in and to the same and all the rights and privileges appertaining thereto, together with the entire goodwill of the business symbolized by the said trademark, the same to be held and enjoyed by Assignee for its own benefit and use and for the benefit of Assignee's successors, assigns, and legal representatives.

IN WITNESS WHEREOF, The Shereth Group, Inc. has signed this document on the 23rd day of October, 1989 by and through its duly authorized officer.

THE SHERETH GROUP, INC.

By_____
    Coby Ethan
    Title: President

ACKNOWLEDGEMENT

STATE OF COLORADO)
COUNTY OF DENVER)

This instrument was acknowledged before me this 23rd day of October, 1989 by Coby Ethan, President of The Shereth Group, Inc.

_____
    Notary Public

TRADEMARK LICENSE AGREEMENT

THIS Agreement is made and entered into this _____ day of
_____, by and between _____
a _____ located and having a place of business at
_____(hereinafter
called "Licensor") and_____
located and having a place of business at_____
_____ (hereinafter called
"Licensee").

WITNESSETH:

WHEREAS, Licensor is the owner of exclusive rights in the
mark_____ (hereinafter "Mark") for (services/products);
and

WHEREAS, Licensee is in the business of manufacturing,
distributing, and selling the products identified and described on
Schedule A, attached hereto and made a part hereof, and desires to
obtain a license from Licensor to use the Mark upon, and in
connection with the manufacture, distribution, sale, and
advertising of said products (hereinafter called "Licensed
Products").

NOW, THEREFORE, for and in consideration of the mutual
covenants and undertakings of the parties hereinafter set forth,
the parties hereto agree as follows:

GRANT

1. (a) Licensor hereby grants to Licensee the non-exclusive
license and right to use the Mark to identify only the Licensed
Products and in connection with the sale, advertising, and
promotion of the Licensed Products, but only within the territorial
limits of the United States, subject to the provisions, conditions,
and limitations set forth in this Agreement. Licensee shall not
use any trademark of Licensor other than the Mark in connection
with the Licensed Products or the sale, advertising, or promotion
of the Licensed Products and shall not use the Mark in connection
with any product or article other than the Licensed Products
without the specific prior written consents of the Licensor. All
rights of every kind and nature exclusive of those specifically
granted to Licensee hereunder are reserved by Licensor for its own
use and benefit.

(b) Licensee acknowledges that its violation of any of
the covenants of this Agreement relating to the use of the Mark,
or its failure to observe any of the limitations upon the license
herein granted, will result in immediate and irreparable damage to

1

Licensor. Licensee admits that there is no adequate remedy at law for such violation or failure, and agrees that in the event of such violation or failure Licensor shall be entitled to equitable relief by way of temporary and permanent injunctions and to such other relief as any court with jurisdiction may deem just and proper.

TERM

2. The period during which this Agreement shall be in effect is the term starting _____, and ending on _____, unless renewed or extended upon mutual written Agreement of Licensor and Licensee, or unless terminated earlier as provided for herein.

ROYALTY

3. (a) For and in consideration of the license and right granted to Licensee by Licensor hereunder, Licensee agrees to pay Licensor, within thirty (30) days after the close of each calendar quarterly period, a royalty in an amount equal to _____percent (_____%) of the "net sales price" of all Licensed Products sold or disposed of by Licensee during such calendar quarterly period. Licensee shall be obligated to pay Licensor a "minimum year fee" of _____ & 00/100 Dollars ($_____) for the period _____, through _____ and for each year thereafter during the life of this Agreement. All royalties in each year received by Licensor from Licensee under this Agreement shall be applied as a credit toward the "minimum yearly fee" and where the total of all such royalties equals or exceeds the "minimum yearly fee", payment of the "minimum yearly fee" shall be deemed to be satisfied. For those years where the total royalties do not equal the "minimum yearly fee", Licensee shall be obligated to pay Licensor the difference between the total of all royalties for the year in question and the "minimum yearly fee". If this Agreement terminates or expires prior to the expiration of any calendar quarterly period, the _____percent (_____%) royalty will be based upon the "net sales price" of the Licensed Products sold or disposed of by Licensee up until the date of termination or expiration and shall be payable to Licensor within thirty (30) days thereafter. For purposes of this Agreement, the term "net sales price" shall mean the price charged by Licensee for the Licensed Products after deducting normal and customary cash and trade discounts actually paid or allowed, returns, allowances, and sales and excise taxes, if any paid or allowed by Licensee. Further, for purposes of this Agreement, any transfer, gift exchange, or other disposition of the Licensed Products to any other party, whether such party be a subsidiary or other related party to Licensee, or whether such party be unrelated to Licensee, shall be considered a transfer for value and thus a "sale or other disposition" of the Licensed Products by Licensee. Such value shall be considered to be the average value received by Licensee from its sales to distributors, dealers, individuals, and

2

any other persons over the sixty (60) days immediately preceding such transfer, gift, exchange, or other disposition, if less than the value actually received, unless Licensee receives the prior written consent of Licensor to make such transfer, gift, exchange, or other disposition. Such written consent shall specifically state the identity of the recipient of the Licensed Products and shall state the exact number and kind of Licensed Products which will be so transferred, given, exchanged, or otherwise disposed of.

(b) During the life of this Agreement Licensee shall keep and maintain accurate and complete books and records showing the quantity, gross sales price, itemized deductions, "net sales price", and the date of sale or other disposition of the Licensed Products sold or otherwise disposed of by or under Licensee and shall permit representatives and accountants designated by Licensor to inspect and copy the same. Licensee shall make said books and records available for inspection and copying by Licensor for a period of two years after the date of termination of this Agreement.

(c) Licensee shall furnish Licensor, within thirty (30) days after the end of each calendar quarterly period, a certificate signed by an officer of Licensee showing the quantity, gross sales price, itemized deductions, "net sales price" and the date of sale or other disposition of the Licensed Products sold or otherwise disposed of by or under Licensee during such calendar quarterly period.

TRADEMARK USE

4. (a) Licensee acknowledges and confirms Licensor's ownership of the Mark as well as its validity and the right of Licensor to control the use of the Mark including the nature and quality of all products identified by it. Licensee further acknowledges and confirms that Licensee will not at any time put in issue the validity of the Mark or challenge Licensor's ownership or rights in the Mark or Licensor's authority to enter into this Agreement with Licensee. In addition, Licensee agrees to faithfully observe and execute all the requirements, procedures, and directions of Licensor regarding Licensee's use of the Mark.

(b) Licensee represents and acknowledges that all use of the Mark hereunder by Licensee shall inure to the benefit of Licensor.

(c) Licensee agrees that neither it nor any distributor, supplier, agent, contractor, or subcontractor for it, or anyone handling said Licensed Products, directly or indirectly, shall have any right to use the Mark or any trademarks of Licensor, except as expressly permitted by this Agreement.

(d) Licensee shall at all times use the Mark in the form

3

283

and style designated by Licensor and in no event shall Licensee produce, procure, or use any artwork, or trademark of Licensor in connection with any sale, distribution, promotion, or advertising of the Licensed Products which have not been approved in advance by Licensor in writing.

(e)   Prior to producing the Licensed Products, their immediate packaging, promotional and advertising material, and the like in quantity Licensee shall submit to Licensor at least two (2) preproduction samples thereof for a written approval of Licensor as to placement of trademark and copyright notices, artwork, appearance, suitability and quality of materials and workmanship. Licensee warrants that all Licensed Products, packaging, promotional and advertising materials shall conform with the preproduction samples which Licensor has approved in writing as provided herein.   Licensor shall not unreasonably withhold such approval. In any case where Licensee uses the Mark or any approved trademark of Licensor, it shall use the same without change in any particular, either as to content or relative position, from that previously approved by Licensor.

(f)   Licensee shall place upon said Licensed Products, including all advertising and promotional materials, packaging materials, and artwork for the Licensed Products such copyright, trademark, and license notices as Licensor may request before the Licensed Products and such material are produced.   Copyright, trademark or other protection relating to the Mark may be obtained only by Licensor at its own expense. Licensee will fully cooperate with Licensor in any action by Licensor for protection of such rights and shall furnish Licensor with all information and specimens which it may require for use in procuring the same.

MANUFACTURING BY OTHERS

5.   In the event Licensee does not itself manufacture all of the items composing the Licensed Products and the distribution and packaging material to be used in connection therewith, Licensee shall arrange for the manufacture of such items by manufacturers, processors, or fabricators.   Licensee shall, in its dealing with such manufacturers, processors, and fabricators, by written Agreement obligate the same to deliver any items on which the Mark is displayed, only to Licensee and not to use the Mark on any items except those delivered to Licensee in accordance with the terms of this Agreement. For this purpose, Licensee shall require that such manufacturers, processors or fabricators agree to a written provision requiring:

> "The Seller shall not manufacture any quantity of the ordered goods in excess of that stipulated in this order and shall not sell or deliver any of said goods except to the Purchaser".

4

PRODUCTION, PROMOTION, SALE AT LICENSEE'S EXPENSE

6. The manufacture, distribution, advertising, promotional activity, and sale of the Licensed Products shall be at Licensee's sole cost and expense and at no cost and expense to Licensor. Accordingly, Licensee represents and agrees that Licensee will pay all the costs and expenses, losses, liabilities, and judgments that may be associated with or arise from Licensee's manufacture, distribution, and sale of the Licensed Products.

REPRESENTATIONS BY LICENSEE

7. Since there is likely to be in the public mind an association between the Licensed Products, packaging materials, and advertising and promotional materials covered hereby and Licensor, Licensee shall not at any time indicate to anyone that Licensor is involved in the manufacture, distribution, and sale of the Licensed Products.

RELATIONSHIP OF THE PARTIES

8. It is the intention of the parties to enter into a licensing Agreement only and nothing herein contained shall be construed to regard the parties as being partners or joint venturers, or to constitute the arrangement herein provided for as a partnership or joint venture.

MERCHANTABILITY OF THE LICENSED PRODUCTS

9. Licensee agrees that the Licensed Products manufactured or sold by it will be of first class merchantable quality consistent with manufacturing standards for such products prevailing in the industry. In no case shall the quality of the Licensed Products be below that set forth in an acceptable sample submitted to Licensor by Licensee as provided under this Agreement.

RIGHT TO INSPECT

10. Licensee agrees to permit designated representatives of Licensor to inspect the manufacturing, shipping, and selling locations where the Licensed Products are produced, shipped, or sold by Licensee, at reasonable times during normal business hours for the purpose of enabling Licensor to determine whether or not Licensee is meeting acceptable standards of quality. Licensee shall immediately notify Licensor of any changes made in the quality of the Licensed Products during the life of this Agreement.

INFRINGEMENT BY OTHERS

11. Licensee shall notify Licensor of any other such products or items of similar nature to the Licensed Products which embody, in any way, the Mark, or any trademarks confusingly similar to the

5

Mark which come to Licensee's attention. Licensor shall have the sold right to determine whether or not any action shall be taken against such infringements, and Licensee shall not institute any suit or take any action on account of any such infringements or imitations without first obtaining the written consent of Licensor to do so.

PRODUCT DEFECTS

12. Licensee represents to Licensor and agrees that the Licensed Products shall be so made such that the Licensed Products and any packaging materials employed in connection with the distribution, advertising, and promotion of the same shall be harmless, non-toxic, and comply in all respects with the provisions of the Consumer Product Safety Act, the Flammable Fabrics Act, the Hazardous Substances Act, and all other applicable laws as well as regulations thereunder including all applicable state and local laws and regulations.

INDEMNITY

13. Licensee agrees to indemnify and hold harmless Licensor against any and all claims, causes of action, suits, damages, liabilities, and/or judgments and settlements including all costs, expenses, and attorney's fees based upon and arising out of Licensee's manufacture, distribution, promotion, and sale of the Licensed Products, or packaging, distribution, advertising materials relating thereto. Licensee shall undertake to conduct the defense of any such suit at its own expense, it being understood, however, that Licensor has at all times the option to participate in, or undertake any litigation involving said matters through counsel of its own selection and at its own expense, subject to the indemnity and hold harmless obligations of Licensee hereunder with respect to such expense. Licensee shall not make any settlement of any claim, suit, or demand for which Licensor may become responsible hereunder without Licensor's written consent which shall not be unreasonably withheld. The indemnity, hold harmless, and defend provisions of this Agreement shall survive its termination or expiration.

INSURANCE

14. Through the life of this Agreement Licensee shall maintain product liability insurance in the following amounts:

Comprehensive General Liability:

Bodily Injury $ each person
                         $ each occurrence

Property Damage $ each occurrence
                         $ aggregate

6

Comprehensive Liability $

Such product liability insurance policy maintained by Licensee shall contain a broad form vendors endorsement specially endorsed to extend such insurance coverage to Licensor. Licensee shall furnish a certificate of insurance to Licensor evidencing the coverage described in this paragraph and the broad form vendors endorsement referred to above as soon as practicable, but not more than thirty (30) days after execution of this Agreement. Such certificate shall provides for at least thirty (30) days' prior written notice of cancellation or substantial change.

SALES TO LICENSOR

15.   During the life of this Agreement Licensee shall sell to Licensor such quantities of the Licensed Products as Licensor may reasonably request at the lowest wholesale price at which the Licensed Products are then being sold in the same quantities by Licensee to others.

TERMINATION

16.   (a)   In the event the Licensee shall, at any time fail to make payments, render reports or otherwise abide by the conditions herein, Licensor shall have the right to notify Licensee of such default and its intention to terminate this Agreement unless such default is corrected by Licensee within thirty (30) days from the date of mailing of such notice. If such default is not corrected within the aforementioned time period, Licensor shall be entitled, without prejudice to any of its other rights conferred by this Agreement to terminate this Agreement at any time thereafter by sending a written notice of termination to Licensee to take effect immediately. Waiver by Licensor of any specific default or breach shall not be deemed to be a waiver of any other or subsequent default or breach.

(b)   In the event that Licensee shall become insolvent, exercise an assignment for the benefit of creditors, go into liquidation, or a trustee is appointed for the benefit of creditors, whether any of the aforesaid events be the outcome of a voluntary act of Licensee or otherwise, Licensor shall be entitled to terminate this Agreement forthwith by giving notice to such effect to Licensee.

(c)   The termination of this Agreement for any reason shall be without prejudice to any of Licensor's rights under this Agreement.

(d)   Notwithstanding termination of this Agreement, the parties shall be required to carry out any provisions hereof which contemplate performance by them subsequent to such termination and

7

287

such termination shall not affect any liability or other obligation which shall have accrued prior to such termination.

(e)   In the event of termination of this Agreement or upon its expiration according to the terms hereof, Licensee shall immediately discontinue all use of the Mark and all trademarks belonging to Licensor and all rights to use such trademarks shall automatically revert to Licensor and Licensee shall promptly execute any and all documents reasonably required by Licensor in connection with such discontinuance and reversion. Notwithstanding the foregoing, Licensee shall have the right to dispose of any then existing inventory of the Licensed Products during but not after the six (6) month period immediately following the date of such termination or expiration and subject to Licensee's obligation to pay Licensor royalty thereon as provided herein. Licensee shall immediately return to Licensor any original artwork provided to Licensee by Licensor hereunder and any plates made from such artwork upon termination or expiration of this Agreement.

ASSIGNMENTS

17. This Agreement shall be binding upon and inure to the benefit of subsidiaries, affiliates, successors, and assigns of the parties hereto. This Agreement shall not be assigned or sublicensed by Licensee without the prior written consent of Licensor and terminates forthwith in the event of any attempt by Licensee to assign it without Licensor's prior written consent.

GOVERNING LAW

18. This Agreement shall be construed and governed in accordance with the laws of the State of _____.

NOTICES

19. All notices and payments provided for in this Agreement shall be given or made by personal delivery or by certified mail return receipt requested to the addresses set forth above for each party to this Agreement, or to such other address as may be designated in writing by each party to the other from time to time. If given or made by personal delivery, notices and payments shall be effective on the date of personal delivery and, if given or made by certified mail return receipt requested, they shall be effective on the date of mailing unless otherwise provided herein.

ENTIRE AGREEMENT

20. This Agreement contains the entire understanding of the parties with respect to the subject matter herein contained. The parties may, from time to time during the continuance of this Agreement, modify, vary, or alter any of the provisions of this Agreement but only by an instrument duly executed by both parties

8

hereto. All provisions of this Agreement shall be severable and no such provision shall be affected by the invalidity of any other provisions. This Agreement shall be interpreted and enforced as if all invalid provisions were not contained herein.

AUTHORITY OF SIGNERS

21. The individuals who sign this Agreement on behalf of the respective parties hereby represent and warrant that they have the right, power, legal capacity and appropriate corporate authority to enter this Agreement on behalf of the corporation for which they sign below.

IN WITNESS WHEREOF, the parties hereto have caused this Agreement to be signed as of the date and year first written above.

_____

By:_____
      Title:

LICENSEE

By:_____
      Title:

9

CONSENT TO USE

A hereby consents to B's use of (*insert B's mark), but only on or in connection with (*insert B's products or services) in the territory described below. This consent is conditioned on B's agreement not use or cause to be used as a mark, corporate name, trade name, or in any manner whatsoever any mark, other than B's mark (*insert B's mark), that is confusingly similar to or a colorable imitation of (*insert A's mark); and, B's agreement not to contest, administratively or judicially, in the United States or elsewhere, the right of A to use, register, maintain, and/or enforce rights in A's mark (*insert A's mark).

In the event B fails to fully comply with all the provisions of this Consent and A institutes action against B for failure to comply and obtains a ruling by a Court or administrative body in A's favor, B shall pay all costs and expenses incurred by A, including reasonable attorney fees.

A releases and forever discharges B of and from any and all claims A has or may have arising from B's use of (*insert B's mark) prior to the date of this Consent. B hereby releases and forever discharges A of and from any and all claims B has or may have arising from or attributable to the subject matter of this Consent.

This Consent is binding on the legal representatives, successors, and assigns of the parties.

The individuals who sign this Consent on behalf of the respective parties hereby represent and warrant they have the legal capacity, requisite power and authority, and power to sign this Consent on behalf of the party for whom they sign.

TERRITORY: A

                                    By_____
                                       Title:
                                       Date:

                                    B

                                    By_____
                                       Title:
                                       Date:

Index